MEDIEVAL DUBLIN IX

In memoriam
Dr Michael Adams (1937–2009)

Medieval Dublin IX

Proceedings of the
Friends of Medieval Dublin Symposium 2007

Seán Duffy

EDITOR

FOUR COURTS PRESS

Typeset in 10.5 pt on 12.5 pt Ehrhardt by
Carrigboy Typesetting Services for
FOUR COURTS PRESS LTD
7 Malpas Street, Dublin 8, Ireland
e-mail: info@fourcourtspress.ie
and in North America for
FOUR COURTS PRESS
c/o ISBS, 920 NE 58th Avenue, Suite 300, Portland, OR 97213.

A catalogue record for this title is available
from the British Library.

ISBN 978–1–84682–171–4 hbk
ISBN 978–1–84682–172–1 pbk

This book is published with the active support of
Dublin City Council/Comhairle Chathair Átha Cliath.

Dublin City
Baile Átha Cliath

Printed in England
by MPG Books, Bodmin, Cornwall.

Contents

Contributors

PETER CROOKS is deputy director of the Irish Chancery Project (funded by the IRCHSS) at the Department of History, Trinity College Dublin, and secretary of the Friends of Medieval Dublin.

SEÁN DUFFY is a Fellow of Trinity College Dublin, and chairman of the Friends of Medieval Dublin.

PETER HARBISON is honorary academic editor of the Royal Irish Academy.

MELANIE McQUADE is a project archaeologist with Margaret Gowen & Co. Ltd.

FRANC MYLES has excavated a variety of sites in Dublin including Nelson's Pillar, Smithfield, and elsewhere in the Liberties.

TRÍONA NICHOLL is a Government of Ireland postgraduate scholar (funded by IRCHSS) in the School of Archaeology, University College Dublin.

GRACE O'KEEFFE is a Government of Ireland postgraduate scholar (funded by IRCHSS) in the Department of History, Trinity College Dublin.

LINZI SIMPSON is senior consultant with Margaret Gowen & Co. Ltd.

CLAIRE WALSH is a director of Archaeological Projects Ltd.

BERNADETTE WILLIAMS holds a PhD from Trinity College Dublin and is editor of *The annals of Ireland by Friar John Clyn* (2007).

Editor's preface

This volume of essays, the ninth in the series, arises from a day-long symposium held in Trinity College Dublin, on Saturday 12 May 2007. Some of the essays are revised versions of papers delivered on the day, and there are several additions: Melanie McQuade and Linzi Simpson did not address the symposium but made their papers available, for which we are very grateful; Claire Walsh spoke the previous year but her paper was held over to this year's volume for technical reasons; while Tríona Nicholl and Grace O'Keeffe spoke at the tenth symposium in 2008.

We are thankful to Dublin's City Manager, Mr John Tierney, and the City Council for their continued support, which allows us to publish the proceedings of the symposia at an affordable price. A contribution to the costs of the symposium was made by the Department of History, Trinity College Dublin. It is also a pleasure to acknowledge again our indebtedness to Ms Margaret Gowen and assorted MGLers for filling many of the pages of this as of every volume in the series, for various favours, primarily IT-related, and for much-appreciated financial support towards the cost of celebrating the launch of the annual volumes.

As ever, the Friends of Medieval Dublin owe a great debt of gratitude to the staff of Four Courts Press for their ongoing commitment to the series. For this reason, news of the death on February 13 of the press's founder and managing director, Dr Michael Adams, is occasion for great regret: to state that Michael Adams's contribution to Irish academic publishing over the last forty years is unparalleled does not come close to capturing the magnitude of the debt owed to him. More importantly, those of us who got to know Michael, or joined him for a glass of rioja and an impossibly hot curry, are just grateful for the privilege, sorry we didn't do so more often, and very sad at the loss of such a unique and lovely man.

Seán Duffy
Chairman
Friends of Medieval Dublin

An early medieval roadway at Chancery Lane: from Duibhlinn to Áth Cliath?

CLAIRE WALSH

INTRODUCTION

This article discusses the results from four archaeological excavations at Chancery Lane, Dublin, carried out by the writer from 2002 to 2006 on behalf of private developers (figs 1–5: location of sites, referred to throughout by their excavation numbers). The archive will be deposited in the Dublin City Archives, where it will be available for consultation. Detailed stratigraphic reports on each site are included in the archive. The finds have been deposited in the National Museum of Ireland.

All the sites had held buildings since at least the eighteenth century, with varying degrees of disturbance into the underlying deposits. Evidence for settlement in the area dates from perhaps as early as the late seventh century. Archaeological deposits dating from the early Anglo-Norman period through to the post-medieval period were also excavated.

Results of archaeological investigation on the west side of Chancery Lane are influenced by the chance survival of early deposits on sites which have been intensively developed since the late seventeenth century. However, evidence for early settlement in the area is strengthening with the level of development and attendant archaeological investigation in recent years. A series of radiocarbon dates from these excavations at Chancery Lane, coupled with an earlier series from Mary McMahon's work at Bride Street (McMahon 2002), provide us with the earliest evidence for inhabitants of Dublin in the historic era, a settlement which $C14$ (radiocarbon) dates strongly suggest precedes the Viking arrival.

Topography
The city centre block from Bride Street to Chancery Lane lies towards the western edge of the ridge south of the Pool, and the lower-lying plain of St Patrick's Park, between the pre-Norman churches of St Michael le Pole (O'Donovan 2008), and St Brigit's. The latter gives its name to Bride Street, the medieval route which led to the Pole Gate and St Werburgh's Street. It was secondary to the main route of St Patrick's Street to the west, but was nevertheless a major route-way in and out of the medieval town. A fording

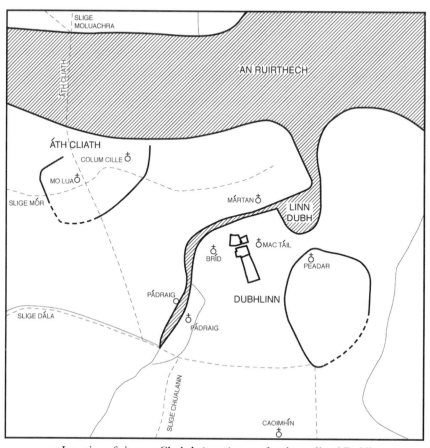

1 Location of sites on Clarke's (2002) map of early medieval Dublin

point over the River Poddle must have been an issue for town access on this
route in the early period, as it was well within the reach of tidal waters.

The sites lie east of the presumed junction of major route-ways of early
Ireland, known as *Slige* (highway), and northwest of the presumed ecclesiastical enclosure at Longford Street/Stephen Street.

Pre-Viking Duibhlinn

There was a monastic settlement at Duibhlinn, the name strongly associated
with the 'pool' (*polla* in some medieval documents), and presumably located
close by. The Annals of the Four Masters record the deaths of abbots of
Duibhlinn in AD 650 and 785. Duibhlinn is the dominant association of the
early references to an ecclesiastical settlement, and Clarke has posited a secular
settlement called Áth Cliath on the northern side of the Poddle, associated
with the major feature of the Liffey ford, in contrast to that of the ecclesiastical
settlement close by the pool.

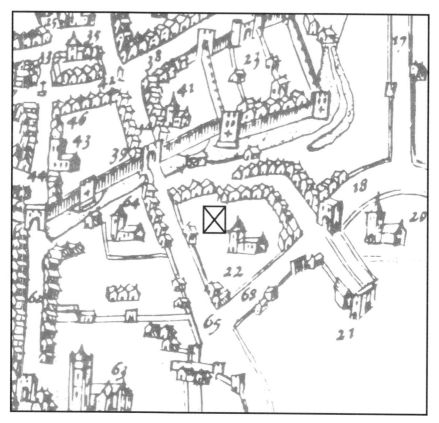

2 Location of sites, approximate, on Speed's 1610 map of Dublin

The large enclosure partly fossilized in the street plan of Whitefriar Street/ Stephen's Street Upper/Stephen's Street Lower still remains a contender for the monastic site. Several churches existed within this large enclosure, one at St Stephen's, and an enclosed church and graveyard at St Peter's (Coughlan 2003).

No enclosure around the church of St Michael has been uncovered to date, and no physical boundary to the graveyard was found in the recent excavations (O'Donovan 2008). There is no evidence as yet that the early church and graveyard of St Michael lie within the monastery of Duibhlinn.

BRIDE STREET/CHANCERY LANE: PRE-VIKING SETTLEMENT

Evidence for early-medieval settlement has been recovered from a site at Bride Street (93E153; see fig 5), excavated in 1993 (McMahon 2002). Radiocarbon dates from two burials at that site yielded dates AD 726–979 and AD 877–1001.

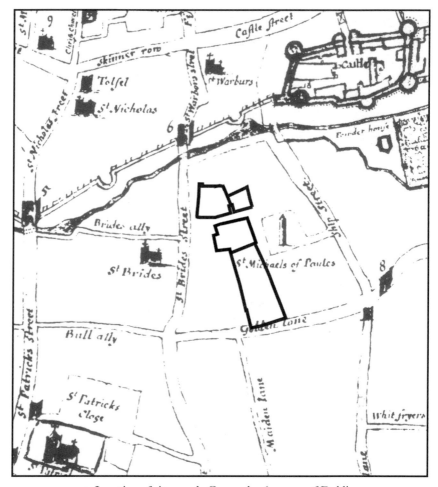

3 Location of sites on de Gomme's 1673 map of Dublin

These burials were not the primary deposits on the site, however, and they post-dated settlement evidence dated to between the eighth and tenth centuries. This archaeological evidence confirmed that an early-medieval settlement existed on the east bank of the Poddle.

The radiocarbon dates for settlement and burial at the Chancery Lane sites 02E1694 and 04E0237, discussed here, indicate still earlier settlement. This close group of dates spans the years AD 680 to AD 964. Unaccompanied adult burial, oriented east-west, was amongst the earliest activity. Four burials in total were recovered, widely spaced, and in shallow graves. A fifth individual is represented by a skull. The posture of some of the individuals indicates that they were, as is the Irish custom, shrouded. The burials were unaccompanied,

4 Location of sites on Rocque's 1756 map of Dublin

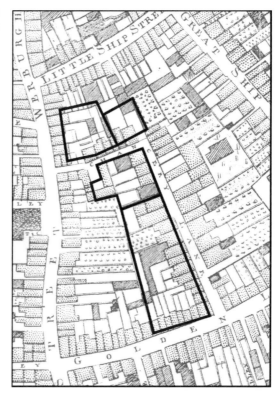

and had no markers or pillow stones. The population represented by this small sample, including the Bride Street group, which consisted of two articulated burials and two other individuals, includes three juveniles, an adolescent, a young adult, two older females and a single adult male, represented by a skull (Sk 22). The two articulated burials at Bride Street had evidence for nutritional deficiency in early childhood. The interment of both Bride Street burials was off the norm – the adolescent was placed prone, and positioned north-south. The older woman had her left arm twisted behind her back. One of the juveniles from Chancery Lane 04E0237 had a marked difference in the bone diameter between the left and right arms – at the age of between nine and eleven, right-handedness had manifested itself in the osteology. This may indicate a high degree of labour. These burials could be considered to be those of marginal individuals, for instance, those without families, the lower classes or even slaves. Burial in an official graveyard is customary in the early-medieval period. The widely spaced burials at Bride Street/Chancery Lane are in stark contrast with the crowded inhumations in the sacred ground close to the church of St Michael (O'Donovan 2008). However, it can be seen that at least five of these burials are aligned very closely with each other and possibly on church ground connected to St Michael's.

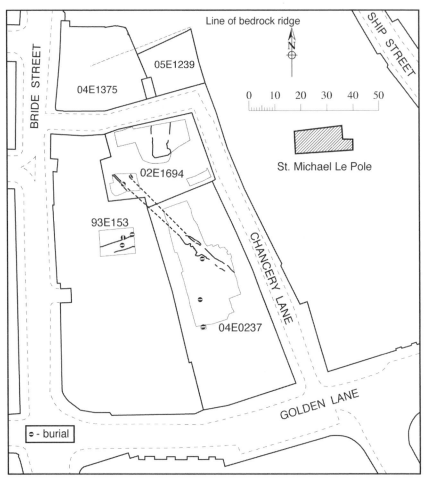

5 Sites excavated, also showing Mc Mahon's 1993 excavation. Early medieval
roads and location of burials indicated.

These burials also contrast with the four outlying burials from the Golden
Lane excavation (O'Donovan 2008) and the warrior burials from South Great
George's Street (Simpson 2005). A male and female burial from the periphery
of the cemetery of St Michael le Pole were Viking, while the other two were
unaccompanied. The male Viking burial from Ship Street Great was placed in
a shallow grave, supine, and oriented west-east. This is an interesting merger
of an accompanied male Viking buried in the Christian tradition (if it is not
merely coincidental). At a site at South Great George's Street, four young
adult male burials were recovered from widely spaced intervals on the site. The
burials were supine, and in shallow graves, oriented variously northeast-
southwest, northwest-southeast, over a cold hearth; north-south, with head to

the south, and west-east, set into an earlier ditch. C14 dating is consistent across the range, clustering at AD 670–880. These single burials may have been marked with cairns, and as is common with pagan Vikings, placed close by the settlement.

CHANCERY LANE PHASES 1 AND 2: THE ROADWAY (FIGS 5–7)

The early-medieval metalled roadway, F27, which extended northwest across both sites at Chancery Lane, is a rare archaeological discovery. It was demarcated by a gully on the northwest side, and on the south side was laid in a shallow trench – a slightly sunken route-way. It does not appear to have been resurfaced. The roadway was, at the very least, a cart track, and indicates the collective organization and probable commencement of property layout in the area. A radiocarbon date with intercepts of AD 808 and 850 was recovered from a pig-bone in the thick silt which overlay the road surface (UB 6337). The date suggests that the roadway may have been disused by the middle of the ninth century. The roadway led northwards down slope and was encountered in the excavation of the adjacent site to the north where the boundary gully of the road cut through an earlier burial (Sk 22: dates for which are as follows: UB-6367 (AMS) @ 2 sigma cal AD 684 (781) 885). The dates suggest that the roadway was laid down shortly after the burial of Sk 22 (see also report by Laureen Buckley, below, who confirms this).

The road F27, which extended northwest/southeast across the site, was set into a wide shallow linear cut, which extended for over 21m northwest-southeast. It had a maximum width of 2.35m with vertical edges rising between 0.06m at its eastern side to 0.12m at the west. The surface of the road was of closely-set sub-rectangular and rounded stones, up to 0.30m in diameter, laid directly onto subsoil. Sections of this metalling towards the southern extent of the road were very fine. The western side of the road was fairly irregular as opposed to the straight edge of its eastern side. However, on this side the roadway was flanked by a gully 0.68m in width which extended parallel to the roadway for 7.42m and would have provided drainage. Where the line of the roadway continued further north into Chancery Lane excavation 02E1694, both sides were demarcated by similar gullies. At the northern limit of the road, the earliest feature was the remains of a burial, F22, consisting only of a skull and mandible. There was clearly some occupation in this area which predated the road. A pit (F43) measuring 1.20m by 1m with a depth of 0.15m had a lower fill of heavily charcoal-stained silt. The upper fill was loam. It was sealed by the metalling.

Discreet areas of metalling overlay subsoil to the west of the roadway. These are extremely truncated occupation surfaces. The metalled surface of the roadway was overlain by a thick deposit of grey silt, which contained occasional flecks of charcoal and marine shell. Animal bone was also recovered in quantities directly off the surface of the road, but was not present through the silt deposit. This thick grey silt – a plough-soil? – with dumped occupation-material on the road surface, indicates disuse of the roadway.

Figure 5 shows the line of the roadway across the sites at Chancery Lane, and a projection of this same feature to the site numbered Chancery Lane 02E1694, where it was excavated in 2002 by the writer. The plan also shows the line of a possibly related feature, F101a, from McMahon's excavation (93E153), described in the excavation report as a channel, filled with brown, very stony, silty clay. Additionally, a structure is suggested on the same orientation as this feature (McMahon 2002, fig. 7) along with other deposits which followed a linear northeast-southwest tangent. The 'channel' at Bride Street (F101a) (interpreted by this writer as a probable roadway) is described thus: 'Several stony, very sterile deposits were found in a slight depression or channel, running in a northeast-southwest direction. The stones were both rounded and angular … It appears that the yellow clay had been cut into and had filled up with, or had been filled up with, these stony layers at some point' (McMahon 2002, 75). The description of this feature, over 2m in width, and its orientation, perpendicular to the extensive roadway at Chancery Lane, suggests that the two are in fact contemporary, and moreover, that this area close to Duibhlinn was laid out in an ordered fashion, with major roads, and the probable development of plots, by the middle of the ninth century. The interpretation of stratigraphy at McMahon's Bride Street site was hampered by excessive later pit-cutting, and the relationship of the probable roadway with the burials, all dated by C14, requires a review.

Land adjacent to a road or route-way was recognized as a valuable asset in the early-medieval period. A law tract distinguishes five categories of road – highway, road, byroad, curved road, and cow-track. The cow-track must fit two cows, one sideways and the other lengthways (Kelly 1997, 391). At 2.35m in width, the roadway at Chancery Lane is considerably wider than the many pathways to houses uncovered within the early-medieval town, being comparable to that of the mid- to late ninth century uncovered at Temple Bar West (Simpson 1999, 21), described by the excavator as a substantial stone road. The projected line southwards of the roadway at Chancery Lane leads to the putative large enclosure at Stephens St/Longford St (see fig. 1). The projected line northwards of the roadway, coincidentally, leads towards the Poddle at Ross Road, where the later-medieval Geneville's Tower is located. It is possible that the later town defences were constructed over an earlier crossing point on the Poddle here, where post-and-wattle fences were present in the river bed (Walsh 2001, 108).

At Bride Street, at least one structure, indicated by a post-and-stake line, and with a hearth, lay along the line of the road (McMahon 2002, 75). Possible

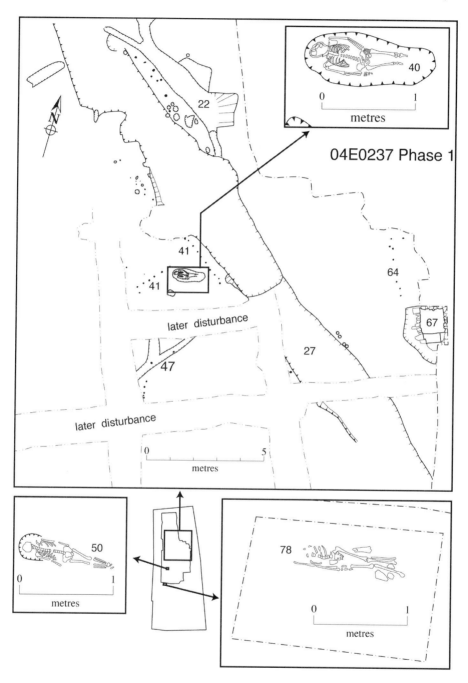

6 Excavation 04E0237, Phase 1

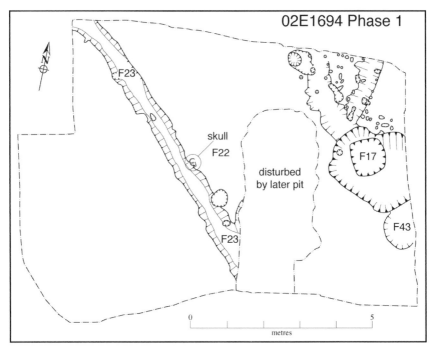

7 Excavation 02E1694, Phase 1 (refer to fig. 5 for location)

structural evidence contemporary with the roadway F27 was recovered from two or three areas along the road at Chancery Lane (fig. 6, 7). On present evidence, this would suggest a late eighth–ninth century date for these sub-rectangular structures indicated by fence lines and post alignments (see fig. 6).

Linzi Simpson's excavation at South Great George's Street has also yielded evidence for early plot layout in this area (Simpson 2005, 50). A large rectangular hall-type building was superseded by metalled surfaces, and further post buildings with hearths were uncovered at the basal layers at this site. The cumulative evidence from all of these sites is of an undefended, widely spread and fairly ordered settlement, on the southeast bank of the Poddle, on the fringes of an ecclesiastical settlement synonymous with that of Duibhlinn.

The archaeological evidence from Chancery Lane argues once again for disparate settlements of early Viking or native Irish, perhaps existing in tandem, in the Dublin area. The earliest settlement in this area may be peripheral to the enclosed monastic site of Duibhlinn to the southeast. That it is of pre-Viking date may be subject to further refining of the radiocarbon dates. Further dates from the cemetery of St Michael's are awaited, where several earth-cut features pre-dated the burials (O'Donovan 2008, 44). There is no indication whatsoever from the burials or from the artefact record that the earliest settlement at Chancery Lane is anything other than native Irish.

McMahon post-dates the earliest phase of occupation by burials, which have a broad date range from the eighth to the tenth centuries. At Chancery Lane, a gully along the western side of the road truncated a burial, dated between cal AD 684 (781) 885 (UB-6367 (AMS). There was more than one phase of burial on the site, with a wide range in dates recovered.

The burials

Three articulated human burials from 04E0237 were contemporary with the period of usage of the roadway. A single burial (F22) was recovered from the excavation of Chancery Lane north 02E1694, while four individuals are recorded from an excavation at Bride Street 93E153, immediately west of the present site (McMahon 2002). All burials have been reported on by palaeopathologist Laureen Buckley.

The three burials from Chancery Lane 04E0237 were all placed in shallow graves, and all were oriented west-east in the Christian practice. All three were unmarked and unaccompanied, and skeleton F78, whose skull was truncated, had some stones lining the grave-cut still *in situ*. The left arm may have been twisted up and extended to the right. The right arm lay deeper.

Skeleton F50, a juvenile, was placed in a shallow grave-cut 0.05–0.10m deep through the metalled surface, F70. No protecting stones were present. Parts of the skeleton were missing, due to later truncation. The position of the arms and legs indicate that the body had been shrouded.

Skeleton F40, a child, was placed in a shallow grave (F42) which cut through subsoil to a depth of only 0.10–0.15m. This body too may have been shrouded. The bone of F40 was in poor condition with the skull badly crushed from overburden.

Samples of human bone returned the following sequence of radiocarbon dates:

> Sk 78: UB-6336 (AMS) @ 2 sigma cal AD 780 (885) 964
> Sk 50: UB-6370 (AMS) @ 2 sigma cal AD 721 (815, 843, 853) 894
> Sk 40: UB-6369 (AMS) @ 2 sigma cal AD 680 (778) 883

The skull from Chancery Lane 02E1694, which burial was truncated by the construction of the roadway, returned the following date:

> Sk 22: UB-6367 (AMS) @ 2 sigma cal AD 684 (781) 885

Burials 22 and 40, with closely paralleled intercept-dates, appear to be contemporary. Both pre-date the presence of early-medieval activity in their respective areas.

Burial 50 post-dates the placement of the metalled surface, which appears to be contemporary with the roadway. In radiocarbon years, the dates form a very close group.

Features associated with the roadway (figs 5, 6, 7)
A series of lines of stake-holes, shallow pits and a gully cut through the soft yellow-brown boulder clay. In the absence of firmer evidence, it is likely that these do not represent more than fence lines, drainage features and perhaps more than one crude hut.

The west line of the road was defined by a linear gully (F23) which was 7.5m in length, 0.60m in width, and had an average depth of 0.30m. The metalled surface of the road partly overlay the silt fill of the gully, indicating more than one period of road construction or maintenance at this section of the road. Also on the east side of site 02E1694, a slot or curving gully (F44) with steep sides and an irregular base cut subsoil to a depth of 0.19m. One side of this slot/gully had a distinctive charcoal lens and an ash fill. The slot was 1.25m in length north-south, and 0.30m in width. The variation throughout the slot suggested that several intercutting features are represented here.

A line of stake-holes F44a, cut into subsoil, extended for a short distance parallel to the west line of the road. The line was incomplete and the spacing was irregular but, at the northern end, a perpendicular row of small stake-holes led westwards. This suggests an enclosed area, possibly an animal pen, or even a structure, in this location, and lying at the same angle as the roadway.

At its northern extent, the road surface (F24) of small pebbles bedded in a green clay was laid over the eastern part of the site. This surface had small pebbles on its eastern edge giving way to larger stones on its western edge with the ground sloping steeply to the north. It had a clear definition for 2m north-south; however, metalling, which appeared continuous with this level, extended over the entire east part of the site.

Iron slag, animal bone and a turned stone weight were recovered off the surface of the metalling.

Further south, a line of stake-holes (F41) extended parallel to the western edge of the roadway for a length of 4.80m. They were driven into subsoil to a depth of 0.05m, and were evenly spaced 10–15cm apart. Six further stake-holes extended perpendicular to the longer line, with a gap of over 2m between the fences. The longer fence line appears to be turning at both ends, suggesting a round-cornered structure. The scant survival of structural features may be evidence for a post-and-wattle structure, oriented on the roadway, measuring almost 5m in width, with a possible internal division on the northern side. A second shorter line of stake-holes continues further north, where there is a second group of parallel stakes (F41a), including also some postholes. These could define a small structure with rounded corners, measuring approximately 4m north-south by 2.5m east-west. No flooring levels, hearth or other associated material remained over this area, but the presence of small structures along the west side of the roadway explains the build-up of occupation material, comprising of butchered animal bone, over the surface of the roadway. In addition, the contemporary metalled surfaces F48/70 had butchered animal bone embedded into them.

F47 was a shallow gully, approximately 0.30m in depth, which extended northwest, perpendicular with the roadway.

At the south-eastern end of roadway F27, a cluster of small stake-holes F64 was driven into subsoil. The stake-holes may delimit the wall of a small structure or perhaps an enclosure.

Immediately south of the stake-hole cluster F64, a stone-lined well F67 was situated on the very eastern edge of the site. The well could not be fully excavated due to safety concerns, as it extended partly into the unshored site baulk. It was a square stone-lined feature, entered by two stone steps at the southern side. The walls were of fairly small dry-stone construction, rammed into the subsoil, and with some clay packing evident. The well extended to a depth of 1.5m, when excavation was halted due to safety concerns. It was infilled with grey silt, which contained only animal bone at the lower level. The later levels had slumped down into the top of the well, and a sherd of medieval pottery was recovered from this.

PHASE 2: TENTH TO TWELFTH CENTURIES

There is scant evidence for direct continuity on the 04E0237 site from the early-medieval through the Viking and later Hiberno-Scandinavian period. There are no finds which are attributable to the well-recorded Hiberno-Scandinavian settlement, with the exception of a possible ring-pin fragment which was recovered in a residual context. However, the excavation of Bride Street and Chancery Lane 02E1694 recorded activity in this area in the eleventh and twelfth centuries (McMahon 2002). The focus of occupation by this period is likely to have been at the church of St Michael le Pole. Also, by this period, the bulk of the population may have relocated within the established embanked town to the north.

Most of the features of this phase are cut into subsoil, and activity is represented by pits. None of the pits had evidence for any function other than rubbish- or cess-disposal. Several regular rectangular pits may have been lined with wood, but there was no survival of organic matter, apart from bone, and no postholes or plank impressions. Artefacts were rare finds.

The roadway of Phase 1 had gone out of use, and was covered over. There are no features which appear to respect the earlier line, except perhaps for a

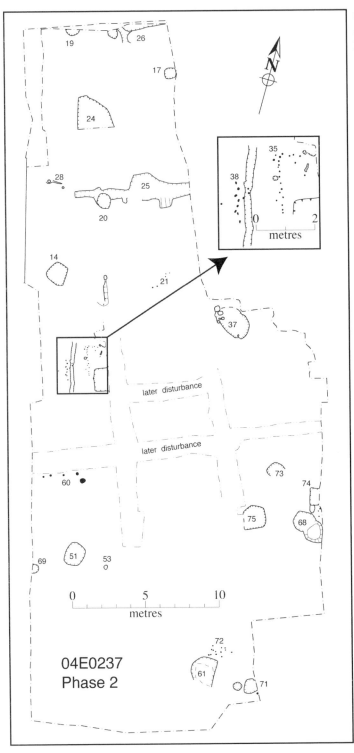

N

metres
0   2

later disturbance

later disturbance

0   5   10
              metres

04E0237
Phase 2

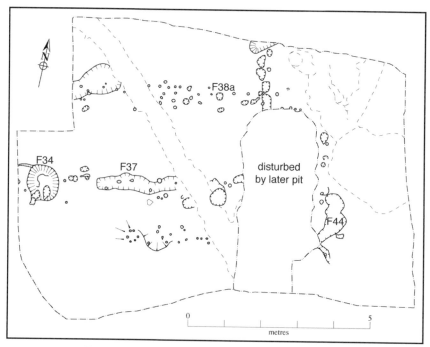

9 Excavation 02E1694, Phase 2 (refer to fig. 5 for location)

small structure, indicated by stakes and posts (F60). In general, the orientation of features appears to lie towards Chancery Lane, and there is the suggestion of plots, measuring approximately 5m in width, from the spacing of gully F25, and clusters of pits and other features.

Few features which were oriented on the alignment of the roadway were uncovered and these are likely to date to the earlier part of Phase 2. Several burnt stake-holes (F21) cut through the surface of the earlier roadway (F27). The orientation of the line, suggestive of a fence, is perpendicular to the roadway, suggesting a lingering of the earlier plot orientation.

Part of a structure measuring over 2.5m in length is suggested by a line of stake-holes and a posthole (F60), which is oriented on the line of the roadway.

At the southern limit of the excavated area, a deposit of dark silty clay, F58/62, overlay subsoil to a depth of 0.25m. It contained no artefacts, with only small fragments of animal bone, charcoal flecks and marine shell. It may be an agricultural or plough soil.

A small structure (F35) is indicated by 21 stake-holes of shallow depth (0.05m) which extended north-south for 2m, where the line turned east. A shallow gully (F38) lay 1m west of the possible structure. The gully extended for 3m north-south parallel to the stake wall. It was 0.10m in width with a depth of 0.07m–10m. The fill of F38 was a dark grey clay silt, with charcoal-flecked silt and sand at the base. Medium-sized flat stones lined part of the base of the gully, which appears to have functioned as a drain. The small structure described by stakes F35 does not respect the orientation of the roadway.

A narrow slot with a posthole cut into the base, F28, was located immediately west of the earlier roadway. The slot and post-holes suggest the entrance jamb of a small structure; however no further structural remains were present in this area. The location of the possible threshold is interesting, placed as it is where the gully F25 terminates.

Many pits are attributed to this level, as they cut earlier features, but contain no pottery. Several pits of this level are extremely regular, and may originally have been timber-lined.

At the northern extent of the road, property fences were uncovered, set at a different angle to the roadway. The property line is suggested by a line of stake-holes, F38a, which extend east-west, a second line which extends southwards from the east end. A putative structure could be suggested by a possible internal division which extends perpendicular to the main east-west line. The northern east-west line, F38a, is the first manifestation of a pre-Norman plot line which was maintained throughout the medieval period.

A rectangular pit (F38) cut through the disused road surface, and was filled with charcoal. The sides of the pit were not oxidized. It is suggested that it may have been a catchment pit beneath a brazier, or a raised hearth. It is possible that it may have been a smith's hearth. Deposits of this level and later can be related to those uncovered at Mary McMahon's Bride Street site.

Churches: twelfth-century records / Anglo-Norman period
All of the churches in the area appear to be pre-Norman foundations. Many are mentioned in Pope Alexander III's list of Dublin churches, 1179 (O'Neill 1950, 3). The accepted date for conversion of the pagan Vikings of Dublin to Christianity is in the reign of Sitric Silkbeard (989–1036) (Bradley 1992, 48). The church of St Brigit was granted to the priory of the Holy Trinity at Christ Church by the family of Mac Turcaill, and is listed in 1179 among its possessions. Documentary sources record that Ascaill Mac Turcaill, the last Hiberno-Scandinavian king of Dublin, held lands around Bride Street in the early twelfth century. The gift of 'Earl Hasgall' to the Holy Trinity is confirmed in 1202 (McNeill 1950, 29). Research by Linzi Simpson has identified the site at Bride Street/Chancery Lane as the large garden, formerly of Ascaill Mac Turcaill, which historically survived into the fifteenth century. It appears to be the same land referred to in 1428 as the 'great garden' in the parish of St Brigit the Virgin and St Michael 'of the poll', also mentioned in 1485 as an orchard, and named in 1488 as 'the Paradise'. The archaeological evidence from Chancery Lane is for continuous cultivation throughout the medieval period, and a section at least was cultivated as late as the seventeenth

century. The fine tilths and later cultivation furrows are indicative of continuous turn-over of the soil, consistent with use as a garden.

Property layout in the Anglo-Norman period
There is a noted change in the orientation of features in Phase 3, where a long
boundary ditch (F45) extends across the site perpendicular to Chancery Lane.
Golden Lane/Crosse's Alley, and Ship Street which leads northwards off it,
are medieval streets. It is extremely likely that Chancery Lane too is a medieval
lane or street, and the plot layout, though tenuous, would certainly support this.

The plot orientation appears to have commenced to change in Phase 2,
which is dated to before the Anglo-Norman period. Indeed, the incidence of
pit digging as an indicator of activity is much higher in Phase 2 than in the
following phase. However, it can still be characterized as low intensity. In the
Anglo-Norman phase, long plots off Chancery Lane are suggested. Alignment
of ditches such as F45 with concentrations of pits, such as F52-F63, may
indicate surviving plot alignments. However, in the area which became the
'Paradise' garden there are very few pits of either date.

PHASE 3: ANGLO-NORMAN

Features of this phase are readily attributable by ceramic analysis. The main
area of stratified deposits lay in the northwest of the site, in an area which was
not cellared in the eighteenth and ninteenth centuries. Several levels of activity
were differentiated.

Level 1
A layer of garden soil F10/F13, sealed the features of Phase 1 and 2 at the
north of the site. The soil had a colour range from light green through yellow
to brown, and was sticky when wet, and compacted when dry. The lower levels
of the soil (F13) contained very few sherds of pottery, and concentrations of
almost articulated animal bone. Characteristically, large pieces of butchered
animal bone were present on the surfaces of the lowest levels, rather than being
deposited into pits – the tendencies of the earlier inhabitants being to deposit
their refuse in middens rather than in rubbish pits. It is likely that this soil
began to form in the Hiberno–Norse period. A similar soil was noted towards
the southern part of the site (see Phase 2, F58/62) however no medieval
pottery was recovered from this material. The northern part of the site
however had evidence of continuous cultivation into the post-medieval period,
and the very small numbers of sherds of pottery may have travelled as the soil
was worked over in successive periods.

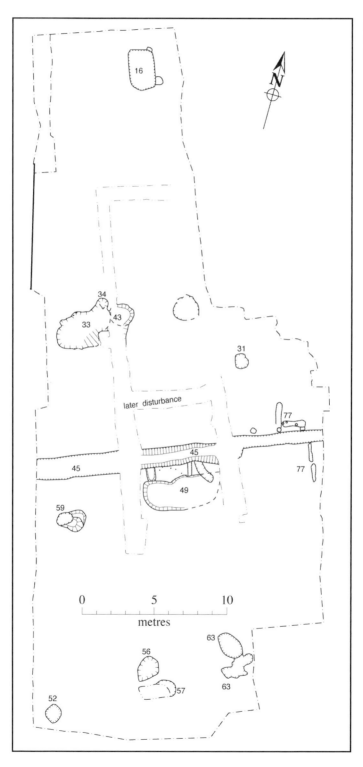

10 Excavation 04E0237, Phase 3

Level 2

This level saw further re-orientation of plot boundaries, which extended parallel to Golden Lane. The long boundary trench, F45, may be a rear boundary trench to plots on Golden Lane, or for a plot oriented onto Chancery Lane.

Level 3

An extensive deposit of tilled soil, F19, sealed all the features of level 3. This was up to 0.20m in depth. No finds of note were recovered from this soil, although butchered animal bone in quantity and iron slag was present.

A localized area of dense charcoal and slag (F20) on the north side of the site was uncovered. This appears to have been used as a base or hardcore for a thin beaten yellow clay floor (F21). This measured 4.10m east-west by 1m north-south and tipped slightly to the north. It was bounded by some flat stones, set in clay on its southern edge. No further structural features were extant.

Several compacted lenses of ash and charcoal overlay the clay floor, suggesting that it may be the remains of a workshop. The possible south wall of the 'workshop' lay along the earlier plot boundary, established by fence line F38a in Phase 2.

This level may relate to the lower level of McMahon's Phase IV (2002, 83) which was dated by ceramics to the twelfth century. These soils on the earlier excavation produced metal-working waste, specifically iron-working, although no features related specifically to that activity were noted.

CHANCERY LANE 02E1694: THE QUARRY

Test excavation of this area had indicated that there was a considerable depth of archaeological soils in this area. The natural contour dropped to the north and east, at the angled corner of Chancery Lane Great with Chancery Lane Little.

Most of the north-eastern part of the site had been dug through by a stone quarry, F40. The upper fills of the quarry were apparent following removal of the later cellars and cleaning of the surface. The quarry measured 12.5m north-south, extending northwards beyond the area of excavation, and 7.5m in width. (Boreholes undertaken on the development sites at the north side of Chancery Lane indicate that the quarry extends into the southern part of that site. The line of the rock ridge exposed to the south of the city ditch is indicated.) The sloping base of the quarry was reached at a depth of approximately 4.80m OD (pavement level lay at *c.*11m OD). The base also sloped from the north towards the south.

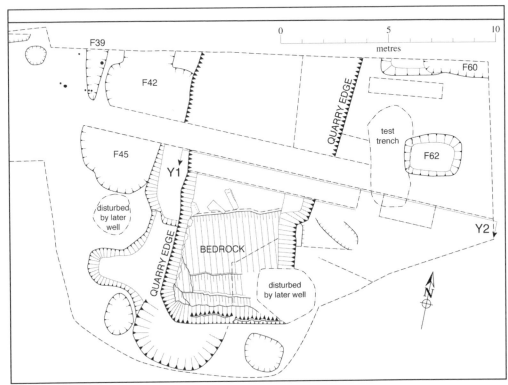

11 Excavation 02E1694, late medieval rock quarry (refer to fig. 5 for location)

The sides of the quarry were regular and vertical, particularly at the southern end, where the fissures initially gave the appearance of coursed masonry. The stone was bedded in sheets aligned northwest/southeast. Several large slabs of limestone which had been quarried had been left at the northern part of the excavated quarry, evidently abandoned by the stone workers.

The lowest fill of the quarry at the southern end was a soft brown silt. This had been permanently waterlogged, and contained many organic finds, which had been thrown into the disused quarry. Amongst the finds from this level was a wooden block wheel and axle, probably from a wheelbarrow. Many shoes from the late-medieval period were recovered from this level.

A thick fill of crushed limestone comprised the bulk of the fill. The crushed stone had a fairly uniform texture, and could represent spoil from the quarry and from stone dressing. It did not contain any finds.

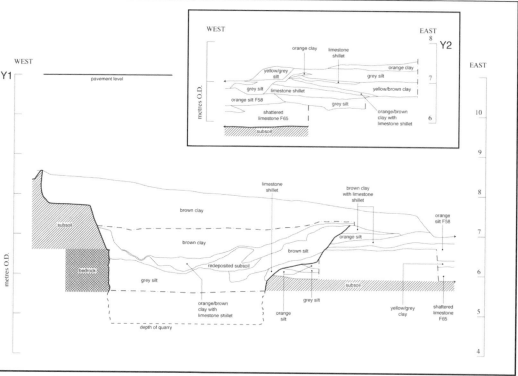

12 Excavation 02E1694, section of late medieval rock quarry (refer to fig. 11 for location)

CHANCERY LANE (ALL SITES): ARTEFACTS SUMMARY

Complete reports on all artefacts, including ceramics by Clare McCutcheon, and animal bone by Dr Emily Murray, are lodged with Dublin City Archives.

Few artefacts were recovered from the early levels at Chancery Lane. None of those displayed any Viking affinities. Two hollow bone cylinders were recovered, along with a fragment of a lignite bracelet.

Only one fragment of a possible ring-pin (6:3) was recovered from a secondary layer. An iron ring-pin was recovered from a Phase 3 context on McMahon's Bride Street excavations.

The medieval finds assemblage includes the usual range of stick-pins, tile and ceramic material, knives and stone objects.

A large quantity of iron slag, including hearth bases or furnace bases, was recovered from the twelfth-century levels in Chancery Lane North. These deposits are related to the deposition of similar material at the Bride Street excavation (McMahon 2002). Several fragments of identifiable portions for the tuyere for a bellows were also recovered.

Textiles

Five textiles were recovered from the quarry fill. A full report has been completed by E. Wincott Heckett. The summary findings are given here.

02E1694:3:1a and b are two pieces of a narrow silk band, made from silk and metal threads, in a variant of tabby weave known as hopsack. There are several stitch holes at one edge of the cloth, implying that originally it had been attached to another cloth. Such bands were used as decorative trimmings on tunics, dresses and vestments, elite garments. The piece is likely to have been imported, thirteenth to fourteenth century.

02E1694:56:104 is a triangular piece of dark coloured silk in a satin weave, with decorative slashing and pinking, dating to *c.*1550–1650AD.

02E1694:64:146 is a lightweight fine woven tabby weave silk, sixteenth to early seventeenth century.

02E1694:64:144 finger looped braid of linen yarn, with aiglet (lace end) secured to one end. The impression where the braid was threaded through an eyelet is still apparent.

02E1694:64:145. Small remnant of knitting in stocking stitch, of linen thread, sixteenth to early seventeenth century.

Leather finds

A catalogue was compiled by John Nicholl. 250 pieces of identifiable leather-work were recovered from late-medieval quarry fills. This includes 25 complete or almost complete shoes. Six shoe types were identified. The styles suggest a date range from early sixteenth century to late seventeenth century.

SKELETAL REPORT

Laureen Buckley

INTRODUCTION

These skeletons were excavated by Claire Walsh in advance of a development at Chancery Lane 04E0 237, Dublin. At this site, two supine, extended skeletons of juveniles were found lying in a west-east orientation and later another adult skeleton was found during monitoring. A skull, F22, was recovered from Chancery Lane 02E1694. The bone was washed by the osteoarchaeologist before examination. A sample of each skeleton was removed for radiocarbon dating and the dates were all within a range from the seventh to the tenth century.

CONDITION OF THE BONE

Although the skeletons and the stray skull were highly fragmented, with the feet of Skeleton 1 from Chancery Lane being removed by a later pit, the bone was in a remarkably good state of preservation with the outer cortex mostly intact. The bodies of the vertebrae, consisting mainly of cancellous bone, had not survived well but the neural arches were almost all present. The ribs also survived in a good state of preservation.

METHODS

Sex of the adult skeletons was determined by examination of morphological features of the pelvis, skull and long bones. The diameters of the head of the humerus and the head of the femur can also be used to determine sex. It is not advisable to attempt to sex juvenile and adolescent skeletons as the sexual characteristics are not defined until after puberty.

The juvenile skeletons were aged by examination of the state of dental eruption and development (Schour and Massler 1944) and also by examining the degree of epiphyseal fusion.

Adults were aged by examination of degenerative features including the auricular surface of the ilium (Lovejoy et al. 1985). Since the burials were from the Early-Christian period, attrition of the occlusal surfaces of the teeth could be used to determine age. In view of the inaccuracy of the various aging methods, it is better to look at the overall degeneration of the individuals to place them in age groups. The age groups used are young adult, up to 25 years, middle adult, up to about 45 years and older adult, over 46 years.

Stature of adults was estimated using the regression equations of Trotter and Gleser (1952, 1958).

RESULTS

The remains of Sk 22 consisted of a skull of an adult male and some cervical vertebrae with part of a right parietal bone only from another adult skull.

A congenital defect was present in Skeleton 1 (F22) in that the dorsal surface of the first cervical vertebrae had not fused together in the mid-line. This spina bifida atlanta is not an uncommon occurrence and would have caused no symptoms.

This individual had attrition on the biting surfaces of the teeth in keeping with what is usually found in the Early-Christian period where bread made from roughly-ground flour was eaten. Although he had two carious teeth the location of the cavities at the neck of the teeth is also what would be expected from the Early-Christian and medieval periods. He also had an abscess in the maxilla caused by bacteria entering the pulp cavity that had been exposed due to excessive attrition. An untreated abscess can become a serious infection as the bacteria can spread through the bloodstream to cause septicaemia throughout the other organs of the body.

Skeleton 1 had been cut through the neck with a linear cut going diagonally from left to right through the third and fourth cervical vertebrae. Since nothing remained from the skeleton below this level, the head had obviously been cut from the body. This must have been done while the vertebrae were still articulated to the skull so it may have been a perimortem cut. However the cut was rougher than has been found in other skeletons in the later medieval period, so either the instrument used to cut the skull off was not very sharp or it happened sometime after death but before decomposition of the flesh.[1]

The other partial skull from Chancery Lane consisted only of a right parietal bone from an adult.

The three articulated skeletons from Chancery Lane consisted of two juveniles and an adult. One of the juveniles was aged 9–11 years at the time of death and the other was aged 4–6 years. The adult skeleton was an early middle-adult female, probably aged 25–29 years at the time of death. The living stature of the female was 155cm, which is entirely in keeping with the average stature of females found in other Early-Christian and medieval populations.

There was no evidence of chronic illness on any of the skeletons from Golden Lane. The only remarkable anomaly was in the development of the bones in one juvenile and the female. In the older juvenile, Skeleton 1, the right arm was more developed than the left arm. Although the length was the same, the diameter of the bones on the right was 2–3mm larger than those on the left. It may indicate that the juvenile was right-handed and that even at such a young age the difference in bone size due to using one arm more than the other was becoming apparent.

In the female the right femur was excessively bowed anteriorly. The bowing was such that the right femur was 2cm shorter than the left. The cause of this is unknown. Excessive bowing is a feature of rickets, but this is unlikely in this case, as both femurs should be bowed if it was due to rickets. There is no bowing on any other bone in the skeleton. It may have been a developmental defect. Whatever the cause, it would have led to serious problems in later life as the limp that would have been present would more than likely have caused early osteoarthritis of the hip or knee joints.

---

1 Claire Walsh adds: this burial was cut through by the construction of the road, F27, so the implement used was probably a wooden shovel.

DESCRIPTION OF SKELETONS

Chancery Lane 02E1694 Skeleton 1 (F22)

This burial consisted of the back of a skull only. The occipital bone, including the basilar part, was virtually complete. Most of the right temporal bone was present and the mastoid area of the left temporal bone also survived. There was a large fragment of the posterior part of the right temporal bone with the lamboid and squamous sutures visible and a smaller fragment of the left parietal bone also from the parietal notch area. The right zygomatic bone and the right side of the maxilla was all that survived from the facial area. The mandible was virtually complete. The upper four cervical vertebrae were present and virtually complete.

Age and sex The mastoid process, posterior zygomatic arch and the external occipital protuberance were all of the male type. The basal-sphenoidal symphysis was fused indicating that the individual was probably over 21 years. The wear on the teeth suggests that he was a mature adult age between 25–45 years.

Skeletal pathology The neural arch of the first cervical vertebra was not fully fused at the dorsal surface. The gap was quite small and would have been closed by ligaments and muscle so that it would not have caused symptoms or been incompatible with life. This condition is known as spina bifida occulta and although it usually manifests itself in the sacrum, it can also occur in the first cervical vertebra, where it is known as spina bifida atlanta.

There was a cut through the left side of the arch of the third cervical vertebra just below the superior articular surface. The cut went diagonally through the body and just below the superior right articular process of the fourth cervical vertebra. Although the cut was linear it was not sharp as is usually seen in weapon wounds from swords. It is possible that this cut occurred after death and this would explain why the rest of the skeleton below this cut is missing. However the fact that the upper four cervical vertebrae stayed in place with the back of the skull means that the possibility that the cut occurred in the perimortem period with a rough instrument cannot be ruled out.

Dentition

```
              A                                  C   C
   P   P   P   P   P   P   PM  PM                      P   P
   18  17  16  15  14  13  12  11              27 28
   48  47  46  45  44  43  42 41   31 32 33 34 35 36 37 38
   P   P   P   P   P   P          P        P   P   P   P
```

P – tooth present
17 – socket missing
C – caries
A – abscess

ATTRITION: there was moderate wear all the teeth except the first molars where attrition was heavy with formation of secondary dentine over the entire surface.

CALCULUS: there were moderate calculus deposits on the buccal and lingual surface of most teeth and on the distal surfaces of the third molars. Deposits were lighter on the lower molars.

CARIES: there was a moderate sized cavity on the distal surfaces of the upper left second molar and on the mesial surface of the upper left third molar, both at the cervical margin.

ABSCESS: there was an abscess at the buccal roots of the upper first molar with an external opening in the alveolus. There was also evidence of periostitis on the alveolus around the abscess.

PERIODONTAL DISEASE: there was a slight degree of alveolar recession around the roots of the lower molars and upper right canine and premolars.

HYPOPLASIA: linear enamel hypoplasia was present on the lower left central incisor, the right canines, upper right first molar and lower left second premolar. This indicates nutritional stress or acute infections during early childhood.

Chancery Lane Skeleton 2

This consisted of most of a right parietal bone in five fragments, with most of the sagittal and coronal sutures present. The lamboid area was missing.

Golden Lane 04E0237, Skeleton 1 (F40)

The skull was highly fragmented but virtually complete with the frontal, parietal, occipital, temporal, zygomatic and sphenoid bones present. The mandible was virtually complete and fragments of maxillae remained. One greater horn of the hyoid bone survived. Although very little remained from the vertebral bodies, the arches of seven cervical, twelve thoracic, five lumbar and four sacral vertebrae remained. There were eleven ribs from each side and most of the manubrium of the sternum was present.

The left and the right clavicle were complete. Both scapulae were fragmented but virtually complete although the glenoid area was missing from the right bone.

The diaphysis of the left humerus was virtually complete although there was some missing from near the proximal end and part of the proximal epiphysis also survived. The right humerus was also virtually complete but fragmented at the proximal end of the diaphysis. The proximal epiphysis of the right humerus was also present. Both radii were virtually complete although slightly fragmented at the distal ends of their diaphysis and the proximal epiphysis of the right bone was present. The ulnae were virtually complete with only slight fragmentation of the distal end of the diaphysis. The left hand consisted of five carpal bones, four metacarpals and five proximal and four middle hand phalanges. The right hand consisted of seven carpals, five metacarpals, four proximal, four middle and two distal hand phalanges.

The pelvis was fragmented but most of the ilia, both ischia and both pubic bones remained. The femurs were virtually complete with all epiphyses present. Part of the left patella survived. Only the proximal third of the left tibia and fibula and the proximal third of the right fibula remained from the lower leg bones.

Skeletal pathology There was no indication of any nutritional deficiency, infection or any other condition on the skeletal remains. The only anomaly observed is that the left arm bones were slightly less developed than the right arm bones. The bones appeared to be the same length but those on the left side had a slightly smaller diameter than those on the right. Although the difference was only 2–3mm it was noticeable. There did not appear to be any pathological reason for this difference so it may be a quirk of development that might have evened out if the juvenile had lived for longer, or it may indicate that the right arm was being used more than the left and that even at such a young age difference in bone development was becoming apparent.

Dentition

U	P	P	P	P	P	P		P	P	P	P	P	P	U
~~17~~ ~~16~~	55	54	53	12	11			~~21~~ ~~22~~	~~63~~	~~64~~	~~65~~	~~26~~	~~27~~	
47	46	85	84	83	42	41		31	32	73	74	75	36	37
U	P		P	P	P	P		P		P	P		P	P	U

U– tooth unerupted

AGE: the permanent first molars had erupted but the second molars, canines and premolars had not. The roots of the second molars were one-quarter formed. An individual at this stage of dental development would be aged 9–11 years.

ATTRITION: there was a moderate degree of attrition on the deciduous molars.

CALCULUS: there were moderate deposits of calculus on the lower lateral incisors, deciduous molars and first permanent molars.

Golden Lane 04E0237, Skeleton 2 (F50)

This skeleton was in poor condition and in a fragmentary state compared to Skeleton 1. The bone was also friable to the touch. Only part of the back of the skull was present. The occipital bone was virtually complete on the left side but little remained of the right side. The posterior part of the left parietal bone with the lamboid suture was also present and the left temporal bone was almost complete. Three loose teeth remained but all that survived from the mandible was the left mandibular condyle.

The vertebral column was fragmentary but virtually complete with seven cervical, twelve thoracic, five lumbar and four sacral vertebrae remaining. The vertebral bodies as well as the arches were present and the arches were fused to the bodies in the sacral and lumbar regions only. Twelve ribs from the left side and eleven from the right side remained and there were two fragments of sternum.

The left clavicle was fragmentary and decayed but virtually complete. The acromion and part of the lateral borders of both scapulae remained but the glenoid areas were missing. The distal two thirds of the left humerus and distal half of the left radius was all that remained from the left arm. The right arm consisted of the distal two–thirds of the humerus and fragments only of the radius and ulna shafts. One carpal, three metacarpals and five phalanges remained from the left hand while the right hand consisted of two fragmented metacarpals and three phalanges.

The left ilium from the pelvis was fragmented and incomplete but the right ilium was complete. Both ischia and the pubic bones were present with the left ischium and right pubis being complete.

Both femurs and tibiae from the leg bones were virtually complete but the distal ends of their shafts were very fragmented. The fibulae were also present but fragmented. Only the talus and calcaneum from each foot and three metatarsals and one phalange from the right foot remained.

Skeletal pathology There was no evidence of disease or trauma on the bones.

Dentition Three loose teeth were found with this skeleton. They consisted of the maxillary deciduous incisors and canine, 61, 62, 63. The roots were complete and there was some wear on the teeth indicating that they had been erupted for some time.

AGE: Since the permanent incisors had not erupted, the juvenile was probably less than 6 years of age at the time of death. A more precise age can be determined from the vertebral column. All the halves of the neural arches have fused together so the individual is over two years. The foramen transversarium are complete in the lower cervical vertebrae and the posterior halves of the axis are also fused so the individual is over 3 years. The posterior halves of the atlas also appeared to be fused so the individual is over 4 years (Scheuer and Black 2000, 218). It is not possible due to incompleteness to determine how much more the vertebrae are developed but the information obtained is sufficient to place the juvenile in the 4–6 years age bracket.

Golden Lane 04E0237, Skeleton 3 (F78)

This skeleton was almost complete apart from the skull and upper cervical vertebrae, which were missing. It was in an excellent state of preservation.

Only a fragment of the anterior part of the left parietal bone remained from the skull. The lower four cervical vertebrae were complete and there were twelve thoracic and five lumbar vertebrae although the arches were missing from the upper thoracic vertebrae. Twelve ribs from the left side and eleven from the right side remained and the manubrium and body of the sternum were complete.

Both clavicles and the right scapula were complete. The humerii were present but their proximal ends were missing. Both radii and the right ulna were complete but the distal half was missing from the left ulna. There were no bones remaining from the left hand but the right hand consisted of all the carpals apart from the trapezoid and the pisiform, all the metacarpals apart from the fourth and three proximal, one middle and one distal hand phalanges.

The pelvis was almost complete with most of the left ilium, all of the right ilium, both ischia and the left pubic bone present. The sacrum was also complete.

Both femurs and tibiae were complete, the proximal end was missing from the left fibula and the shaft of the right fibula was also present.

Sex and age The sciatic notches, sub-pubic angle, sub-pubic concavity and ventral arc of the pubic bones were of the female type. All the bone measurements were in the female range.

The epiphyses at all the long bones were fused but the epiphyseal line was still faintly visible at the proximal femur and tibia. The sternal end of the clavicle was fused. The auricular surface of the ilia indicates an age of 25–29 years and this is in accordance with the epiphyseal fusion. This individual can therefore be put in the early middle-adult age range.

Skeletal pathology There was no indication of infectious disease or trauma on the skeleton. The only deformity was in the right femur, which was excessively bowed anteriorly compared to the left femur. The bowing was such that there was a difference of 2cm in length between the left leg and the right leg. There was no bowing of the tibiae and they were the same length.

Anterior bowing of the femur occurs in rickets, a vitamin D deficiency disease. However it is usually bilateral and the tibiae are usually affected as well. It is unlikely that rickets caused the bowing of one femur. The cause of this deformity is unknown but it may be a congenital defect. Because of the defect the stature was estimated using the left femur only using the equations of Trotter and Gleser (1952, 1958).

ACKNOWLEDGMENTS

Site supervision at Chancery Lane was carried out by Brian Hayden. The drawings are by Conor McHale. Excavations were facilitated by John Fleming Associates (Chancery Lane 02E1694); Rhatigans (Chancery Lane 04E0237) and Temple Construction (Chancery Lane 04E1375 and 05E1239).

BIBLIOGRAPHY

Clarke, H. 1990 The topographical development of early medieval Dublin. In H. Clarke (ed.), *Medieval Dublin: the making of a metropolis*, 52–69. Dublin.
— 1998 Proto-towns and towns in Ireland and Britain in the ninth and tenth centuries. In H. Clarke, M. Ní Mhaonaigh, and R. Ó Floinn (eds), *Ireland and Scandinavia in the early Viking Age*, 331–80. Dublin.
— 2002 *Dublin, part 1 to 1610*. Irish Historic Towns Atlas. Royal Irish Academy. Dublin.
Kelly, F. 1999 *Early Irish farming*. Early Irish Law Series, vol. IV. School of Celtic Studies, Dublin Institute for Advanced Studies. Dublin.
Lovejoy, C., Meindl, R., Pryzbeck, T. and Mensforth R. 1985 Chronological metamorphosis of the auricular surface of the ilium: a new method for the determination of adult skeletal age at death. *American Journal of Physical Anthropology* 68, 15–28.
McNeill, C. 1950 *Calendar of Archbishop Alen's register, c.1172–1534*. Royal Society of Antiquaries of Ireland. Dublin.
McMahon, M. 2002 Early medieval settlement and burial from outside the enclosed town: evidence from archaeological excavations at Bride Street, Dublin 2. *Proceedings of the Royal Irish Academy*. 102C, no. 4.
O'Donovan, E. 2008 The Irish, the Vikings and the English: new archaeological evidence from excavations at Golden Lane, Dublin. In S. Duffy (ed.), *Medieval Dublin VIII: Proceedings of the Friends of Medieval Dublin Symposium 2006*, 36–130. Dublin.
Ó Floinn, R. 1998 The archaeology of the early Viking Age in Ireland. In H. Clarke, M. Ní Mhaonaigh, and R. Ó Floinn (eds), *Ireland and Scandinavia in the early Viking Age*, 131–65. Dublin.
Schour, I. and Massler, M. 1944 The development of the human dentition. *Journal of the American Dental Association*, 28, 1153–60.
Simpson, L. 1999 *Director's findings: Temple Bar West*. Temple Bar Archaeological Report 5. Dublin.
Simpson, L. 2005. Viking warrior burials in Dublin: is this the *longphort*? In S. Duffy (ed.), *Medieval Dublin VI: Proceedings of the Friends of Medieval Dublin Symposium 2004*, 11–62. Dublin.
Trotter, M. and Gleser, G.C. 1952 Estimation of stature from long bones of American Whites and Negroes. *American Journal of Physical Anthropology*, 10, 463–514.
Trotter, M. and Gleser, G.C. 1958 A re-evaluation of estimation of stature based on measurements of stature taken during life and long bones after death. *American Journal of Physical Anthropology*, 16, 79–123.
Walsh, C. 2001. Dublin's southern town defences, tenth to fourteenth centuries: the evidence from Ross Road. In S. Duffy (ed.), *Medieval Dublin II: Proceedings of the Friends of Medieval Dublin Symposium 2000*, 88–127. Dublin.

Dublin's famous 'Bully's Acre': site of the monastery of Kilmainham?

LINZI SIMPSON

INTRODUCTION

This article examines the evidence for the origins of a well-known graveyard at Kilmainham in Dublin, known as 'Bully's Acre', which is located at the western end of the grounds of the seventeenth-century Royal Hospital, Kilmainham, now the Irish Museum of Modern Art (figs 1–2). New evidence came to light in the late 1980s after archaeological excavations by the late Paddy Healy established the presence of features at the site which were most likely to be related to the medieval church of St John the Baptist. His death in December 2000 unfortunately prevented Paddy from publishing these results and they are presented here in fond tribute to him.

The excavation was carried out between 1989 and 1991 and was part of a road-widening scheme being carried out along the South Circular Road at Kilmainham (archive lodged with National Museum of Ireland). This involved the removal of a section of the western boundary wall of the graveyard and a narrow strip within the line of the wall measuring approximately 80m north-south by 8.50m wide (fig. 3). The discovery during the monitoring programme of a medieval ditch sealed by eighteenth-century burials led to full-scale excavation which produced numerous finds, both medieval and post-medieval in date. In 2002 the writer, of Margaret Gowen and Co. Ltd, was commissioned by the City Archaeologist, Dr Ruth Johnson, to prepare an excavation report to accompany this artefactual collection for submission to the National Museum of Ireland (Simpson 2004). This article concentrates on the medieval aspects of that excavation report.

BULLY'S ACRE: AN EARLY CEMETERY?

The enclosed wooded graveyard at Bully's Acre, encompassing 3.6 acres, survives almost intact, perched on a prominence and overlooking the River Liffey and the Phoenix Park to the north. This northern landscape, however, has been considerably altered by the construction of the Great Southern and Western railway (a goods line was completed in 1847 and a passenger terminal in 1848), which cut a swathe through a natural gravel ridge, along the southern

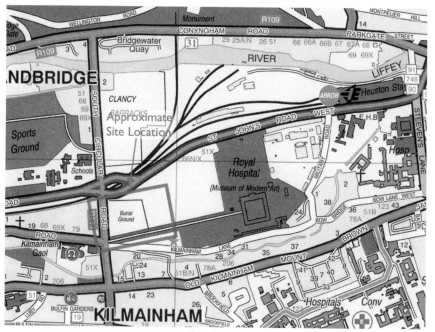

1 Site location

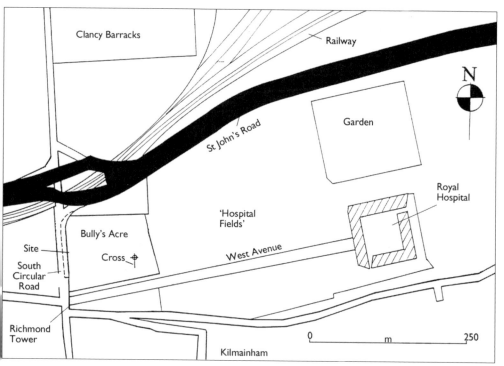

2 Detail of site

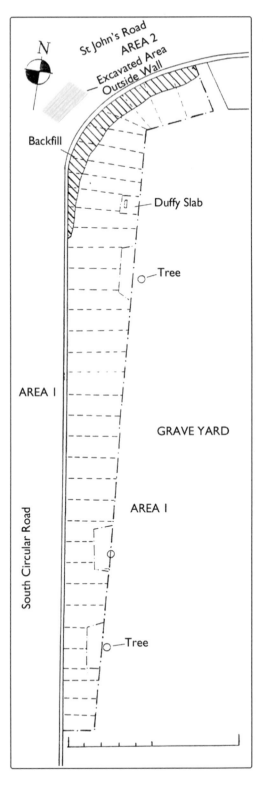

3 Overall plan of excavated area

Plate 1 The site, looking north; photo by B. Ó Ríordáin

banks of the Liffey (O'Brien 1998, 35). Bully's Acre was originally a more extensive cemetery but was divided in two by the construction of the avenue leading to the Royal hospital (from what is now the South Circular Road) in the late seventeenth century (fig. 4). The separated southern section then became the Officers' Burial Ground. A second individual burial-ground is positioned further north, on the other side of Bully's Acre but this is more modern in date, opened in 1800 for privates and non-commissioned officers. The last burial in this cemetery can be dated to 1954 (Murphy 1989, 16).

The graveyard at Bully's Acre has had something of a chequered past, as extensively charted by Murphy and Kenny in their detailed publications on the subject, especially Kenny, a work of exceptional merit (Murphy 1989; Kenny 1995). It is best known as the burial-ground or cemetery attached to the Royal Hospital of Kilmainham founded in 1681 for 'old and infirm soldiers', a function it continued to serve until 1922 (Murphy 1987, 43; Kenny 1995, 84). It was always known that the graveyard was earlier in date, however, as one of the surviving grave-slabs in the Officers' Burial Ground records the death of a member of the Hackett family in 1652, twenty-nine years before the hospital was established (see Murphy 1989, 17 for drawing and list of inscriptions). Not only that, but Charles McNeill attempted to push the origins further back

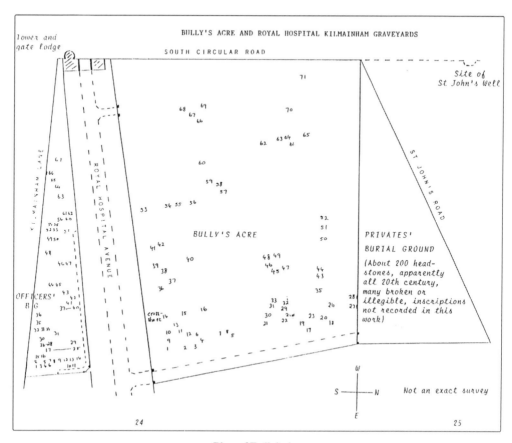

4 Plan of Bully's Acre

still when he speculated that the medieval church of St John the Baptist, recorded in the documentary sources, was located at the site of the later cemetery (McNeill 1924, 19: fig. 5). This church was attached to the priory of the order of the Knights Hospitallers, whose Dublin house was founded in the early 1170s in the fields to the east of Bully's Acre, towards and possibly including the site of the Royal Hospital. The priory at Kilmainham was the main Irish house of this powerful and influential order and it held considerable lands in the area, extending as far west as Palmerstown.

There are at least two strong indications, however, that Bully's Acre may be a site of even greater antiquity, perhaps the Early-Christian monastic site of Kilmainham (a corruption of *Cell Maignenn*, frequently referred to in the early Irish annals and other sources) (Lennox Barrow 1985; Kenny 1985). Firstly, the graveyard contains a massive decorated stone, possibly a cross shaft or grave-marker, which has been dated to between the ninth and eleventh century (Harbison 1992, 130) and, secondly, there was originally a holy well attached to

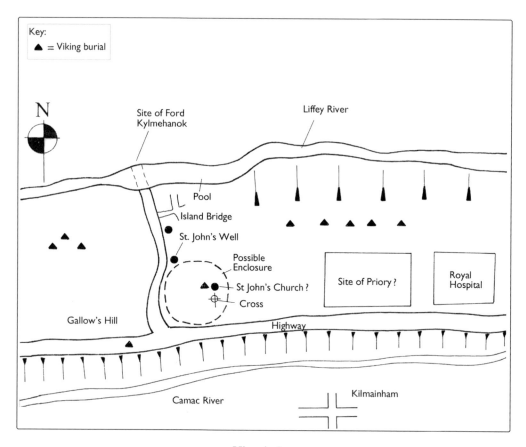

5 Historical map

the cemetery, just outside the northeast corner of the graveyard. Other incidental evidence attesting to its possible antiquity includes the reputed discovery of a collection of Viking coins and a sword at the base of the cross shaft and the (albeit undoubtedly apochryphal) tradition that Brian Bóruma (or 'Boru') and his son Murchad were buried under the shaft after the battle of Clontarf in 1014 (Kenny 1985).

This combination of evidence, then, certainly alerts the researcher to the possibility that Bully's Acre is probably considerably earlier in date than the seventeenth century and was assuredly in existence before the establishment of the Royal Hospital. The importance of the excavation under discussion is that it has produced the first archaeological evidence to support the theory that there was medieval activity at Bully's Acre most likely to be associated with the church of St John the Baptist. If this is the case, this establishes an ecclesiastical presence on the site ranging back to the late 1170s, which brings us one step closer to possible earlier origins.

THE MONASTERY OF 'CILL MAIGNENN'

Bully's Acre lies a short distance to the west of the old town of Kilmainham, which flanks the western approach to the city of Dublin, overlooking a crossing in the Liffey valley to the north (figs 5&6). The ancient settlement of Kilmainham is thought to have originally centred on the monastic establishment founded, according to Ware, sometime in the seventh century by St Maigniu, whose feast day is December 18 (Kenny 1995; Falkiner 1906–7). Not much is known about this monastery although it has been recorded that it was famed for its hospitality and that it had a sacred perennial fire known as 'Maigniu's fire', which is described in the account of the eponymous saint's *Life* (Kenny 1995, 18).

Although the precise site of the monastery is not known, Bully's Acre is certainly a good contender, when taking into account the combined evidence, such as it is, and in the absence of a firm rival site. It is on a prominent location, on top of a ridge, with sweeping views all around, and is on the main route to Dublin, where the early ecclesiastical settlement of Duibhlinn was located. The Liffey was fordable a short distance to the northeast at an early crossing place recorded in the medieval documentary sources as 'Kylmehanok', which can be located just west of the present Sarah Bridge, built *c*.1791 (figs 5&7). The early name for the ford was Cell-mo-Shamóc, the name derived from an early church thought to have been located on the north side of the Liffey somewhere near Islandbridge (Ó Floinn 1998, 134).

The cross shaft

The physical evidence at Bully's Acre includes, as already mentioned, the colossal decorated stone, 3m high, which may be the shaft of a cross and is located in the southeast corner of graveyard (see Appendix A for description). It is known that the stone was re-erected after it fell in the late eighteenth century but was probably replaced at or close to its original position, as its sheer weight would have militated against it being moved any great distance (it was recently broken in three pieces but has since been repaired). The stone is of granite and has been dated by Peter Harbison to between the ninth and the eleventh century, the latter date perhaps suggesting that the monastery struggled on for some time after the Viking invasions, although there is no evidence for this in the documentary sources. The stone is clearly important, not only from an art-historical point of view, but also in folk memory, as local tradition has it that, as mentioned previously, after the battle of Clontarf in 1014, Brian Bóruma and his son Murchad were buried under the cross, although the annals record that they were buried in Armagh (Falkiner, however, states that it was Murchad and the latter's son Tairdelbach who were buried here: Falkiner 1906–7, 279; O'Brien 1998, 43).

The cross was recorded in article in the *Dublin Penny Journal* in 1832, which was possibly written by the famous antiquarian George Petrie and he

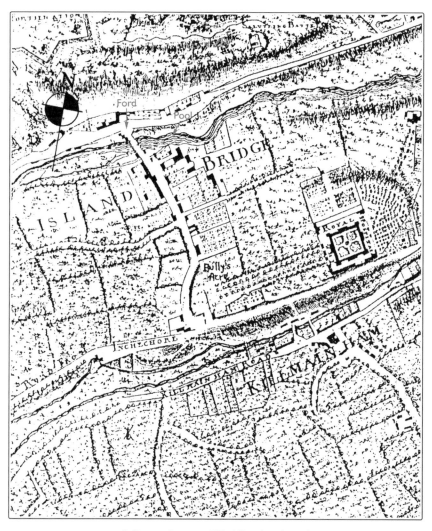

6 Rocque's map of Dublin, dated 1756

states that, when the shaft was being re-erected in 1792 after it fell, a number of coins of the Viking kings of Dublin were found at the base of it, along with a sword (known as 'O'Brien's sword') of the same period (Falkiner 1906–7, 279; Kenny 1995, 27). Healy records that these items were put on display in the Royal Hospital but that when the inmates were transferred to Chelsea in 1927 the artefacts were sent over with them and, as a result, cannot now be located. An iron bell, now in the National Museum of Ireland, was found during the railway works at Kilmainham and was probably also associated with the monastery (see Kenny 1995, 28 for photograph).

A monastic enclosure?

It is certainly of note that the stone is positioned on what appears to be a distinct bank or rising ground running along the southern boundary of the graveyard. Although this may have been associated with the construction of the avenue to the hospital in the seventeenth century, it is confined to the eastern end of the graveyard and does not continue westwards. It is therefore possible that this bank or raised ground represents the remnants of an internal enclosing feature and that the stone may have functioned as some sort of boundary stone, delineating the bank. Most striking is John Rocque's map of Dublin, dated 1756, which may preserve the shadow of a much larger enclosure, preserved in the semicircular curve of the road to Islandbridge (now the South Circular Road), bordering the cemetery on the western side (fig. 6). The curving boundaries on this side are most distinct especially when compared to the eastern side, which is devoid of any such similar characteristics, the regimented nature of the field systems there perhaps suggesting that they were laid out anew during the construction of the hospital and avenue. It is probably not coincidental, either, that the curving section of the road terminates at the northern boundary of Bully's Acre, at the precise location of the holy well (see below).

This type of topographical survival is common at important ecclesiastical centres where the presence of the enclosure is transferred into surrounding topographical features such as field systems or roadways, which prove more enduring than the monastery itself (Swan 1983). Rocque's map suggests that the original enclosure, if that is what it reflects, was probably approximately 200m in diameter, which fits within the general parameters of other large monastic sites in Ireland, for instance at Dunshaughlin, Co. Meath where the internal enclosure was 210m in diameter (Simpson 2005, 228). The complex may even have had an outer enclosure, as there are traces of a second delineation preserved in the curving field boundaries on the western side of the road.

The holy well of St John

The position of St John's holy well, then, may lend credence to the suggestion that there was an early ecclesiastical focus to the site of Bully's Acre (fig. 5). The dedication to St John can presumably be related to the foundation of the medieval priory but the original dedication was possibly to St Maignenn (Kenny 1995, 52). The presence of the well also raises the possibility that there was a predecessor to the later medieval St John's church. The fact that the church was inconveniently sited some distance from the priory complex, and that it also served a parochial function, may suggest that it had already existed, and was subsequently adopted by the order of Knights Hospitallers at the time of the Anglo-Norman invasion. A sixteenth-century description of the building describes a southern 'chapel' attached to the main building, which may just possibly refer to an earlier building (see below).

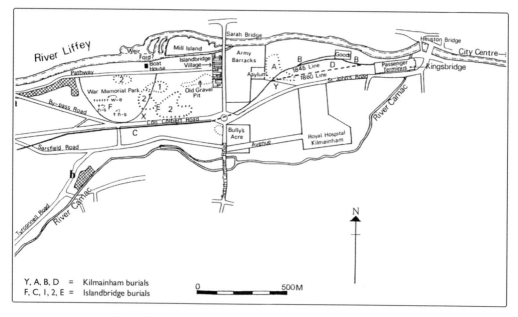

7 Plan of Islandbridge/Kilmainham burials, after O'Brien 1998

VIKING-AGE KILMAINHAM

The Viking burials

That the ninth-century Viking incursions impacted heavily on the Kilmainham area was most spectacularly demonstrated during the ground-moving works for the railway project in the mid-nineteenth century, and later on during the construction of the War Memorial Park in 1933. The excavations exposed the remains of numerous Viking burials extending along the natural gravel ridge that forms the southern bank of the river Liffey (fig. 7). The spread was extensive, stretching from Heuston station at Kilmainham, north of the Royal Hospital, as far west as the Memorial Park at Islandbridge, a distance of some 1.5m km (Wilde 1866–9). The detailed work done by O'Brien has established that the railway works produced seventeen burials, fifteen of which were of male and two female, while a total of eighteen burials were recovered at the Memorial Park, sixteen of which were of male, two female (O'Brien 1998, 37–8). These interments were accompanied by numerous grave goods including swords, shield bosses and knives, as well as decorative jewellery, some of which could be dated stylistically to the ninth century (Graham-Campbell 1976, 40).

In addition to these numbers, O'Brien has also calculated that discoveries of individual swords and other objects in the general vicinity probably indicate the presence of an additional sixteen male burials, bringing the total up to forty-nine (ibid., 40). The discovery of these individual swords, however, suggests that the Viking burials were not confined to the riverbank but extended a further 450m south at least, as far as Bully's Acre. We know this as the find-spot for a Viking sword, discovered in 1740, and recorded by Hubbard Smith as somewhere close to the stone cross marking the fabled burial place of Brian Bóruma's son (O'Brien 1998, 43). As O'Brien has noted that such finds are usually indicative of Viking warrior graves, this suggests that there was a burial somewhere in this location, perhaps deliberately interred in the monastic enclosure. The collection of coins, also reputedly found in this location, may possibly have been grave-goods associated with the burial, the massive stone shaft perhaps a marker for the grave (Kenny 1995, 26).

A second sword, which was purchased by the Royal Irish Academy in 1851, was also probably found at or close to Bully's Acre, suggesting the presence of a second Viking warrior grave in the immediate vicinity. The find spot was described as 'Mr Drum's field near Kilmainham', which is vague and hard to pin down. However, we know that the Cullens of Gallow's Hill (where Kilmainham Gaol stands) held the burial-ground and adjoining land in the 1730s and that they are recorded as renting lands to a Mr Drum after 1785, which is presumably the derivation of the place-name 'Drum's field' (ibid. 49–50; Murphy 1989, 10). The Drums were evidently a well-known family as they also had an ale house at Kilmainham.

In her detailed work on locating the burial find-spots of the Kilmainham/ Islandbridge burials, O'Brien has suggested that they may have been deliberately interred in two pre-existing early Irish cemeteries, one at Kilmainham, on the west side of Heuston Station, and the other at Islandbridge at the Memorial Park, the Vikings taking advantage of existing native settlements including their graveyards and simply reusing them (O'Brien 1998, 40–1: fig. 7). The suggestion that Bully's Acre represents the monastery of Kilmainham, however, places the ecclesiastical enclosure some distance (at least 800m) from the passenger terminal (Heuston Station) and it is unlikely that a cemetery attached to the monastery would have extended this far. In addition to this, the identification of two Viking male burials close to if not at Bully's Acre probably suggests that, instead of confining the burials to two individual areas, the burials should be viewed as a general spread, evidently most concentrated along the southern riverbank of the Liffey but with other burials extending southwards up the ridge, perhaps with some reuse of the putative monastic enclosure at Bully's Acre. Between the Heuston passenger terminal and the Islandbridge memorial park stands the military barracks now knows as Clancy Barracks, and perhaps there are no 'linking' burials between Heuston and Islandbridge for the simple reason that they were removed at the time of its construction in *c*.1857.

This combination of concentrated and dispersed burial pattern is similar to the spread of burials found along the Poddle valley, on the southern side of the medieval city. Burial finds to date in this location, although limited in number, consist of individual male warriors at Cork Street, Bride Street and Kildare Street with a concentration of five burials at the south-western side of the 'Black Pool' at South Great George's Street (four) and Ship Street Great (one), all of which can be dated to the ninth century (Simpson 2005). More recently, four additional burials have been found at Golden Lane, lying just outside (10–30m) an Early-Christian cemetery at the church site of St Michael le Pole (O'Donovan 2008, 50–2). Two of the burials were found with associated grave-goods, one of which was a warrior burial and also dated to the ninth century. The other skeleton was a female (ibid.). This spread of burials may have continued eastwards as burial mounds are recorded in eastern suburb of Dublin, at Hoggen Green (from Old Norse *haugr*, a mound) along the south bank of the Liffey, a short distance from South Great George's Street. At least two of these burial mounds survived into the seventeenth century, one of which is documented as containing burnt and scorched human bone (Duffy 2005a, 354). In addition to this, a find in the early nineteenth century included two Viking swords, four spear-heads, a shield umbo and a silver buckle, presumably originally associated with burials (Bradley 1992, 53).

This dispersal-pattern was first mooted by Ó Floinn who envisaged the interments as 'grave fields that are strung out on both sides of the Liffey, some of which were located on the sites of earlier pre-historic or Christian cemeteries, and which for the most part are located close to water' (Ó Floinn 1998, 137).

Ninth-century encampment at Bully's Acre?

The findings certainly raise the very distinct possibility that a large ninth-century Viking encampment (what the annals might call a *longphort*) was positioned somewhere in the locality of Kilmainham and the site at Bully's Acre. It has long been argued that the cemetery at Kilmainham/Islandbridge was attached to the historically-recorded *longphort* stated in the annals to have been set up at Dublin in 841. Bully's Acre is in a similarly prominent location, was ecclesiastical in function, is also close to the strategic crossing on the river and, perhaps more importantly, not far from a large natural pool at Islandbridge, on the south side of Sarah Bridge. The Liffey was tidal as far as this pool and was thus presumably navigable for the keel-less Viking vessels, which may have docked there, as they did in the 'Black Pool' of Duibhlinn further downstream (Simpson 2005, 35). It may be the case that the pool at Islandbridge served as a focal point for an early Viking settlement, which was positioned further south at Bully's Acre.

The strategic location of Kilmainham close to the ford ensured it witnessed many battles and skirmishes in the Viking period and earlier. In 1013 Brian Bóruma's son Murchad is recorded in the Annals of the Four Masters as plundering from Glendalough to Kilmainham, burning the entire country after which he camped at Dublin, laying siege unsuccessfully to the town (Falkiner 1906–7, 279). The following year Brian himself is recorded as having burnt Kilmainham just before the epic battle of Clontarf. The lands at Kilmainham probably remained in ecclesiastical hands throughout the Hiberno-Norse period, making it a suitably prestigious choice for the grant of land to the Hospitallers in the late twelfth century. It was also a militarily strategic site, situated as it was on the western approach to the city. Hence, the famous battle of Dublin in 917, in which the high-king Niall Glúndub lost his life in conflict with Vikings, was in fact fought at the ford of Cill-mo-Shamhóc near Islandbridge.

THE PRIORY OF THR KNIGHTS HOSPITALLERS

In 1170 Leinster was overrun by Anglo-Normans under Richard de Clare, earl of Pembroke (Strongbow), acting at the behest of the dispossessed king of Leinster, Diarmait Mac Murchada. Hard on their heels came various religious establishments anxious to gain a foothold in the newly-won territory. The order of Knights Hospitallers of St John of Jerusalem first arrived in what is now Co. Wexford in 1172 and soon afterwards Strongbow (whose family had close ties with the order) granted them extensive lands centred at Kilmainham (Gwynn and Hadcock 1970, 333). Pope Innocent III confirmed the possessions of the order in 1212, which, by this date, had property in nearly every province in Ireland (apart from Connacht). Their main stronghold, in terms of land, however, remained in Co. Wexford. Their main function was to provide alms for the poor and hospitality for pilgrims but they were a military order, amply demonstrated on many occasions, as for example in 1274, when Prior William Fitz-Roger commanded a contingent of the English army that travelled into the fastness of Glenmalure in the Wicklow mountains to suppress the rebellious O'Byrnes and O'Tooles (Falkiner 1907, 297). The order was divided into preceptories (there were approximately twenty after 1312), which farmed and managed the extensive lands, grouped under individual priories. However, Kilmainham was the main house and the seat of the conventual prior; thus, although it was also a preceptory under its own preceptor, all other preceptories in Ireland were subject to it (Gwynn and Hadcock 1970, 333).

St John's of Kilmainham
Although the original charter of the house does not survive, James Ware has suggested a foundation date of *c*.1174 (ibid.). However, a later dispute may

throw some further light on the date of the original grant (Gilbert 1870, 495–501; idem, 1889–1944, I, 160–63). The dispute involved property along the Liffey, which the citizens claimed had been granted to them as part of the grant of the city's liberties, but which the prior claimed had formed part of their own original grant. It has been plausibly demonstrated that the first peramabulation of the boundaries, within which the liberties had effect, took place at the time of Henry II's visit to Dublin in 1171–2 (Duffy 2005b, 95–117). This may suggest that the hospital was founded shortly thereafter, when the boundaries as then fixed were still relatively new.

Their grant was considerable, stretching as far west as Palmerstown, and including Chapelizold on the north side of the Liffey. Kilmainham was also an attractive location, as it marked the western limit of the liberty of the city and was thus not subject to the jurisdiction of the hundred court of the city. This border location, however, was to result in many clashes with the latter throughout the medieval period, most notably with regard to the Liffey and the rights pertaining to it, as mentioned above. A partial register (of the chapter acts) of Kilmainham house does exist but this records events that are much later than the foundation, dating to between 1326 and 1339 (McNeill 1943, 111; Lennox Barrow 1985, 108).

The priory complex

A good description of the house and its possessions can be gleaned from the documentary sources related to the dissolution of the monasteries in the sixteenth century, when it is recorded that the prior was seized of

> the said priory with all its buildings, and three gardens, and an orchard walled with stone, four towers erected on the said walls; one tower on the northlands over the bridge crossing the river Lyffe, which gardens and orchards were reserved for the use of the hospital, 260 acres of arable land, the demesne, annual value £13: 12 acres of meadow, a large wood containing 42 acres on the north of the river, another wood of 10 acres of underwood, and 260 acres of pasture and briars.

The inquisition also lists additional possessions including a mill of the Liffey, a fulling mill on the Camac, a salmon weir with nets on the river, as well as the rectories of Chapelizod, Ballyfermot, and Palmerstown (ibid.; Falkiner 1906–7, 284–5).

This record describes the encastellated nature of the complex, a common type associated with the Hospitallers, as their priories were usually laid out as fortified residences or castles with an emphasis on towers and enclosing walls. A description gleaned from the documentary sources by McNeill provides even greater detail and describes an inner and outer enclosure with a castle and precinct wall (and postern gate), as well as a gate tower and corner towers and an outer ditch. Within the precinct there were various residences, private apartments for permanent guests and a chapel, as well as a prison. The priory also had a great hall (McNeill 1924, 18–19).

The properties surrendered by the priory at its dissolution totalled 10,000 acres of land, as well as various properties including castles and mills (Gwynn and Hadcock 1970, 335). The buildings of the priory itself were reported to be among the best in Ireland and were valued at £725, an enormous sum. This was confirmed by the fact that on 7 April 1541 they were considered suitable as a residence for the king's deputy in Ireland (ibid.).

The site of the priory
The exact site of the complex is not known. The most important cartographic source, the Down Survey map (by Robert Gilder, 1655–6), depicts it to the east of what is now the South Circular Road and to the north of the town of Kilmainham but this map is notoriously difficult to scale (fig. 8). A source dated to 1681 sheds some light on the situation, noting:

> on the west side of the said ground [the Royal Hospital, Kilmainham] had been formerly a large pile of buildings which consisted of several quadrangles but now all ruinous and most of the foundations dug up: there only remained standing in the year 1680 part of the walls of the chapel, the stones whereof were taken down and carefully removed to the new hospital and wholly used in the building of the present chapel of the same (Kenny 1995, 43).

This description has it categorically that the priory complex lay to the west of the Royal Hospital, and thus it was located in the fields between Bully's Acre on the west and the Hospital on the east. However, in 1979, during refurbishment of the Hospital, medieval masonry was exposed within the build, which raised the possibility that some of the priory survived the demolition and was incorporated within the new hospital (ibid.). This is highly plausible as the reference above makes clear that there were several quadrangles originally attached to the priory. It is also possible that it may suggest reuse of the original stones, as per the reference above, since the priory buildings must have been the main source of stone.

The position of the main complex, however, to the west of the Royal Hospital supports the theory of Childers and Stewart, writing a history of that institution in 1921, in which they record that the site of the priory was along the crescent of a hollow located in the 'Master's Fields' ['the hospital fields'] as they could see traces of foundations there (Childers and Stewart 1921; Kenny 1995, 89). This location was partially confirmed in 1948 when excavations were carried out 'towards Bully's Acre' by Gerhard Bersu, where he found floor

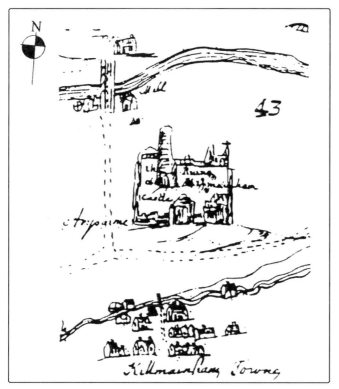

8 Down Survey, dated 1655–6

slabs and a well, in addition to a stone wall and fragments of medieval tiles (ibid., 90).

The church and cemetery at Kilmainham
The documentary sources record that the priory had both a church and chapel servicing the community. The chapel was dedicated to St Mary and this is probably the building with a cross depicted on the Down Survey map (1656), in the northeast corner of the quadrangle. The church, however, appears to have been far larger in size and is named in the documentary sources as St John's of Kilmainham, the dedication presumably taken from the priory. In an extent (or list of properties and possessions) in 1541 it was recorded that

> The church annexed to the site is the parish church, and is, at present, too large. Part of it, namely the chapel on the south, can be thrown down without loss, and this ought to be done, as the parishioners owing to their extreme poverty are unable to maintain the church and what would remain is sufficient to them (Kenny 1995, 35).

This reference suggests that the church was a substantial building and this is confirmed in the documentary sources, as in 1330 when there were a total of ten chaplains perpetually appointed to it. By 1572 the church of St John was roofless while St Mary's chapel was in use as a stable, its steeple 'being broken'. St John's was finally demolished in 1612 but the walls of St Mary's chapel within the complex were recorded as still standing in 1680 (ibid., 35, 37–8).

McNeill suggested that the church site was close to the cross shaft, placing it at Bully's Acre, some distance west of the priory. This was based on the fact that it was recorded that when the Viking sword was found near the cross shaft in *c.*1740 is was 'on a tiled floor, near the site of the old Priory of Kilmainham' (O'Brien 1998, 39) A number of medieval floor tiles were recovered from this area and were exhibited in 1859 at a meeting of the Royal Irish Society. These tiles were recorded as

> dug up under the portion of an ancient cross at the cemetery known as 'Bully's Acre' near the Royal Hospital of Kilmainham. The types of the ornamentation of these tiles, originally, no doubt, forming a portion of the flooring of the church of the Knights of St John … (Anon. 1858–9, 444).

The case for the location of St John's at Bully's Acre is strengthened by the fact there does appear to have been a graveyard at Kilmainham and this was presumably attached to John's church. A reference is preserved in the early fourteenth-century Justiciary Rolls to the effect that two criminals, executed for murder, were

> taken down as dead from the gallows and carried in a cart to Kilmeynan to be buried, [but] were found alive and took refuge in the church there.

The men sought sanctuary in the church and were eventually pardoned (Mills and Griffith 1905–50, III, 219). Apart from the intriguing circumstances that could result in two men not dying on the gallows and making their escape to Kilmainham, the reference is important in two other aspects. It demonstrates that there was a graveyard at Kilmainham but, more importantly, that it may have been a common burial ground, as both men were criminals. This fits in with the later history of Bully's Acre, which was always considered a paupers' graveyard.

The priory in the sixteenth and early seventeenth century
The priory, however, was to suffer the same fate as all the rest of the ecclesiastical establishments during the Dissolution when it was surrendered by its prior, Sir John Rawson (Gwynn and Hadcock 1970, 335). It was briefly restored in the 1550s under Queen Mary but was taken back into government hands shortly afterwards and the buildings repaired for use in the summer

9 Excavated area and fosse

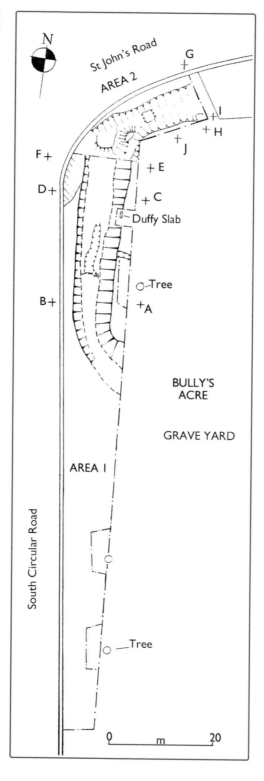

months by the Irish administration. By the 1660s the former priory (the buildings of which were ruinous) and its land were to form part of the great Phoenix Park laid out by the newly-created Lord Lieutenant of Ireland, the Duke of Ormonde (Kenny 1995, 40–2).

THE ROYAL HOSPITAL

In 1677 Ormonde started to put in train plans for a hospital for retired soldiers and in 1680 King Charles II directed that a hospital be built for the aged and maimed soldiers of the army of Ireland, 'near the old ruinous building commonly called the Castle of Kilmainham' (ibid., 43). Thus the lands at Bully's Acre were not to remain as part of the Phoenix Park but to be given over for the new hospital. The remaining complex, including the castle and the chapel attached, was then demolished, an event that was recorded by the diarist John Dunton, who, on visiting Kilmainham in 1698, commented that 'there are no marks of the convent of the priors now to be seen' (ibid.). The hospital continued as a home for retired soldiers until 1927, after which time it was taken over by the Garda Síochána as their headquarters. In 1949, however, the buildings were deemed to be structurally unsound and were converted into a storage facility until their complete refurbishment between 1980 and 1984, at the behest of the then Taoiseach, Charles Haughey, to provide the new home of the Irish Museum of Modern Art.

BULLY'S ACRE IN THE EIGHTEENTH CENTURY

The colourful history of the graveyard is well documented in the eighteenth century and was very familiar to the citizens of Dublin, mainly because it was a communal graveyard, where many of the poorer classes were buried. In addition to this, the celebrations, which took place at the holy well on the feast of St John (24 June), achieved carnival-like status and were a huge social event for Dubliners, with hundreds camping out in the fields (Murphy 1989, 7–8). Not surprisingly, the Royal Hospital officials considered this a great nuisance and a report in 1737 by the committee of Royal Hospital governors recorded that the hospital fields were 'generally by day and night full of idle and disorderly people, the grass is trod and the cattle stray' (ibid., 8).

Eventually, in 1755, a Major General Michael O'Brien Dilkes, then Master of the hospital, applied to the magistrates to have the 'nocturnal revels' ended and to enclose Bully's Acre within stone walls (the latter of which was not carried out at this time). Other drastic measures included levelling some of the existing graves and removing the headstones, which dramatically altered the burial-ground. By 1795 Bully's Acre had evidently fallen into a bad state of repair as it was voted a 'public nuisance' while the grand jury noted that, in this 'once highly venerated repository for the dead', shocking scenes were exhibited, including 'swine devouring human bodies while in the most pernicious state of putrefaction, and the torn remains of males and females left exposed to public view' (ibid., 10–11). The result was a decision to enclose the cemetery with a high wall, which by 1795, was duly carried out.

Bully's Acre was also infamous as a favourite haunt of the 'body-snatchers' in the eighteenth and the early nineteenth century and this added greatly to the notoriety of the graveyard. The bodies were stolen for use in the anatomy schools (before donation was made legal by the Anatomy Act of 1832) and Bully's Acre was the preferred source, mainly because it had a plentiful supply of paupers, whose graves were less likely to be guarded at night. When cholera hit Dublin in 1832 a total of 3,200 hurried burials took place in the graveyard, forcing the Board of Health for the city of Dublin to close it down the same year because of the 'many bodies lying exposed, without any covering' (ibid.).

The holy well of St John was removed during the railway works to the north of the site and, although it was discovered several times, it is now lost, the most likely site being on the west side of Islandbridge Road, opposite Bully's Acre.

THE EXCAVATION

Introduction

The excavation was located on the western side of Bully's Acre, along the South Circular Road boundary, which was widened on the eastern side by approximately 8.50m (fig. 9). The existing stone boundary wall was demolished in advance of the works, exposing a strip of land formerly in the graveyard, which measured approximately 80m north-south by 8.50m in width at the northern end, narrowing to 4m in width at the southern end. Paddy Healy divided the excavation into two areas. Area 1 represented the north-south section along the South Circular Road, and Area 2 the east-west section at the northern end, along St John's Road.

Summary of findings

The medieval phase was represented by the construction of a substantial ditch, which was cut into subsoil, sometime in the mid-thirteenth/early fourteenth century (fig. 10). It may originally have formed some part of an enclosure feature and it evidently functioned for a considerable period of time, as it was only infilled in the mid-seventeenth century, suggesting that it had been continually re-established throughout the centuries. At this time it was backfilled with demolition masonry, which was identified by Healy as being

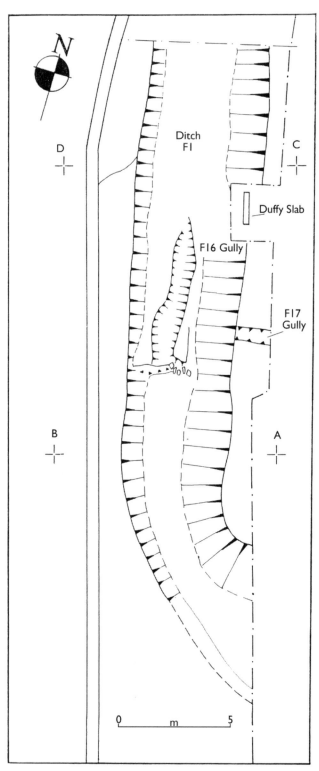

10 Detail of fosse

medieval in date and can presumably be related to the demolition of the medieval church of St John's in 1612.

The area was then left open for a period of time and a sod layer gradually accumulated but was eventually sealed by 3m of what Healy termed 'burial soil', which contained disarticulated human remains, as well as fragments of headstones, the result, no doubt, of Dilkes's 'levelling' operation. However, inhumation continued at the cemetery, as at least four other burials survived *in situ* dating to the eighteenth and nineteenth centuries, as well as a mass grave related to the cholera epidemic noted above. The remains of an eighteenth-century pier were also located on the southern side of the graveyard, presumably marking an early entrance.

The medieval period

The ditch F1 As stated previously, the excavation of Area 1 revealed the remains of a substantial ditch or fosse, F1, which could be dated to the thirteenth/fourteenth century and was located at the northern end of Area 1, representing the earliest activity on the site (figs 9 and 10). It was orientated north-south but curved eastwards at the southern end, raising the possibility that it may have formed part of some sort of enclosing feature, the western side of which was at least 27m in length. The northern end was truncated and did not survive.

Plate 2 The medieval ditch, F1, looking north; photo by B. Ó Ríordáin

Plate 3 The medieval ditch, F1, looking south; photo by B. Ó Ríordáin

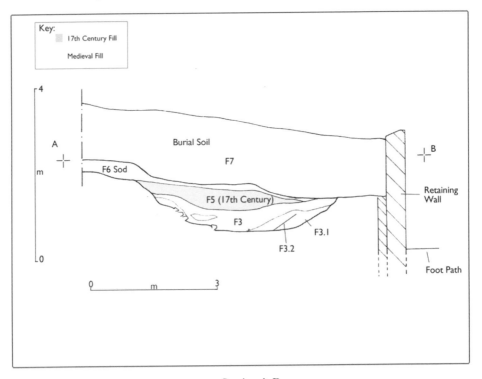

11 Section A–B

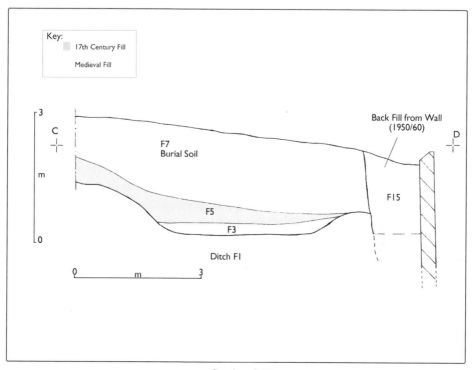

Key:
- 17th Century Fill
- Medieval Fill

12 Section C-D

This ditch measured, on average, 5m in width at the upper level, narrowing to 3m in width at the base (figs 11–13). It was not deep, measuring only 1m to 1.50m along the eastern side and approximately 0.65m on the western side but the evidence suggests that it had been substantially truncated at the upper levels. The surviving width at the base may indicate that this was originally a very substantial feature, which could have been up to 8m in width based on a conservative depth of 2.50m. The ditch was cut into natural grey gravel/clays marking a break in slope from east to west, which reflected a drop in the ground level of approximately 0.60m (from east to west). Thus the ditch was positioned along a ridge bordering slightly higher ground to the east (the graveyard proper).

The water channels That the ditch originally held or channelled water is suggested by the presence of a gully, F16, which extended along the base of the ditch and was at least 6m in length (fig. 10). It was substantial in size, measuring 0.60m in width but was only 0.20m in depth; the profile suggested it was natural feature created by running water (from south to north). The ditch then gradually began to silt up, as was demonstrated by the sand and silt layers deposited on either side. The ditch was also fed externally as a second gully, F17, which was outside the line of the ditch, fed directly into it (fig. 10).

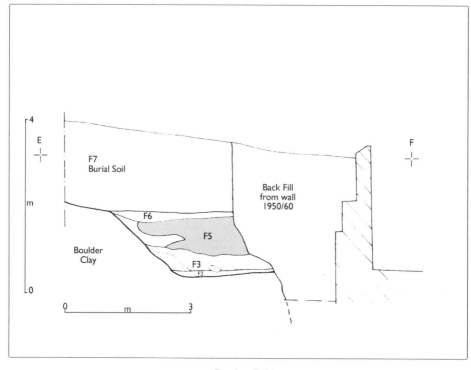

13 Section E-F

The deposits, F2, F3 and F5 The primary fill at the northern end of the truncated ditch was a lens of fine white sandy mud, F2, which was deposited sporadically along the base, presumably by the water in the ditch (fig. 13). This deposit was up to 0.10m in depth and contained inclusions of charcoal, iron and slag fragments, oyster and mussel shell as well as considerable assorted animal bone. Fragments of pottery and medieval floor tiles dated the layer to the thirteenth/fourteenth century. Lenses of sand and silt were also recorded lining the sides of the ditch and Healy suggests that these were 'natural deposits which resulted from growth and decay over a period of four centuries'. The layer F3.1 was made up of gravel and sand, which accumulated along the western side of the ditch and included lenses of silt and mud (fig. 11). This was a sizable depth, at over 0.40m in depth and was probably indicative of a substantial volume of water. The lens F3.2 was similar in type and depth and was described by Healy as 'black organic silt with small stones'.

These sand and silt deposits were then sealed by the main fill of the ditch F3, which was up to 0.60m in depth and described by Healy, as 'a homogenous black compacted silty clay and ash deposit, which contained flecks of shell and snail'. The inclusions of ash deposits are indicative of fires or hearths and may

Plate 4 The fill of the ditch F1 and burial soil, looking northeast; photo by B. Ó Ríordáin

have been related to either industrial or domestic occupation close by. Elsewhere in the ditch Healy describes this deposit as 'a black organic gravely soil', which evidently included lenses of sand and gravel, some of which were concentrated along the bottom of the ditch. This ditch fill, F3, produced a series of finds including animal bone, oyster shell, a large amount of thirteenth-/fourteenth-century pottery (mainly of red fabric with green glaze, including jug handles), a whetstone with groove(s), antler tines, numerous pieces of iron slag and part of a furnace tray. Other artefacts also included worked flint (used for cutting or scraping), as well as fragments of hard white cementatious mortar.

Discussion The physical evidence of a ditch at Bully's Acre throws up interesting possibilities about conditions in the medieval suburb of Kilmainham in the thirteenth and fourteenth centuries. The ditch was probably originally substantial in size and may have had some sort of defensive function, perhaps enclosing the church. There is no doubt that the Anglo-Norman colony in Ireland was in contraction by the late thirteenth/early fourteenth century which saw the hinterland of Dublin under ongoing threat from the resurgent Irish, based in the Leinster mountains (Simpson 1994,

208–10). Their continual raiding attacks resulted in a significant depopulation and considerable swathes of land were rendered waste (Lydon 1994, 151–89). The city itself did not escape, as revealed in the surviving 'extent' of the archiepiscopal manor of St Sepulchre, compiled in 1326. This demonstrated that even this manor, the caput of which was practically within the city (the present-day Kevin Street Garda Station incorporates part of the palace) was in a near derelict state, and the hall chamber castle and kitchen are mentioned specifically as being ruinous and the prison 'now broken and thrown down' (Simpson 1997, 31). The moat or ditch at Bully's Acre may therefore have had a defensive element, constructed in the late thirteenth/early fourteenth century around the church at precisely the same time that the English colony in Ireland was experiencing difficulties.

What must also be taken into account, however, is that finds from the ditch at Bully's Acre are suggestive, not only of an ecclesiastical presence (the floor tiles), but of a possibly lay community living close by if not at the site. The iron and bronze slag, as well as the furnace bottom, is a clear indication that there was some sort of metal-working taking place in the immediate vicinity while the antler tines are waste products of bone working, possibly bone-comb making. In addition to this, the large amount of pottery and butchered animal bone recovered is also another settlement indicator.

Taking this evidence into account it may be the case that what survives at Bully's Acre is the remains of a 'moated site', a settlement type which emerges in the thirteenth and fourteenth centuries in response to the worsening political climate (Simpson 1994, 216–17). The basic defining feature was a square or rectangular platform containing the homestead, which was surrounded by a water-filled moat, often with an internal or external bank. In Ireland, the sites are usually located in rural frontier situations while in England they are often associated with church or castle sites. The site at Bully's Acre, while in the shadow of the great priory, was, nevertheless, in an exposed frontier position, on the western flank of the city and vulnerable to the 'smash and grab' raids of the rebellious Irish, under the leadership of O'Byrne and O'Toole. It is possible that there were other similar types of defended sites dotted around the immediate suburbs, outside the city walls.

Truncation and backfilling of the ditch, seventeenth century
The ditch was significantly damaged when the ground level was reduced and the remaining section of the ditch was backfilled, an activity that can be dated to the seventeenth century. The fill (F5) consisted of masonry rubble, which, Healy suggested, was the remains of the church of St John, which was demolished, according to the documentary sources in 1612 (figs 11–13). These rubble deposits measured between 0.60m and 1m in depth and was described by Healy as 'masonry rubble and loose mortar in which were found numerous medieval

Plate 5 Excavation area, looking south; photo by K. Weldon

Plate 6 Excavation area, looking north; photo by K. Weldon

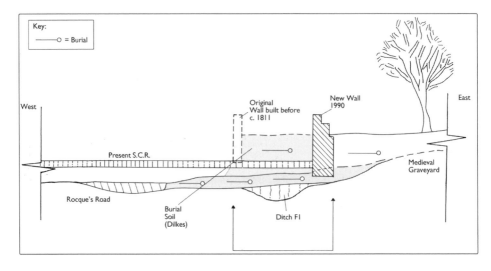

14 Schematic section

decorated floor tiles'. Healy describes the layer as having significant amounts of 'small building stones', which suggested to him that the larger ones had been picked out for reuse, perhaps during the construction of the Royal Hospital.

The stone recovered from the ditch had clearly originated in some masonry structure as many had large mortar fragments attached. The mortar was a hard white cement-like medieval mortar, which contained small pebble inclusions, measuring 1mm in diameter (description from sample, which forms part of the collection). The masonry and rubble deposits from the church may also have been put into a large pit at the northern end of the site in Area 2, as Healy records a section at this end, which indicates that the ground was disturbed to at least 3.60m in depth (not illustrated). The lowest level or primary deposit, F10, is described in the section as a 'deposit of small stones and mortar', which was up to 0.44m in depth and this was sealed by a second deposit of masonry, F11, which was of similar depth. The similarity in these deposits may suggest that they can be equated to the upper fill of the ditch, F5.

The graveyard deposits were dated to the eighteenth century and there was no evidence of medieval burials in the small area examined. The infilled truncated ditch appeared to have lain fallow for some period, since a soil layer, 0.10m in depth, had gradually accumulated which sealed the ditch and formed the topsoil elsewhere.

The eighteenth-century cemetery
The burial soil This old sod was subsequently sealed by the introduction of the 'burial soil' (F7: see below), which can probably be related to the levelling operation carried out by Dilkes in the mid-eighteenth century as part of the

Plate 7 Excavation area, looking northwest; photo by K. Weldon

Plate 8 Standing stone, looking west; photo by K. Weldon

works to enclose the graveyard. This 'burial soil' contained a large amount of disarticulated remains and fragments of headstones and was a consistent 2m in depth. Interestingly, some of the bones still had traces of lime on them and this can be tied directly to Dilkes, as it is recorded that he spread lime to decay the bones quickly.

Dilkes appears to have levelled the main burial-ground area to the east of the excavation site and pushed the deposits down the natural slope, towards the west. In doing so, medieval deposits must have been disturbed as the burial soil contained a large number of medieval finds. The newly-infilled area was then used for burial as was demonstrated by the survival of four intact burials (one in a coffin) cutting through the soil deposits to almost the old ground level (F14), at the northern end of the site (in Area 2).

The 'body snatchers' Healy also found numerous pits, which contained dumps of cut and sawn human bones in an area outside the site to the west, under the present South Circular Road, confirming that the graveyard possibly originally extended as far as the curving boundary depicted by Rocque. These were clearly the end product of the 'body snatchers' much referred to in the documentary sources who evidently reinterred the corpses having made off with what was required of their bodies. A mass grave of men, women and children was also unexpectedly found during the monitoring, which could be related to the cholera epidemics of the nineteenth century.

The finds
The excavation produced a large number of artefacts, which were predo-minantly eighteenth century in date but included a significant assemblage of medieval finds suggesting the presence of a site of some importance. Most dominant was the collection of pottery consisting, for the most part, of green-glazed local ware, distinctive for its orange fabric and mica inclusions, and datable to the thirteenth and fourteenth centuries. Imported wares were not well represented and were confined to several small sherds of Saintonge. Far more important in terms of establishing the type and significance of the site was the assortment of eighteen fragments of ceramic floor tiles recovered from the ditch. The majority were line-impressed, which can be dated generally from the early fourteenth to the sixteenth century, while one was a two-coloured tile, probably of thirteenth-century date (Lennon 2004). The tiles are evidently high-status as they can be compared directly with similar examples found in Dublin at Christ Church cathedral, St Audoen's church, St Mary's abbey, St Nicholas church, St Patrick's cathedral and St Saviour's friary. Other parallels include the Dominican friary in Drogheda, Kildare cathedral, Great Connell priory, Co. Kildare, and Bective abbey, Co. Meath (Eames and Fanning 1988, 89–91).

Plate 9 Detail of standing stone; photo by K. Weldon

Plate 10 The graveyard, looking west; photo by K. Weldon

Plate 11 Looking east, with the hospital in the background; photo by K. Weldon

The lower ditch-fill also produced slag fragments, charcoal and a furnace bottom, which is suggestive of some sort of metal-working in the immediate area in the medieval period. Other artefacts included a horse-shoe, a pair of antler tines, bronze slag and iron slag as well as numerous shells (mussel and oyster) and butchered animal bone. The most predominant find of the upper fill of the ditch were the cut stone fragments, which clearly originated from a medieval building, presumably the church of St John. Healy records a number which had 'splayed sides and were possibly of thirteenth-century date', and scaled pencil drawings identify at least ten separate fragments. In his notes he specifically mentions two pieces of cut limestone as likely to have originated in St John's church as they were part of a window mullion with an engaged column, which, he suggests may originally have been from a chapel window. The current location of this cut stone is not known but it may have been reburied in the graveyard as part of the programme of works.

CONCLUSIONS

The importance of the excavation at Bully's Acre cannot be over-emphasized, primarily in the evidence it provides for medieval occupation, which in turn, allows us to extrapolate about possible earlier origins for the site. Although the physical remains are limited to some sort of defended enclosure and occupation of the site, the artefacts from this feature highlight the fact that this graveyard, as suspected for some time, has much earlier origins, which take us back into the thirteenth/fourteenth century at least and possibly much earlier. The most significant finds were the cut-stone masonry fragments and the medieval floor tiles, the latter almost exclusively indicators of ecclesiastical sites, providing the first piece of significant evidence that the church of St John was located at the cemetery. These reveal that the church was evidently a substantial building and expensively furnished in the interior as the tiles can be compared directly to similar examples found at some of the most important ecclesiastical buildings in Ireland.

Having established that Bully's Acre is probably the site of St John's church, serious consideration has to be given to the possibility that the church was reoccupying the site of the Early-Christian monastery of Cell Maignenn, recorded in the documentary sources. The tentative enclosure, the holy well and, perhaps most importantly, the ancient cross-shaft, all combine to suggest as much, especially in the absence of an obvious rival site. The continuing importance of Kilmainham is reflected in its subsequent history throughout the Viking and Anglo-Norman periods. Also, the possibility that the Viking burial fields, hitherto thought to be confined to the banks of the Liffey, may possibly have extended some distance southwards up onto the ridge, is of

Plate 12 The 'hospital fields'; photo by K. Weldon

Plate 13 The avenue, looking east, with the south wall of the graveyard on the left;
photo by K. Weldon

Plate 14 Medieval cut stone loose in ha-ha on north side of the avenue; photo by K. Weldon

crucial importance in understanding the widespread and extensive nature at Viking presence at Kilmainham and Islandbridge. The presence of at least one Viking burial within Bully's Acre is also significant as it suggests the deliberate reuse of the high-status Early-Christian church as a place of burial in the Viking period. Finally, the takeover of the church of St John by the Knights Hospitallers was also most likely to have been a calculated decision, being the conscious adaptation by Dublin's new Anglo-Norman masters of the prestigious site of Cill Maignenn; incorporation of the site into the priory complex was no doubt a deliberate act, which reflected on the status of the priory of the order of the Knights Hospitallers and also served to establish their dominance in the area.

FUTURE DIRECTIONS

The site of the priory remains one of the most important and, as yet, un-investigated archaeological sites in Dublin that urgently requires a focused and discrete research strategy or framework, which can allow us to plan for the future of the site.

Unusually, the site of the priory has not been touched by the massive building programme of the 'Celtic Tiger' and remains an open public green-space today. This could be investigated as part of a research framework using non-invasive methods such as geophysical survey or ground-probing radar, in combination with archaeological assessment and investigation, which could help establish the exact site of the priory, in advance of any redevelopment of the lands.

It should be noted that the stone-revetted ditch or 'ha-ha' feature along the northern side of the avenue (leading from the cemetery to the Hospital) includes medieval cut stone. This material urgently requires to be surveyed and recovered.

ACKNOWLEDGMENTS

The author would like to thanks Kevin Weldon for all his work on the post-excavation project, most notably his efforts with the figures and plates of the original archive. He also produced all the accompanying figures for this article. Thanks are also due to Nuala Hiney who was responsible for the finds, to Dr Ruth Johnson for commissioning the work, and Lindsay Rafter for the graphics. Margaret Gowen and Co. Ltd, as always, supported this article.

Plate 15 Burial F4, with slab; photo by B. Ó Ríordáin

Plate 16 One of the burials; photo by B. Ó Ríordáin

Plate 17 Mass
grave; photo by
B. Ó Ríordáin

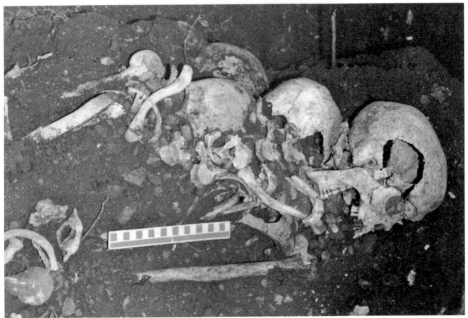

Plate 18 Mass grave; photo by B. Ó Ríordáin

Plate 19 Skull with hole from anatomical studies; photo by B. Ó Ríordáin

Plate 20 Coffin handles; photo by B. Ó Ríordáin

APPENDIX A
DESCRIPTION OF THE CROSS SHAFT

(by Patrick Healy (†))

At the top of the shaft are the remains of the round hollows in the angles of the arms and what appears to be a fragment of the ring. The two broader faces are decorated, one with an interlace of broad bands in large circular loops, of rather Scandinavian type, ending in two tassles. There are some errors in the overlapping. On the opposite face is a single band down the centre of the panel, ending in a pair of spirals. This band divides at the top into two strands, and it is probable that the two strands were twisted together to form one rope. This feature of a band down the centre of the panel can be seen at Kilgobbin, Co. Dublin where it ends in two leaves and also as Kilfenora, Co. Clare, where there are two twisted ropes which divide at the top as at Kilmainham, while at bottom they form a large triangular panel, which has been identified by Fergus O'Farrell as the outline of a box tomb, probably of the founder.

APPENDIX B
EXAMINATION OF HUMAN REMAINS FROM BULLY'S ACRE, KILMAINHAM, DUBLIN 8

(by Máire Delaney M.B. (†))

(Dated 12 December 1990; personal communication between L. Simpson and Máire Delaney (†) in 2002)

Ms Delaney stated that a large number of skeletons came from a large mass-grave that was found unexpectedly during the monitoring programme. The skeletons were excavated and reinterred that day in a garden attached to the National Centre for Arts and Culture, at Kilmainham hospital. Ms Delaney had a collection of pathology specimens (presumably from this grave); these are housed in University College, Dublin. She indicated that the mass grave was associated with the cholera epidemic of 1832.

Condition: Fragmented and disarticulated due to damage while being lifted. It was not possible to determine which bones came from which body.
Preservation: Very good while *in situ*.
Burial rite: Most were extended, supine, inhumations orientated with the head to the west. At least one of the groups was found where there was no attempt at alignment and bodies were closely packed. Some bodies were buried in coffins, some without. There was a very high density of burial with much disturbance of older burials by subsequent ones.
Age at death: Remains of all ages from infancy to old age were represented.
Sex: Both sexes were represented.
Nutrition: Appears to have been adequate in most cases. A soft diet seems to have been common.
Pathology: There are several cases of a) infection of the bone, b) osteoarthritis c) periodontal disease, d) carries, e) indication of mild vitamin D/calcium deficiency.

Trauma: There are two healed fractures of long bones and a healed broken nose.
Comments: This is a unique opportunity to excavate a city cemetery of this period.
With correct archaeological excavation, the information could provide a very valuable
picture of the lifestyle and health of the working people of Dublin.

APPENDIX C
REPORT ON MEDIEVAL FLOOR AND ROOF TILES
FROM BULLY'S ACRE, KILMAINHAM, DUBLIN 8
(E598)

(by Máire-Anne Lennon, formerly of Margaret Gowen & Co. Ltd)

Introduction A total of fourteen fragments of line-impressed floor tiles, one two-
coloured floor tile, and two line-impressed roof tiles, were recovered from the
excavation at Bully's Acres, Kilmainham Road, Dublin 8. None of the tile was found
in situ. The tiles are described using Eames and Fanning's typology and the letter 'L'
indicates the category of line-impressed tile while the letter 'T' indicates a two-colour
tile. The number, which follows the letters, refers to the decorative motif on the tile.

There are three main types of decorative techniques classified by Eames and
Fanning (1988), two-colour, line-impressed and relief. The majority of the medieval
floor tiles recovered from Bully's Acre (E598) are line-impressed, with the exception of
one tile fragment, which is a two-coloured tile fragment. Line-impressed tiles are dated
from the early fourteenth century to the sixteenth century while two-coloured tiles are
slightly earlier, dating predominantly to the thirteenth century.

The distribution of medieval floor tiles was mainly confined to the areas of Anglo-
Norman influence in Ireland and it is most likely that the earliest examples were
imported into Ireland through trade. These decorative techniques were then adopted
through the establishment of a local industry. Unlike England, there is a lack of
decorated floor tiles in secular buildings and the majority of floor tiles come from
ecclesiastical sites dotted around the Leinster area.

Line-impressed floor tile Line-impressed floor tiles were manufactured from
earthenware clays, which were formed in a mould and then covered in sand. It was
shaped and laid out to dry on wooden boards or on the ground. When the clay was
partially dry the decoration was stamped into the tile face using a large stamp, which
covered the tile and was struck with a hammer. The tile was then covered with a lead
glaze and fired in a clay-walled kiln. Only two types of lead glazes were commonly
used: a lead glaze, and a lead glaze to which copper and brass were added (Eames and
Fanning 1988, 13). This could produce a total of six colours:

- Yellow (tile coated with a white clay or slip and a lead glaze)
- Brown (applying lead glaze directly to the red tile body)
- Light green (tile coated with a white clay or slip and glazed with a lead glaze with
  added copper)
- Dark green (applying a lead glaze with added copper directly to the tile body)
- Olive green (applying lead glaze directly to a grey tile body)
- Black (applying high copper lead glaze to a red or grey tile body)

Two-coloured tile Two-coloured floor tiles were manufactured in a similar way to line-impressed tiles. The decoration was stamped into the tile face and the cavities were then filled with white clay. After firing, the white clay turned yellow, with the red colour of the tile body turning brown. This resulted in a two-colour faced tile.

Line-impressed floor tile

E598:774:L76: This design comprises of a foliate spray within a circular band with alternate four foils and Is. The decoration is set diagonally and would have originally formed part of a four tile unit. The tile is of red earthenware clay with a grey core and has an olive green glaze. It measures 62.3mm x 60.1mm x 19.5mm thick. In Dublin this tile type is found at Christ Church cathedral, St Audoen's church, St Mary's abbey, St Nicholas's church, St Patrick's cathedral and St Saviour's friary. This type was also found on the site of the Dominican friary in Drogheda (Eames and Fanning, 1988, 91).

E598:613:L47: Two fragments of floor tile were assigned this number. The decoration on the smaller one is unidentifiable. The decoration on the larger fragment is a variant of L46. It consists of a four foil within an anti-clockwise scroll. This floral design would have fitted together with other tiles like a jigsaw to make a larger recurring overall pattern. Both tiles are made of red earthenware clay with a grey core. The smaller fragment measures 54.4mm x 35.5mm x 20mm thick. The larger fragment measures 62.5mm x 61.7mm x 19mm thick. They both have an olive green glaze. This tile type is found on sites including Christ Church cathedral, St Patrick's cathedral, excavations at High Street, Dublin, Kildare cathedral, and Great Connell priory, Co. Kildare (Eames and Fanning 1988, 89).

E598:765:L73: This design is a variant of L72. It consists of a double outlined quarter foil, which is set within quarter circles. The design is placed centrally with the corner decoration forming part of a larger overall pattern. The tile is made from red earthenware clay with a grey core. It measures 68.8mm x 53.8mm x 18.5mm thick and has a brown glaze which darkens towards the centre. This tile type is found at St Mary's abbey, St Patrick's cathedral, St Saviour's friary, all in Dublin, and Bective abbey in Co. Meath (ibid., 91).

E598:299:L6: Only a small fragment of this tile remains. The leaf design may possibly be the remains of a tile depicting a lion face with leaves (see **E598:46**). The tile is of red earthenware and has a brown glaze. It measures 61mm x 39mm x 21mm.

E598:46:L6: This design is a lion face surrounded by leaves. It would have formed part of a four tile design depicting four lion faces within a circular band. Christian tradition has long connected the authors of the four Gospels, Mathew, Mark, Luke and John, with four living creatures, which surround God's throne. Mathew is represented as a human/angle figure, while Mark is a lion, Luke is an ox and John is an eagle. This tile fragment has been over-fired but sections of black glaze can still be seen. The tile measures 108.3mm x 81.2mm x 21mm thick. This tile type is well represented on a variety of sites including Christ Church cathedral, St Patrick's cathedral, Fishamble Street, Dublin Castle, Wood Quay, all in Dublin. Outside Dublin, it occurs on sites such as the Dominican friary in Drogheda and Mosney church in Co. Meath (Eames and Fanning 1988, 86).

E598:359: L78: This design consists of a circular band with alternate four foils and Is. The design is set diagonally to form part of a four tile decoration depicting circular band enclosing an eight foil. The tile is of red earthenware with a dark green glaze. It measures 108.5mm x 76mm x 22mm thick. This tile type is found at a variety of sites such as Christ Church cathedral, Dublin Castle, Wood Quay, St Patrick's cathedral, St Mary's abbey, St Saviour friary and Glasnevin, all in Dublin. Other examples outside Dublin have been found at Kildare cathedral and the Dominican friary, Drogheda (Eames and Fanning 1988, 91).

E598: unnumbered floor tile 1: L47: The decoration on this tile is a variant of L46. It consists of a four foil within an anti-clockwise scroll. This floral design would have fitted together with other tiles like a jigsaw to make a larger recurring overall pattern. The tile is made of red earthenware and has a light green glaze. It measures 76mm x 52mm x 19.5mm thick. This tile type is found on sites including Christ Church cathedral, St Patrick's cathedral, High Street, all from Dublin, and Kildare cathedral and Great Connell priory (Eames and Fanning 1988, 89).

E598: unnumbered floor tile 2: L76: This design comprises of a foliate spray within a circular band with alternate four foils and Is. The decoration is set diagonally and would have originally formed part of a four tile unit. The tile is of red earthenware clay. It measures 79mm x 65.3mm x 19.2mm thick. It has a dark green glaze. In Dublin this tile type is found at Christ Church cathedral, St Audoen's church, St Mary's abbey, St Nicholas church, St Patrick's cathedral and St Saviour's friary, all in Dublin. It was also found on the site of the Dominican friary in Drogheda (Eames and Fanning 1988, 91).

The following floor tiles were unidentifiable: E598:76; E598:683; E598: unnumbered floor tile 3; E598: unnumbered floor tile 4; E598: unnumbered floor tile5.

Two-colour floor tile
E598: unnumbered floor tile 6: T212: This simple design consists of a circular band with roundels. It would have been part of a four tile design linking the circular band. This tile type is found at Christ Church cathedral, Dublin and Graiguenamanagh abbey, Co. Kilkenny.

E598:158: unidentifiable: this tile appears to belong to the two-coloured tile category. It does not appear to have a relief or impressed decoration. The remains of a slip decoration on the tile face may add to this assumption. The tile is made of red earthenware with a grey base. It measures 68.3mm x 49mm x 23.2mm thick.

Roof tiles
Only two fragments of roof tile were also found at the Bully's Acre site. These tiles had line-impressed decoration but the decoration was unidentifiable.

E598:684, E598: unnumbered tile 7. Line-impressed roof tiles, which were unidentifiable.

BIBLIOGRAPHY

Anon. 1858–9 Proceedings, November meeting 1859. *RSAI Jn.* 11, 441–50.

Ball, F.E. 1906 *A history of county Dublin*. Part IV. Dublin.

Bradley, J. 1992 The topographical development of Scandinavian Dublin. In F.H.A. Aalen and Kevin Whelan (eds), *Dublin city and county: from prehistory to present*, 43–56. Dublin.

Childers, E.S.E. and Stewart, R. 1921 *The story of the Royal Hospital of Kilmainham*. London.

Duffy, S. 2005a A reconsideration of the site of Dublin's Viking *thing-mót*. In Tom Condit and Christiaan Corlett (eds), *Above and beyond: essays in memory of Leo Swan*, 351–60. Bray.

— 2005b Town and crown: the kings of England and their city of Dublin. In R. Britnell, R. Frame and M. Prestwich (eds), *Thirteenth century England, X*, 95–117. Woodbridge.

Eames, E. and Fanning, T. 1988 *Irish medieval tiles*. Dublin.

Falkiner, C.L. 1906–7 The hospital of St John in Jerusalem in Ireland, *RIA Proc.*, 26C, 274–317.

Graham-Campbell, J. 1976 The Viking-age silver hoards of Ireland. In B. Almqvist and D. Greene (eds), *Proceedings of the seventh Viking congress, Royal Irish Academy, Dublin*, 39–74. Dublin.

Gilbert J.T. (ed.) 1870 *Historic and municipal documents of Ireland AD 1172–1320*. London.

— (ed.) 1899–1944 *Calendar of ancient records of Dublin*. 19 vols. Dublin.

Gwynn, A. and Hadcock, R.N. 1970 *Medieval religious houses, Ireland*. Dublin.

Harbison, P. 1992 *The high crosses of Ireland: an iconographical and photographical survey* Vol. 1. Bonn.

Kenny, C. 1995 *Kilmainham: the history of a settlement older than Dublin*. Dublin.

Lennon, M. 2004 Reports on medieval floor and roof tiles from Bully's Acre, Kilmainham, Dublin 8. In L. Simpson, 'Stratigraphic reports for Bully's Acre, Kilmainham Dublin 8 (E598) and Con Colbert Road/Memorial Park (E497)', 47–50. Unpublished report lodged with the Department of the Environment, Heritage and Local Government (National Monuments Section) and the National Museum of Ireland. Dublin.

Lennox Barrow, D. 1985 The Knights Hospitaller of St John of Jerusalem at Kilmainham. *Dublin Historical Record* xxxvii, no. 3, 108–12.

Lydon J. 1994 Medieval Wicklow–'a land of war'. In K. Hannigan and W. Nolan (eds), *Wicklow: history and society*, 151–89. Dublin.

McNeill, C. 1924 The Hospitallers of Kilmainham and their guests. *RSAI Jn.* 54, 15–30.

— (ed.) 1943 *Registrum de Kilmainham*. Dublin

— 1950 *Calendar of Archbishop's Alen's Register c.1172–1534*. Dublin.

Mills, J. and Griffith, M.C. (eds) 1905–50 *Calendar of the justiciary rolls of Ireland 1295–1314*, 3 vols. Dublin.

Murphy, S. 1989 *Bully's acre and Royal hospital Kilmainhan graveyards: history and inscriptions*. Dublin.

O'Brien, E. 1998 A reconsideration of the location and context of Viking burials at Kilmainham/Islandbridge. In Conleth Manning (ed.), *Dublin and beyond the Pale: studies in honour of Patrick Healy*, 35–44. Bray.

O'Brien, R. and Russell, I. 2005 The Hiberno-Scandinavain site of Woodstown 6, Co. Waterford. In *Recent archaeological discoveries on national road schemes 2004: proceedings of seminar for the public, Dublin, September 2004*, 111–24. Dublin.

O'Donovan, E. 2008 The Irish, the Vikings, and the English: new archaeological evidence from excavations at Golden Lane, Dublin. In S. Duffy (ed.), *Medieval Dublin VIII*, 36–130. Dublin.

Ó Floinn, R. 1998 The archaeology of the early Viking Age in Ireland. In H.B. Clarke, M. Ní Mhaonaigh and R. Ó Floinn (eds), *Ireland and Scandinavia in the early Viking Age*, 132–65. Dublin.

Saint James's Graveyard Project 1988 *St James's graveyard, Dublin: history and associations.* Dublin.

Simpson, L. 1994 Anglo-Norman settlement in Uí Briúin Cualann 1169–1350. In K. Hannigan and W. Nolan (eds), *Wicklow: history and society*, 191–236. Dublin.

— 1997 Historical background to Patrick Street excavations. In Claire Walsh (ed.), *Archaeological excavations at Patrick, Nicholas and Wintavern Streets, Dublin*, 17–33. Dingle.

— 2004 Stratigraphic reports for Bully's Acre, Kilmainham Dublin 8 (E598) and Con Colbert Road/Memorial Park (E497). Unpublished report lodged with the Department of the Environment, Heritage and Local Government (National Monuments Section) and the National Museum of Ireland. Dublin.

— 2005 Viking warriors in Dublin: is this the *longphort*? In S. Duffy (ed.), *Medieval Dublin VI*, 11–62. Dublin.

— 2005 The ecclesiastical enclosure at Dunshaughlin Co. Meath: some dating evidence. In T. Condit and C. Corlett (eds), *Above and beyond: essays in memory of Leo Swan*, 227–38. Bray.

Swan D.L. 1983 Enclosed ecclesiastical site and their relevance to the settlement patterns of the first millennium AD. In T. Reeves-Smyth and F. Hammond (eds), *Landscape archaeology in Ireland*, 269–80. BAR British Series, 116. Oxford.

Wilde W.R. 1866–9. On the Scandinavian antiquities lately discovered at Islandbridge, near Dublin. *RIA Proc.*, 10C, 13–22.

The lost coronation oath of King Edward I: rediscovered in a Dublin manuscript

BERNADETTE WILLIAMS

The coronation oath of Edward I, as present in the Dublin Dominican Annals of Pembridge, is as follows.[1]

> Edwardus, filius Regis Henrici, per Fratrem Robertum Kilwardby, Ordinis Predicatorum, Archiepiscopum Cantuariensem, die Sancti Magni, martyris,[2] in ecclesia Westmonasteriensi unctus est in Regem Anglie, et coronatus est, presentibus magnatibus totius Anglie, cujus professio sive juramentum tale fuit: Ego, Edwardus, filius et heres Henrici Regis, profiteor, confiteor, et promitto, coram Deo et Angelis ejus, amodo et deinceps legem et justitiam, pacemque Sancte Dei Ecclesie, populoque michi subjecto [sine] respectu [servare] sicut cum consilio fidelium nostrorum invenire poterimus; Pontificibus quoque Ecclesie Dei condignum et canonicum honorem exhibere ut ab Imperatoribus et Regibus ecclesiis sibi commissis collata sunt inviolabiliter conservare, Abbatibus et vasis dominicis congruum honorem secundum fidelium nostrorum [consilium] sicut Deus me adjuvet et Sancta Dei Evangelia.[3]

This oath, if it is in fact the genuine article, is the only record in existence of the coronation oath of Edward I. In 1941, H.G. Richardson had said that it would be very difficult to add anything to the early history of the coronation oath 'unless, which seems unlikely, some altogether fresh documents are discovered'.[4] It appears that a fresh document has come to light in these Dublin Dominican annals.

---

1 Bodl. MS Laud 526; TCD MS 584; J.T. Gilbert (ed.), *Chartularies of St Mary's abbey, Dublin: with the register of its house at Dunbrody, and annals of Ireland*, 2 vols (RS 80, London, 1884), ii, 317. Bernadette Williams, 'The Dominican annals of Dublin', in Seán Duffy (ed.), *Medieval Dublin II: proceedings of the Friends of Medieval Dublin Symposium 2000* (Dublin, 2001), pp 142–68. I am most grateful to Professor Brian Scott and Professor Seymour Phillips for their interest and helpful guidance in the matter of this oath.   2 The feast of St Magnus is 19 August: Christopher Cheney (ed.), *Handbook of dates for students of English history* (Royal Historical Society, Guides and Handbooks, 4, revised by Michael Jones (Cambridge, 2000). This is the correct date: Michael Prestwich, *Edward I* (London, 1988), p. 90. Richardson gives the date of the coronation as 18 August: H.G. Richardson, 'The English coronation oath', *Transactions of the Royal Historical Society*, 4th ser., 23 (1941), 143.   3 The square brackets are as found in J.T. Gilbert's Latin edition, Gilbert (ed.), *Chartul. St Mary's, Dublin*, ii, 317.   4 Richardson, 'The English coronation oath',

A debate raged between the twentieth-century historians centred round when a fourth clause (which was present in the 1308 oath) was conceived and whether it had actually been included in the oath of 1274. Richardson constantly reiterated his theory that the fourth clause had been present in the 1274 oath, but this claim was hotly contested and in the end the consensus of historical opinion – up to and including the last word on the subject – is that Richardson was not convincing on several counts.[5] The lack of a record of the coronation oath of 1274 resulted in historians concentrating at great length on the coronation oath of 1308. Robert Hoyt, who wrote two articles on the oath of 1308, said:

> Few problems in medieval constitutional history, and perhaps none in English constitutional history, have occasioned more irreconcilably different interpretations than the problem of the meaning and significance of the coronation oath of 1308.[6]

A great deal of the proof of the authenticity, or otherwise, of this Dublin-sourced oath is connected to the belief by Richardson that there was a fourth clause included in the oath of 1274. This fourth clause is not present in the

Trans. Royal Hist. Soc., 4th ser., 23 (1941), 129. **5** Books and articles which refer to the coronation oath of Edward I are as follows: Bertie Wilkinson, 'The coronation oath of Edward II', in J.G. Edwards, V.H. Galbraith & E.F. Jacob (eds), *Historical essays in honour of James Tait* (Manchester, 1933), pp 405–16; H.G. Richardson and G.O. Sayles, 'Early coronation records', *Bulletin of the Institute of Historical Research*, 13:39 (1936), 129–45; 14:40 (1936), 1–9; Percy Ernst Schramm, *A history of the English coronation*, trans. L.G. Wickham Legg (Oxford, 1937); H.G. Richardson and G.O. Sayles, 'Early coronation records. Supplementary notes', *Bull. Inst. Hist. Research*, 14:42 (1937), 145–8; H.G. Richardson, 'Early coronation records', *Bull. Inst. Hist. Research*, 16:46 (1938), 1–11; P.L. Ward, 'The coronation ceremony in mediaeval England', *Speculum*, 14:2 (1939), 160–78; H.G. Richardson, 'The English coronation oath', *Trans. Royal Hist. Soc.*, 4th ser., 23 (1941), 129–58; B. Wilkinson, 'The coronation of Edward II and the Statute of York', *Speculum*, 19:4 (1944), 445–69; H.G. Richardson, 'The "Annales Paulini"', *Speculum*, 23 (1948), 630–40; idem, 'The English coronation oath', *Speculum*, 24:1 (1949), 44–75; E.H. Kantorowicz, 'Inalienability: a note on canonical practice and the English coronation oath in the 13th century', *Speculum*, 29 (1954), 488–502; R.S. Hoyt, 'The coronation oath of 1308: the background of "les leys et les custumes"', *Traditio*, 11 (1955), 235–57; idem, 'The coronation oath of 1308', *English Historical Review*, 71 (1956), 353–83; H.G. Richardson, 'The coronation in medieval England: the evolution of the office and the oath', *Traditio*, 16 (1960), 111–202; Raymond Foreville, 'Le sacre des rois anglo-normands et angevins et le serment du sacre [XIe-XIIe siècles]' [The divinity of Anglo-Norman and Angevian monarchs and the sacramental oath (11th–12th centuries)], *Proceedings of the Battle Conference on Anglo-Norman Studies*, 1 (1978), pp 49–62; János M. Bak, *Coronations: medieval and early modern monarchic ritual* (Berkeley, CA, 1990). In this volume there appeared three articles of great value, namely, J.M. Bak, 'The introduction: coronation studies – past, present and future', pp 1–15; A. Hughes, 'The origins and descent of the fourth recension of the English coronation', pp 197–216; David J. Sturdy, '"Continuity" versus "change": historians and English coronations of the medieval and early modern periods', 228–45. **6** Hoyt, 'The coronation oath of 1308: the background of "les leys et les

oath that appears here. In 1949 Richardson stated that, although there is a fairly full account of the ceremony, there is no mention of the oath and he states that 'the chroniclers are, as usual, disappointing'.[7] But in 1960, after, presumably, someone had brought to his attention the account of the oath in Camden's *Britannia*, Richardson made a mistake by instantly dismissing this account as a fabrication, stating in a footnote, 'this is not in the original [Marlborough] manuscript but is a fabrication by either William Howard or more probably by Camden'.[8] But Richardson was quite mistaken; Camden was not using Marlborough for his source but rather Pembridge.

Before the authenticity of this record of the pivotal 1274 oath can be considered, it is most important that the manuscript in which it can be found is discussed and evaluated. The oath is taken from the *Annales Hiberniae ab Anno Christi 1162 usque ad annum 1370*; these annals, as extant, are to be found in two manuscript transcripts, one in the Bodleian Library, Oxford, as Laud MS Misc. 526 and the other in Trinity College, Dublin, MS 584. A Latin edition was also included in the *Chartularies of St Mary's abbey, Dublin*, volume two, as edited by J.T. Gilbert for the Rolls Series in 1884. Both of these manuscripts are mid-fifteenth-century copies of the original annals and neither presents the appearance of being a working document; that is to say there are no marginalia, no corrected errors, no spaces left for names to be inserted, et cetera. At the conclusion of the year 1347 in the TCD manuscript is a rubricated note, which states 'Hic finitur cronica Pembrig.'[9] The author of these annals was John de Pembridge who was prior of the Dominicans in Dublin from 1329 to 1333 and then again prior at some period between 1341 and 1343.[10] The claim that his contribution to the annals ended in 1347 is entirely credible because up to and including the year 1347 virtually each year is only identified by the words Anno Domini followed by the year in Roman numerals. From the following year, 1348, the method of dating changes and the regnal year is added to the dating of each year. From internal evidence it is quite clear that the annals are Dominican and of Dublin origin until 1347 and it is equally clear that they continue to be Dominican and Dublin from that year to the last entry in 1370. This Dominican provenance could clearly be a vital ingredient in the search for the truth regarding this oath.

John de Pembridge ceased writing at the end of 1347. We can determine, from internal evidence, a small time-period within which he was writing his

custumes'", *Traditio*, 11 (1955), 235.   7 Richardson, 'The English coronation oath', *Speculum*, 24:1 (1949), 49.   8 H.G. Richardson, 'The coronation in medieval England: the evolution of the office and the oath', *Traditio*, 16 (1960), 172n53a.   9 TCD MS 584, fol. 34v. For identification of Pembridge as John de Pembridge see Bernadette Williams, 'The Dominican annals of Dublin', in Seán Duffy (ed.), *Medieval Dublin II: proceedings of the Friends of Medieval Dublin Symposium 2000*, (Dublin, 2001), pp 154–5.   10 Philomena Connolly (ed.), *Irish exchequer payments, 1270–1446* (Dublin, 1998), pp 337, 342, 345, 351, 357, 408. I am most grateful to the late Dr Phil Connolly for all her help and assistance in

annals. Pembridge was writing after 1316, because when he recounts that the stones of his priory were used to strengthen the defences of the north part of the Dublin quays against the Bruce invasion, he can state that later the king ordered that the priory should be restored as before. Also there is an entry in 1308 in which he refers to the Dublin mayor, John le Decer, and mentions that he was subsequently buried with the Franciscans, but as John le Decer died in 1332 Pembridge was obviously writing the 1308 entry in, or after, 1332. Finally, in 1343, when Pembridge reports the arrival in Ireland of Ralph Ufford on 13 July 1343, he can report, in advance, that the weather became bad on Ufford's arrival and did not improve until after the death of Ufford, and Ufford died in 1346 – as Pembridge himself reports. Pembridge ceased writing at the beginning of the outbreak of the Black Death in Dublin. According to the Franciscan *Annals of Friar John Clyn of Kilkenny*: 'the Black Death began near Dublin and Drogheda and the cities of Dublin and Drogheda were almost destroyed and emptied of inhabitants'. He adds that in the Franciscan friary of Dublin twenty-three friars died. The friars were particularly susceptible to the plague as they lived in the towns and ministered to the people, and indeed Clyn tells us that in Kilkenny the confessor died with the confessed.[11] If Pembridge was in Dublin he was in great danger. However, Pembridge could also have been in Drogheda in 1348 as the chapter of the Dominicans was held there that year.[12] The odds against Pembridge surviving in either place were not good.

In all of the discussion concerning the unknown oath of 1274 no one considered the identity of the person who crowned Edward I in 1274. Pembridge gives, correctly, the date of the coronation as the feast of St Magnus, 19 August, and, also correctly, gives the officiating prelate as the then archbishop of Canterbury who was Friar Robert Kilwardby of the Order of Preachers. Kilwardby had been provincial of the Dominicans of both England and Ireland from 1261 to 1272; unlike the Franciscans, the Irish Dominicans were not a separate custody. Kilwardby was chosen by Pope Gregory X to fill the see of Canterbury, vacant for two years. Subsequently, four years after the coronation in 1274, Pope Nicholas III made Kilwardby cardinal bishop of Porto and Santa Rufina. Kilwardby duly resigned his archbishopric and left England in July 1278. He took with him valuables belonging to the diocese, as well as his official registers, possibly because he was hoping to pursue the interests of Canterbury in the curia.[13] He died a year later in Viterbo in 1279. The registers were never recovered, although his successor John Peckham did try.

How much reliance can we place on the veracity of this account of the oath in Pembridge? Firstly, a Dominican issued the oath and it is found in a

this matter.   11 Bernadette Williams (ed.), *The Annals of Ireland by Friar John Clyn* (Dublin, 2007), pp 246–52.   12 BL MS Add 4789, fol. 206r.   13 Simon Tugwell, 'Kilwardby, Robert (*c.*1215–1279)', *Oxford Dictionary of National Biography* (Oxford University Press, 2004) [http://www.oxforddnb.com/view/article/15546, accessed 18 Feb. 2008].

Dominican annal. Secondly it is presented as a formal item and stands alone in the text as such. Religious men, as indeed all medieval people, placed great emphasis on the importance of oaths. Oaths were taken before God on the gospels and were not treated lightly. There is even mention in two English documents of the ceremony of laying the text of the oath on the altar.[14] It is therefore highly unlikely that a Dominican would take the wording of an oath lightly. This is the only coronation oath in these annals.

There are a few occasions in Pembridge's annals when extreme formality, similar to that of the oath of 1274, is used. One is in 1320 when Pembridge is recounting the launching of the first university in Dublin. A second time that a formal note enters the annals is the account of the accusation against Roger Outlaw, prior of Kilmainham and head of the order of St John of Jerusalem (the Knights Hospitaller) in Ireland, and sometime justiciar and chancellor of Ireland, who was defamed by Bishop Ledrede on the grounds that he was a supporter of heresy in the case against Alice Kyteler. Despite the solemn account, there are no formal words included. The third time was in 1341 when the king revoked all grants made in the royal name stretching back an entire generation, an action which left Dublin and indeed Ireland in turmoil. A parliament was held and we are told that the magnates, together with the mayors of the cities, sent messengers to the king complaining 'that from henceforth they would not tolerate the land of Ireland to be ruled by his ministers as before'.[15] And then a document in French is included giving an account of the complaints.[16]

The 1274 oath stands alone. How did the oath reach Dublin? Either the oath reached Ireland fairly soon after the coronation or was brought to Ireland at a later date. It is impossible, on the available evidence, to determine how and through what agency the oath came to be in our annals. Various possibilities can be suggested but unless firm evidence is forthcoming they all remain just vague possibilities. Pembridge might have been English, not Anglo-Irish, and have brought the oath with him when he came to Ireland. But this theory is hard to validate. If true, one would expect to find that Pembridge was a royal clerk in England in this period and also that he would display in his writings a greater interest in English matters. So, on balance, and at this moment in time, Pembridge himself is not a prime possibility, but of course cannot be ruled out altogether.

A superior possibility is a Hotham connection. There are two Hothams to be considered, the elder William de Hotham (*c.*1255–98), a Dominican friar

14 H.G. Richardson, 'The coronation in medieval England: the evolution of the office and the oath', *Traditio*, 16 (1960), 125 n. 68.   15 For discussion, see Robin Frame, 'English policies and Anglo-Irish attitudes in the crisis of 1341–1342', in James F. Lydon (ed.), *England and Ireland in the later middle ages: essays in honour of Jocelyn Otway-Ruthven* (Dublin, 1981), pp 86–103.   16 There is also the account (1345) of the Justiciar Ralph Ufford giving two separate writs to William Burton; we are given an account of what was in

who was also the head of the Dominican order in England and Ireland and became archbishop of Dublin in 1296, but never came to Ireland.[17] The second is his nephew John, later bishop of Ely. William de Hotham (the uncle) was a trusted royal administrator but also a committed Dominican. His close association with Edward I and his involvement with Edward I's attempted conquest of Scotland was probably instrumental in advancing the spread of the Dominicans in Scotland. Hotham was with the king in Wales, Gascony and Flanders, acted as arbiter in Scottish affairs and was involved in peace negations between France and England. Hotham went to Rome in 1289 to seek a dispensation for the proposed marriage of the king's son, Edward, to Margaret of Scotland. All of these events, including the marriage of Edward to Margaret of Scotland, are included in the annals. But one must also consider that there may have been a naturally greater interest in Edward as, from 1254, Edward I was lord of Ireland.

Hotham died at Dijon in 1298 and this brings us to his nephew John, later bishop of Ely, who was with him at the time and acted as one of his executors.[18] John de Hotham was following in his uncle's footsteps as a royal administrator. He was already connected with Ireland from an early period; in 1291 he was attorney for the earl of Pembroke and later for Piers Gaveston and as early as 1305 he was a baron of the Irish exchequer. He was successful in Ireland securing many benefices and appointments. In 1314 Hotham was in Ireland to see how much money could be raised for the king and was soon to be heavily involved in the defence against the Bruce invasion.[19] Later he was also involved in the appointment of Alexander Bicknor as archbishop of Dublin. All that can be said is that there is a considerable interest in the king's affairs in this period in the annals, more so than in later periods, for which information from Hotham could account. Here is a man who could have been in possession of material belonging to his Dominican uncle William de Hotham; he was present at his death and had prayers said for his uncle at Welbeck abbey (and also for the countess of Pembroke, Gaveston, and John Wogan, erstwhile justiciar of Ireland); he was also his uncle's executer and was frequently in Dublin. Additionally, John de Hotham could also, independently, have acquired historical material which contained the oath and left it with the Dominicans in Dublin. When one considers who his uncle was, his loyalty to the Dominicans

the two differently-worded writs, but not the exact words. **17** A grant to Queen Eleanor, mother of King Edward, was witnessed by William de Hotham as provincial prior of the Friars Preachers. Queen Eleanor left 165 pounds for a number of Dominican houses and further money in her will to William de Hotham: A.G. Little, 'Provincial priors and vicars of the English Dominicans', *English Historical Review*, 33 (1918), 519–25. **18** M.C. Buck, 'Hotham, John (*d.* 1337)', *Oxford Dictionary of National Biography*, Oxford University Press, 2004 [http://www.oxforddnb.com/view/article/13851, accessed 26 April 2007]. **19** J.R.S. Phillips, 'The mission of John de Hothum to Ireland, 1315–1316', in J.F. Lydon (ed.), *England and Ireland in the later middle ages* (Dublin, 1981), pp 62–85.

and their loyalty to him, must have been a given fact. It is also more than probable that when he was in Dublin itself John de Hotham stayed with the Dominicans. It may even have been through Hotham's intercession that the king ordered the restoration of the Dominican priory after the damage occasioned by the Bruce invasion. As will be patently obvious, this Hotham/ Dublin/Dominican/oath connection is all mere conjecture but it highlights both the possibilities and problems associated with such searches.

Professor Seymour Phillips has suggested to me another possibility. He points out that the Dominicans were the confessors of Henry III, Edward I and Edward II,[20] and suggested that if such a confessor could be found, who had Irish connections or links with someone else with an Irish connection, it would be a most useful line of research.[21]

This paper is a very exploratory exercise, the main function of which is to bring to public attention the presence of an English coronation oath of 1274 in a Dublin annal. Historians better able and better qualified in this subject-matter are required to analyze, dissect and pronounce as to whether it is genuine or not.

---

20 One of Henry III's most trusted councillors was his Dominican confessor, John of Darlington (*d.* 1284); after the battle of Evesham, Henry wrote an impassioned letter to Kilwardby asking for John to be returned to his service, as being one of the few people trusted by both sides.   21 Reginald Dennis Clarke, 'Some secular activities of the English Dominicans during the reign of Edward I, Edward II and Edward III', *Bulletin of the Institute of Historical Research*, 10 (1933), 189–90. I am grateful to Professor Seymour Phillips for this reference.

Archaeological excavations on the site of Meakstown Castle, Finglas, Co. Dublin

MELANIE McQUADE

INTRODUCTION

In autumn 2006 archaeological excavation (05E044ext.) was carried out by the writer prior to residential development in the vicinity of the recorded site of a sixteenth-century castle (Record of Monuments and Places DU014–020) in the townland of Meakstown (fig. 1), Finglas, Dublin 11. The site is situated on relatively flat pastureland at an elevation of 70m OD. It lies just over 1km to the northeast of the medieval monastery town of Finglas at National Grid 313590/ 240960. The site is bounded to the south by St Margaret's Road and lies a short distance to the northeast of the junction with Jamestown Road which leads south to Finglas. The land is drained by the Santry River which flows *c*.1.5km to the north of the site.

There are no upstanding remains of the castle the 'site of' which is recorded on the 1843 Ordnance Survey map on the opposite (southern) side of St Margaret's Road (fig. 3). The castle lands, however, probably extended into the development area which lay within the northern part of the constraint circle that illustrates the location of the castle on the RMP map. St Margaret's Road and Jamestown Road are both depicted on Rocque's map (1758) (fig. 2) and may be considerably earlier in date since a number of medieval sites are located in the wider area and there is an early-medieval ringfort (RMP: DU014–022) just north of St Margaret's Road and east of the site (fig. 1). Prior to development the site was within an area of farmland. The adjacent lands to the south and east of the site have recently been developed as high-density housing.

The area of excavation measured 80m east-west and a maximum of 30m north-south. Excavation was directed by the writer (during September and October 2006) and was carried out on behalf of Durkan Residential Ltd. Three levels of settlement activity were identified on site, which have been dated to the prehistoric, medieval and post-medieval periods. This paper focuses on the medieval occupation, which appears to suggest a small nucleated settlement comprising at least three timber buildings and a contemporary enclosure that fronted onto St Margaret's Road. A later phase of medieval occupation is characterized by a series of ditches representative of property boundaries.

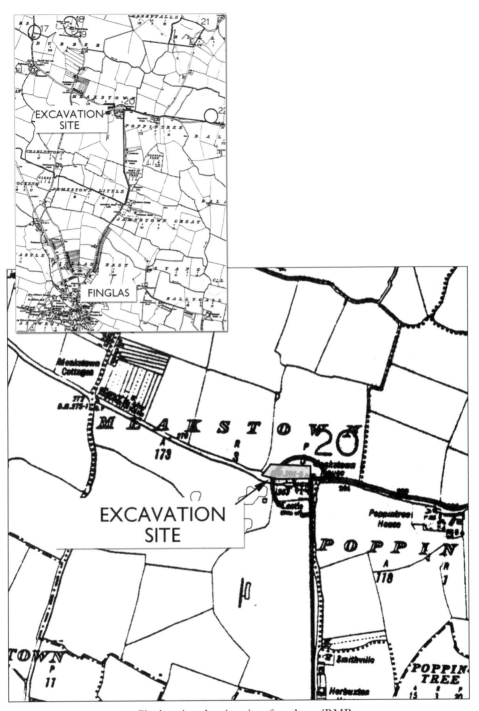

1 Site location showing site of castle on/RMP

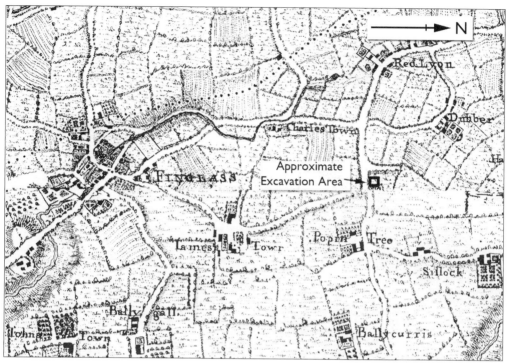

2 Site location shown on Rocque's map of 1758

Dating is based primarily on the pottery, which is predominantly late twelfth to fourteenth century. Some sixteenth-century finds were recovered during excavation but *in situ* post-medieval features date from the eighteenth and nineteenth centuries.

ARCHAEOLOGICAL AND HISTORICAL BACKGROUND

The excavation site was located to the north of Finglas, a town which built up around the monastery founded by St Cainnech (Canice) in AD 560. Finglas was one of the earliest and most important parishes in Dublin. Its name is an anglicized form of *fionn glaiss*, or clear stream, referring to the stream that flows through the village and into the Tolka River, and possibly also referring to the holy well on Mellowes Crescent. Early-medieval settlement in the wider area is evident from the ringforts at Balcurris (RMP DU014–022), approximately 1km to the east of Meakstown (fig. 1), and at Coldwinters (RMP DU014–016) and Newtown (RMP DU014–006; 007) further to the northeast.

The arrival of the Vikings off the coast of Ireland in the late eighth and early ninth century and their raids on the hinterland of Dublin must have been a threat to the monastery at Finglas. However, within a few years of their arrival the Vikings had settled at the Áth Cliath site at Dublin and their presence in the Finglas area is attested by the recent discovery of a Viking burial there (Kavanagh 2007, 139). In the twelfth century the monastery at Finglas became a parochial church. Following the Anglo-Norman invasion the lands passed to Strongbow and in 1171 Dublin was besieged by Ruaidrí Ua Conchobair (O'Connor), the king of Connacht and high-king of Ireland. Ruaidrí set up camp at Finglas, but it was successfully attacked two months later by a body of 600 Anglo-Normans aided by Irish allies. The following year King Henry II is said to have set up a base for his archers in Finglas. Under the Anglo-Norman settlement, the lands belonging to the early-Christian church of Finglas, like those of Tallaght and Clondalkin, were confirmed to the archbishop of Dublin. They formed part of one of his most valuable manors (Ball 1920, vi, 84).

Finglas subsequently began to emerge as an important manor town. In 1228 the Archbishop set up residence there. During his time there were nineteen burgesses in Finglas and it became a favourite location for 'big house' dwellers such as Dublin's merchant aldermen and legal families. However, the borough status of Finglas was never confirmed and is only recorded as being among the archbishop's boroughs in historical records, like those of Tallaght, Clondalkin or Swords (Bradley 1998, 129).

A number of archaeological excavations have been carried out within the town of Finglas. These have recorded medieval settlement evidence in the form of ditches and gullies (McConway 1997, 33; Halpin 1998, 56).

Two castle sites are recorded within Finglas. One lies to the northwest of the old St Canice's church and the other, known as 'Cardiff Castle', to the west of the village. The latter may have been removed as early as AD 1700 (Maher 1932) and is specifically marked on the 1837 OS six-inch map as 'Cardiff Castle (Site of)'. The area has since been extensively developed and no trace of the castle remains. Settlement evidence in the wider area includes the recorded sites of two other castles. One in the townland of Dubber (RMP DU014–018) *c.*1km to the northwest of Meakstown Castle is accessed via a road leading northwards from St Margaret's Road (fig. 1). The other castle was located at Cappogue (RMP DU014:027) *c.*2.5km to the northwest of Finglas and recent archaeological investigations on that site have uncovered evidence for medieval settlement dating from the twelfth to the fourteenth century (McQuade 2009).

MEAKSTOWN CASTLE

The recorded castle at Meakstown (RMP DU014–020) was erected in the later part of the sixteenth century (Adams 1881, 492). The 'Hearth Money Rolls' record that in 1641 it was inhabited by Sir John Stevens, the governor or

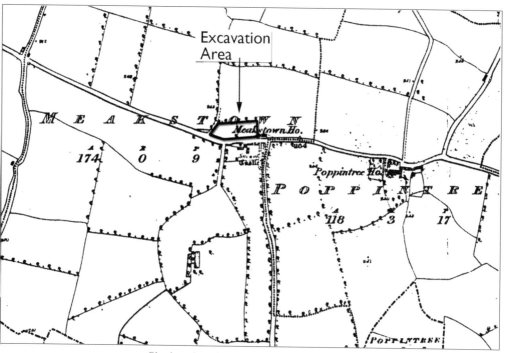

3 Site location shown on 1843 edition OS Map

constable of Dublin Castle. It was later occupied by none other than Sir James Ware, the noted scholar and antiquarian and auditor-general of Ireland. The original form of the building is not clear. It may have resembled a tower house since castles of that type continued to be built until *c.*1650. In the later sixteenth century semi-fortified houses with defensive elements and surrounding bawn walls came into fashion and such buildings were often built on an elaborate tower house plan (Forde-Johnston 1977, 175; Sweetman 1995, 42). The first known description of the castle is found in the Civil Survey which dates from almost a hundred years after its construction (1654–6). The survey describes Ware's Meakstown holdings in some detail:

> There is upon ye premises a dwelling house of Brick with other office houses therto belonging-as a barne & a stable. Also an orchard and Garden Plott Valu'd by ye Jury at 300 li. (Simmington 1945, 202).

The townland of Meakstown is not marked on the Down Survey map and Ware's house is not precisely identified. John Rocque's map of 1758 does not show Meakstown townland, nor is the castle illustrated but a house is depicted near the excavation site (fig. 2). A building is marked at the same location on Taylor's map of 1816 which shows another structure on the southern side of the road. 'Meakstown House' is shown on the 1843 Ordnance Survey map on the northern side of the road, at the same location as the building on Taylor's map (fig. 3).

Several archaeological investigations were carried out within the confines of the recorded 'site of' Meakstown Castle (RMP DU 014–020) on the southern side of St Margaret's Road. A series of wall foundations, linear ditches, a cobbled surface and a stone-lined well were uncovered (Birmingham 1999; Swan 1999; E. O'Donovan pers. comm.), some of which were probably associated with the ancillary buildings related to Ware's seventeenth-century dwelling.

THE EXCAVATION

This site was first occupied during the prehistoric period, when at least two pits and two ditches were dug for drainage purposes on the eastern end of the excavation area. The exact date of these features was not established but stray finds of Neolithic (*c.*4000–2500 BC) and Early Bronze Age date (*c.*2500–2200 BC) were recovered during excavation (McQuade 2007). Several millennia passed before the next datable evidence for settlement here during the medieval period. Three phases of medieval activity were evident from the stratigraphic sequence of features on site. The pottery assemblage indicates that these phases were closely dated, suggesting that the site was occupied on a continual basis from the late twelfth to the fourteenth century. Sixteenth-century artefacts from the site were all *ex situ* but indicate activity in the environs at that time. The post-medieval features on site are all eighteenth- and nineteenth-century in date and probably relate to the occupation of Meakstown House.

Phase 1

During the first phase of medieval occupation there were two foci of activity on site. On the western end the remains of three wooden structures were apparent. On the east side of the site were the partial remains of a sub-rectangular ditched enclosure within which was a stone yard, an associated drainage ditch, and a series of refuse pits.

Structures 1–3
The truncated remains of three structures, which may have been houses or farm buildings, were located on the western end of the site and two of them were set perpendicular to what is now St Margaret's Road suggesting that it may have been a medieval route.

The eastern structure (Structure 1) was highly truncated but appears to have been rectangular in plan. It was defined by a foundation trench (F51) which may have supported wooden sill beams and a wall built of planks. This

Plate 1 Structure 1 slot trench F51 post–ex

Plate 2 Stone spread F63 from north

trench was set more or less parallel to St Margaret's Road and each end curved southwards suggesting that the original structure was perpendicular to the road. The trench (F51) was *c*.9.50m north from the present line of the road and measured at least 12.90m long (east-west). This suggests that Structure 1 measured *c*.9.50m by 12.90m. The eastern arm of the trench (F51) was truncated by the Phase 2 boundary ditch (F49) but its western arm terminated just 1.50m from the return. This terminus could have marked an access point or could represent a change of construction at this location. The foundation trench (F51) was between 0.65m and 0.75m in width and varied from 0.15m to 0.35m in depth (pl. 1). It was filled by F52, mid-grey brown silty clay with frequent inclusions of stone and domestic waste comprising sea shell, animal bone fragments and occasional charcoal flecking. Numerous sherds of Leinster Cooking-ware, various Dublin-type wares and an iron nail were recovered from this fill. Within the structure was a small stone spread (F63) which measured 4.10m by 2.10m (pl. 2) and an overlying occupation deposit (F62). These were both truncated to the south by the large post-medieval boundary ditch, F59 (fig. 4). Leinster Cooking-ware, various Dublin-type wares and several metal pieces including a corroded iron loop staple, a knife blade and a fragment of a strap or binding were recovered from the deposit.

Structure 2 fronted onto St Margaret's Road and was located 8m to the west of Structure 1 (fig. 4). Its plan-form could not be determined since its foundations had been truncated to the south by the post-medieval ditch, F59. The northern wall of Structure 2 was defined by a curvilinear trench (F44/F48) which was located *c*.8m from the road and indicates that this was the maximum length of the structure which was 7m in width. The trench (F44/48) measured 0.60m in width and between 0.30m and 0.35m in depth. Structure 3 was set just 0.50m north of Structure 2 and was truncated by modern disturbance, which blurred both its western and northern ends, but its surviving south-eastern corner was rounded and suggests that the building was sub-square or sub-circular in plan. It was defined by a curvilinear trench (F68) which indicates that the structure had a diameter of *c*.9m. The trench (F68) ranged from 0.48m to 0.57m in width and was between 0.18m and 0.23m in depth.

The foundation trenches of Structures 2 and 3 were both filled by silty clay which could have formed from structural remains that had decayed *in situ*. The foundation trench of Structure 2 contained snail shell, animal bone fragments, sherds of Leinster cooking-ware, various Dublin-type wares and an iron nail, finds similar to those recovered from the slot trench (F51) of Structure 1. In contrast, there were no finds or inclusions within the fill of the trench (F68) which defined Structure 3. However, its proximity and morphological similarity to Structure 2 suggest that it was probably more or less con-temporary. There was no evidence for any internal features within either of

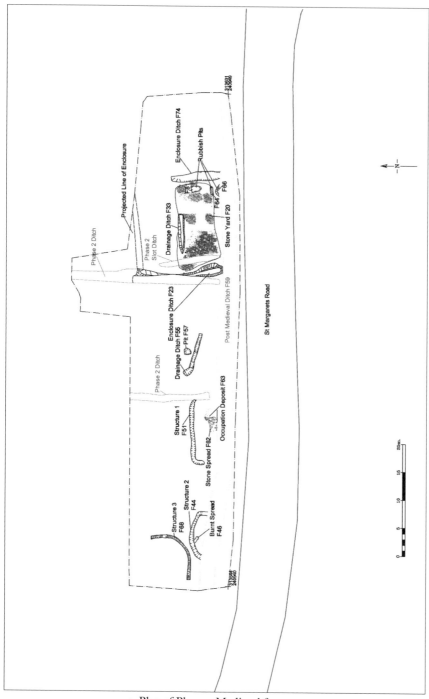

4 Plan of Phase 1 Medieval features

these structures, although this may be due to truncation. A small (0.80m by
0.60m) spread of burnt material containing animal bone and shell (F46)
partially overlaid trench F44/F48 and probably post-dates Structure 2. Sherds
of Dublin-type wares recovered from this deposit date to the medieval period.

The enclosure

The ditched enclosure on the eastern end of the site was heavily truncated but
appears to have been sub-rectangular in plan. Its original dimensions are
estimated at *c.*15m north-south by an estimated 17m east-west. The western
extent of the enclosure was delimited by the ditch (F23) and its eastern edge
was defined by the ditch, F74. Both of these ditches were orientated roughly
north-south, perpendicular to the road (fig. 4). There was no evidence for
northern or southern enclosing ditches but the northern part of the site had
been heavily truncated and the southern ditch of the enclosure could have
been truncated by the post-medieval boundary (F59) that ran along the
southern extent of the site.

The surviving portion of the western ditch (F23) measured 15.10m in
length and was between 0.80m and 2.20m in width. It varied in depth from
0.30m to 0.46m and had one level of silty clay fill (F24) which had occasional
flecks of charcoal and varied in colour from light brown grey in the northern
end of the ditch to dark grey in the south.

The eastern side of the enclosure was delimited by the ditch (F74) which
cut an earlier undated ditch on roughly the same alignment (McQuade 2007).
The ditch (F74) was truncated to the south by the post-medieval boundary
ditch (F59) and survived for a length of just 9.00m (fig. 4). The northern
terminal of the ditch was well defined and could mark an entrance point to the
enclosure. The ditch was between 0.83m and 1.33m in width and was up to
0.30m in depth. It was filled by yellow grey silty sand (F78), which was sealed
by brown clay (F75). Sherds of Leinster cooking-ware and various Dublin-
type wares, dating from the late thirteenth to the fourteenth century, were
recovered from both of the enclosure ditches (F23 and F74) which also
contained fragments of animal bone and shell.

Internal features

Stone yard Within the southern area of the ditched enclosure was a sub-
rectangular stone surface (F20) measuring 15m east-west by 7m wide (fig. 4;
pl. 3). It consisted of a single layer of randomly set limestone and sandstone
pebbles which were bedded on a very thin layer of small pebbles and gravel.
These had been set on the subsoil and the eastern extent of the surface partly
overlaid a prehistoric ditch (McQuade 2007).

Drainage ditch The north-western edge of the stone yard (F20) was delimited
by an east-west oriented ditch (F33) which ran more or less parallel to St

Plate 3 Phase 1 stone yard F20 and Phase 2 linear drain F21 (mid-ex) viewed from west

Margaret's Road (fig. 4). This ditch was 7.10m in length, between 0.26m and 0.90m in width, and ranged in depth from 0.05m to 0.31m. It was filled by two layers of grey brown silty clay with occasional animal bone fragments, flecks of charcoal and charred plant remains. The presence of snail shells within each level of fill suggests that the ditch had contained water and it probably functioned as an open drain which kept the yard free from surface water. Sherds of Leinster cooking-ware and various Dublin-type wares were recovered from the yard (F20) and the ditch (F33). A prehistoric flint scraper recovered from the ditch was clearly residual, since it was found alongside medieval pottery.

Rubbish pits There were three rubbish pits (F81, F64 and F66) set closely within the eastern end of the enclosure just west of the ditch, F74. The pits ranged from 1.40m to 2.00m in length and were between 0.40m and 0.90m in width. They were relatively shallow, measuring between 0.07m and 0.24m in depth. The pits were filled with silty clays which contained domestic refuse in the form of animal bone, shell and charcoal flecks. Finds from these pits include a corroded piece of an iron horse shoe and sherds of Dublin-type wares and Leinster cooking-ware.

External features
Drainage ditch A small drainage ditch (F55) was located on a wet part of the site to the west of the ditched enclosure (fig. 4). This ditch was similar in size

to the open drain (F33) within the enclosure. It measured 6.10m in length (northwest-southeast) and was between 0.60m and 1.20m in width. The western terminal may have acted as a sump since it was noticeably wider and almost twice as deep (0.40m) as the rest of the ditch. The fill of the ditch was brown grey silty clay (F56) within which were occasional sea shells, animal bone fragments and flecks of charcoal. Several sherds of Leinster cooking-ware and various Dublin-type wares were recovered from the ditch.

Rubbish pit There was a sub-circular rubbish pit (F57) on the centre of the site a short distance to the north of the drain, F55. This pit measured 1.20m by 1.05m and was 0.30m in depth. It was filled with silty sands which contained fragments of shell and charcoal as well as sherds of Dublin-type wares and Leinster cooking-ware.

Phase 1 discussion

The first phase of medieval activity was characterized by the truncated remains of three structures on the western end of the site and a heavily truncated ditched enclosure on the east. The structures and the enclosure were set perpendicular to St Margaret's Road, suggesting that it may have been built on the line of an earlier, possibly medieval, route.

Structure 1 appears to have been a large rectangular building (c.12.90m x 9.50m) whose long axis fronted onto the road. All that remained of this structure was the northern foundation (F51) but it is possible that further remains could have been removed by the post-medieval boundary ditch (F59) that ran just 4m to the south of the slot trench (F51). At 12.90m this structure was longer than most house foundations recorded from the medieval period. However, it was only marginally longer than the 12m stone-built structure at Lady Castle, Co. Kildare (Fallon 2006, 247) and was not as long (14.5m) as the larger house excavated at Bouchier's Castle, Co. Limerick (Cleary 1982). Structure 1 may have been a large house or barn and the internal stone spread (F62) and occupation deposit (F63) are indicative of activity within the building. The domestic nature of the finds from these features indicates that, if Structure 1 was not a dwelling, it was not far removed from one.

Structure 2 was a smaller building located to the west of Structure 1, whose southern extent had been truncated by the post-medieval boundary ditch (F59). The curving northern wall of this structure and its location from the road indicate maximum dimensions of 8.50m by 7m. These compare with measurements recorded for other houses of this period (which average c.8.90m x 6.40m). Structure 3 was also heavily truncated but its remains indicate that it was similar in size with an estimated diameter of 9m.

Each of the three structures was defined by slot trenches which could have supported sill-beams typical of the timber-framed buildings generally recorded on Anglo-Norman sites. A further indication that these structures were constructed of wooden planks was the dimensions of their trenches (F44/F48 and F68) which compared with those of the slot trenches for the plank-built structures excavated at Cookstown, Co. Meath (0.50m to 0.70m in width and between 0.20m and 0.40m in depth) (Clutterbuck 2007).

The sub-rectangular enclosure on the east end of the site may have functioned as a haggard within which was a stone yard (F20). Two tentative entrance points to the enclosure are suggested by distinct terminals at the southern end of its western ditch (F23) and the northern end of the eastern ditch (F74). However, since the full extent of the enclosure was not established, its access points cannot be determined with any certainty. The absence of structural remains within the enclosure could be due to truncation of the site, since the presence of a drainage ditch (F33) and a series of rubbish pits (F81, F64 and F66) indicate that it was occupied. Stone yards or surfaces similar to F20 have been recorded at contemporary settlement sites excavated at Blackcastle, Co. Kildare, Nangor, Co. Dublin, Merrrion Road, Co. Dublin and Tullykane, Co. Meath where they were not always associated with structures (Sleeman and Hurley 1987, 101; Doyle 2002, 136; Baker 2008; Baker forthcoming).

Phase 2

During Phase 2 property boundaries were marked by two linear ditches which ran perpendicular to the road. The eastern ditch (F10) marked a revised boundary which cut through the phase 1 enclosure ditch (F23). A slot trench (F21) and a stone-lined drain (F26) within the eastern property cut the Phase 1 stone yard (F20). While a re-cut (F43) facilitated the continued use of the Phase 1 drainage ditch (F33) that ran along the northern edge of the yard (F20).

Property plots
The two boundary ditches (F10 and F49) indicate that there were at least three separate properties on the excavation area: a central property between the two ditches, one to its east, and another to the west. Both of the boundary ditches were truncated at their northern end and consequently the length of the properties was no longer evident. The central property was 20m wide, but since the outer boundaries of the eastern and western properties were not identified their widths could not be determined. However, they were likely to have been similar to that of the central property.

The eastern boundary ditch (F10) cut through the western edge of the Phase 1 enclosure ditch (F23) and was oriented north-south (fig. 5; pl. 4). The northern end of the ditch had been truncated by later activity on site but it survived for a length of 27.50m, its southern terminal was located *c*.4m north of the road. The ditch was between 0.70m and 1.60m wide and had a depth of between 0.40m and 0.90m (pl. 5). The profile of the ditch varied along its

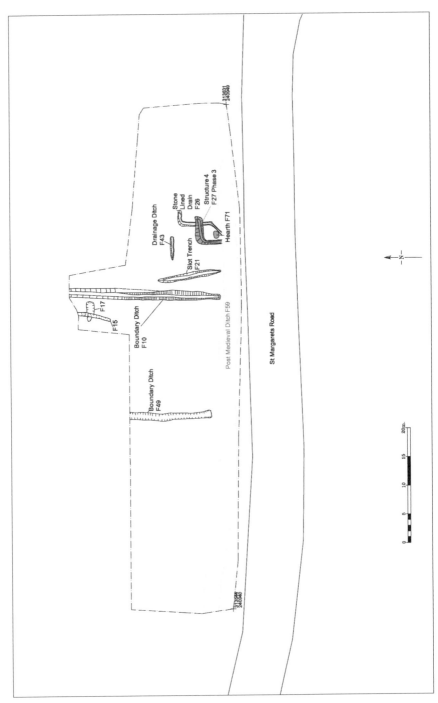

5 Plan of Medieval features Phases 2 and 3

Plate 4 Phase 1 ditch F23 and Phase 2 ditch F10 viewed from north

Plate 5 South–facing section of enclosure ditch F10

length from U-shaped to V-shaped. Four different fills were contained within
the ditch, indicating that it filled in gradually. Snail shells in the basal fill
probably accumulated in the open ditch over a period of time after it was first
dug. This fill (F31) was re-deposited subsoil which may have washed in from
the sides of the ditch. The second and third fills (F30 and F12) were yellow
brown clays, with varying amounts of stone. The uppermost fill (F11) was dark
brown sandy clay. Domestic waste in the form of animal bone fragments and
sea shell had become incorporated into the upper three fills. Pieces of worked
flint, metal artefacts, sherds of Leinster cooking-ware and various Dublin-type
wares were recovered from the ditch. The flints included a barbed and tanged
arrowhead of a type typically used during the Final Neolithic/Early Bronze
Age (*c.*2500–2200 BC). It was clearly residual in this context and may have been
disturbed from the prehistoric features on the site. The metal finds all came
from the upper fill of the ditch and included an iron arrowhead, a ferrous knife
blade, several nails and a fragment of a double loop copper alloy buckle which
dates from the fifteenth or sixteenth century.

The western boundary ditch (F49) was on the same north-south alignment
as the eastern ditch (F10). As mentioned earlier, its northern end was
truncated by modern disturbance but the remaining section was 14.74m long
and its southern terminal was *c.*6m north of the road (fig. 5). The ditch (F49)
varied from 0.80m to 1.20m in width and it was up to 0.31m in depth. It was
filled by F50 light grey silty clay with inclusions of sea shells and flecks of
charcoal. Sherds of Leinster cooking-ware as well as Dublin-type coarse and
fine-wares were recovered from the fill along with a knife blade fragment.

Eastern plot
A linear slot trench, a drainage ditch and a stone-lined drain were evident
within the eastern plot.

Slot trench
A linear slot trench (F21) cut the Phase 1 stone yard (F20) a short distance to
the east of the boundary ditch (F10) (fig. 5). This trench was on roughly the
same north-south alignment as that ditch and was more or less perpendicular
to the road. Its southern terminal aligned with that of the boundary ditch
(F10) and it measured 11.55m in length. The trench was between 0.58m and
1.04m in width and was concave in profile increasing in depth from 0.10m at
the northern end to 0.25m at the south. The slot trench appears to have
supported some form of structure which could have been part of a building no
other foundations of which remained. Alternatively it may have held a free-
standing fence-line. The trench was mainly filled by F22, grey brown pebbly
clay, and a yellow brown silty fill, F37, was confined to its northern end.
Occasional inclusions of charcoal flecks, animal bone and sea shell were noted
in each of these fills. Sherds of Leinster cooking-ware and various Dublin-type

Plate 6 Phase 2 Stone lined drain F26 from south

wares were recovered from the trench and corroded pieces of iron knife blades were found in the upper fill.

Drainage ditch

A linear re-cut (F43) was made into the western end of the Phase 1 drainage ditch F33. The re-cut ditch lay a short distance to the east of the slot-trench F21 and may have been associated with the structure supported by that trench (fig. 5). The drainage ditch (F43) was 4.10m in length, 0.80m in width and 0.19m in depth. It was filled by F34 grey silty clay with charcoal flecks, occasional fragments of animal bone and sea shell. Sherds of Leinster cooking-ware and Dublin-type wares, a lozenge shaped flint arrowhead and iron nails were recovered from the fill. The arrowhead was typical of the kind used in the Neolithic period (*c.*4000–2500 BC) and was clearly residual in this context.

Stone-lined drain

A stone-lined drain (F26) was located a short distance to the east of the drainage ditch (F43), where it cut the north-eastern corner of the Phase 1 stone surface (F20) and cut through an earlier prehistoric ditch (McQuade 2007). The drain was S-shaped in plan (running westwards, southwards and then curving westwards again). The northern part of the drain was aligned with the ditch F43 and it curved well before the terminal of that ditch (fig. 5). The second curve in the drain was probably designed to avoid a structural feature but no traces of such survived there. The drain (F26) was truncated to the south by the post-medieval ditch (F59) but survived for a length of 9.15m. The cut for the drain was 0.55m in width and an average of 0.26m in depth. The base and sides of the cut were lined with limestone pieces which averaged 0.30m x 0.20m x 0.20m. The top of the drain was capped with similarly-sized slabs (pl. 6). This drain was filled with mid-brown sandy clay (F25), which contained fragments of animal bone and Leinster cooking-ware.

Central property
The only features remaining within the central property that appeared to be contemporary with its boundary ditches (F10 and F49) were a small gully and an associated pit.

Gully and pit
There was a small linear gully (F15) on the northern end of the site, within the central property. This gully was 5.60m in length (north-south), between 0.42m and 0.88m in width and up to 0.33m in depth. A shallow pit (F17) was cut into the centre of the gully. Both of these features were filled by grey silty clay and it is likely that they were filled in at the same time. Sherds of Leinster cooking-ware and an iron nail were recovered from their fill.

Phase 2 discussion

During Phase 2 there were at least three properties on the site which were set out perpendicular to St Margaret's Road, lending further support to the suggestion that the road marks the line of an earlier route-way. The properties were defined by two linear ditches which terminated 4m and 6m north of the road, but whose northern extents had been truncated. These defined a central property measuring 20m in width and although the outer ditches of the two flanking properties were not identified these properties were probably of a similar size. The eastern boundary ditch (F10) was dug to a greater depth than the enclosure ditch (F23) which it replaced and in some places it was twice as deep. This suggests that the earlier ditch was not only re-aligned but was also reinforced and strengthened. The remains of a building or a fence of plank construction within the eastern property were indicated by the slot-trench (F21). The re-cut drainage ditch (F43) and the distinctly curved stone-lined drain (F26) within that property were further indicators that one or more structures may have occupied this plot although no further remains of such survived there. Other examples of stone drains were excavated on medieval settlements at Bouchier's Castle, Co. Limerick and Piperstown, Co. Louth where they were believed to have carried animal waste. The Piperstown drain was a large straight structure (8m long and 1.25m wide) which was located within a dwelling house (Barry 2000). The stone-lined drain at Bouchier's Castle led from the corner of the house to a pit outside it. In size and plan it was more like the drain from Meakstown, measuring 0.70m in maximum width. It also had a distinct curve and was almost U-shaped in plan (Cleary 1982). It was not clear exactly where the stone-lined drain at Meakstown ran to or from but the curves in the drain may indicate the location of a former building or some other feature which left no archaeological remains.

Phase 3

The third phase of medieval activity was evident from the remains of what appears to have been a rectangular timber house fronting onto St Margaret's Road on the eastern end of the site. The foundation trench (F27) of this structure cut through the Phase 2 stone-lined drain (F25).

Possible sill-beamed house
The remains of the rectangular building (Structure 4) were defined by an inverted L-shaped trench (F27), which would have supported the sill beams of its western and northern walls (fig. 5). No remains of the eastern wall survived but the extant foundation-remains indicate that the structure measured at least 4.60m in width (east-west). Its full length could not be determined since the foundation trench (F27) was truncated to the south by the post-medieval ditch, F59; however, the northern trench was set *c*.8m from the road and this indicates the maximum possible length of Structure 4. The truncated remains of a small hearth (F71) internal to this structure indicate that it was a dwelling. The hearth was defined by an area of fire-reddened clay (0.70m by 0.50m), with frequent inclusions of charcoal and was located a short distance from the western wall. As with the other structures on this site, there was no evidence for the roof, but it was probably constructed of sod or thatch.

The foundation trench (F27) measured between 0.87m and 1.46m in width and between 0.25m and 0.38m in depth. It was filled by F28, grey brown clay silt with occasional stones, animal bone fragments and flecks of charcoal. Sherds of Dublin-type ware and Leinster cooking-ware were recovered from the fill along with a copper alloy buckle of a type dating from *c*.1250–1400, a heavily corroded iron nail and a fragment of human femur. This was the only human bone recovered from the site and had clearly been re-deposited from its original burial which was presumably somewhere nearby.

Phase 3 discussion

The remains of a rectangular dwelling house (Structure 4) mark the third and final phase of medieval occupation on the east of the site where the ditched enclosure had been. The length of the northern wall trench (4.60m) suggests that this structure was slightly narrower than many of the excavated house foundations from this period which average *c*.8.90m by 6.70m (see Ó Ríordáin and Hunt 1942; Barry 2000; Foley 1989; Opie 2000; Baker forthcoming). However, examples of narrower buildings just 3m and 3.50m wide are known (Fallon 2006; Clutterbuck 2007). The rounded terminals of the trench bare comparison to those recorded for other Anglo-Norman structures, such as Bouchier's Castle, Co. Limerick and Tullykane, Co. Meath (Cleary 1982 and Baker forthcoming). Furthermore the dimensions of the foundation trench at Bouchier's Castle (which was up to 1m in width) are similar to those of the foundation trench F27. Interestingly, the hearth within the houses excavated at Piperstown and Bouchier's Castle was positioned in the western and southwest parts of those structures respectively, while Structure 1 at Jerpointchurch had a central hearth (Barry 2000, 119; Cleary 1982, 78–80; Foley 1989).

Phase 4: eighteenth to nineteenth century occupation

Post-medieval activity was represented by a series of stone-lined drains and linear drainage ditches on the centre of the site and the remains of a curving masonry wall on the east end. Ceramics manufactured between the sixteenth and twentieth centuries were recovered during the excavation but all of the pottery from sealed contexts dates from the eighteenth and nineteenth centuries.

Stone-lined drain
A large stone-lined drain (F19) ran down the centre of the site and was fed from the east by a smaller, partially stone-lined drain (F29) (fig. 6; pl. 7). The main drain (F19) measured 26m in length (north-south), 0.75m in width and 0.26m in depth. The sides of the drain were lined with cut limestone blocks and occasional red bricks and it was capped with large limestone flags. Mortar adhering to some of the stone blocks, indicates that they had been re-used from an existing structure. The drain was dated to the eighteenth-nineteenth century by sherds of black glazed red earthenware and sherds of post-medieval tiles recovered from it.

Drainage ditches
A linear ditch (F53) was located to the west of the large stone-lined drain (F19) and was on the same north-south alignment. It measured 7.60m in length and was between 0.60m and 1.20m in width. The ditch had a depth of 0.36m and sherds of cream ware and post-medieval roof tile were recovered from it. Another north-south oriented ditch (F72) was cut into the northern end of this ditch (F53). The silty fill and presence of snail shells within both of these ditches indicate that they served as drains.

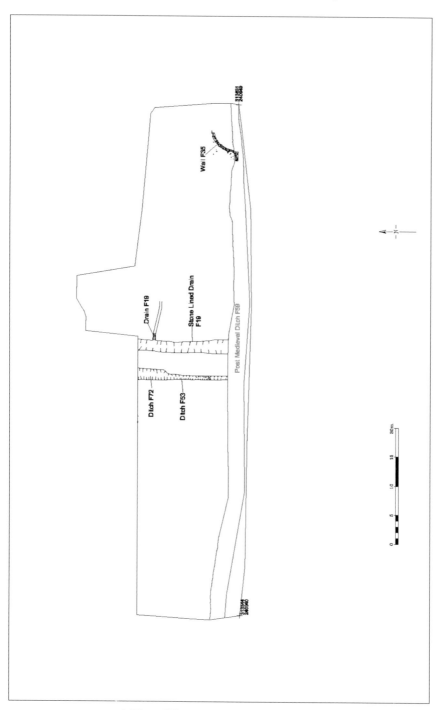

6 Plan of Phase 4 post-medieval features

Plate 7 Post-medieval stone-lined drains F19 and F29

Boundary ditch
A substantial boundary ditch (F59) ran along the southern extent of the site
parallel to St Margaret's Road. It cut the southern end of the aforementioned
ditch (F53) and also cut several medieval features. This boundary ditch (F59)
measured 2.80m in width and 0.58m in depth. Medieval and post-medieval
pottery and clay pipe fragments were recovered from it.

Masonry wall
The foundation-remains of a curving masonry wall (F35) were uncovered on
the south-eastern end of the site. The wall was built over the fill of the
boundary ditch (F59). It was probably a garden feature associated with
Meakstown House which is shown at this approximate location on the
Ordnance Survey map (fig. 3). The wall was semi-circular in plan and was a

well faced randomly coursed construction which consisted of two courses of limestone blocks bonded by lime mortar. It measured 7.20m in length and 0.45m in width.

Phase 4 discussion

Sixteenth-century artefacts found during excavation suggest a continuity of activity in the area from the medieval period. However, these sixteenth-century finds were all *ex situ* and no features contemporary with the construction or occupation of Meakstown Castle during the late sixteenth century were identified within the excavation area. In fact the post-medieval features uncovered on site were all dated to the eighteenth and nineteenth centuries and most of them are likely to relate to the occupation of Meakstown House and farming of the surrounding land.

SUMMARY DISCUSSION

During the thirteenth century much of the lands surrounding Finglas were part of the manor held by the archbishop of Dublin. The excavation site at Meakstown almost certainly fell within that manor and the manorial centre probably focussed around the town of Finglas to the south of the site. At that time the practice of open-field farming, which had been introduced by English settlers, was widespread in eastern Ireland. This practice was characterized by large common fields which were divided into strips for peasant holdings (Otway-Ruthven 1951; O'Connor 1998, 69; O'Keefe 2000, 61–2). Manorial records for Finglas dating to 1326 imply the use of large fields on a three-field system. Under this system crops of wheat and oats were grown in rotation and between these crop-cycles the field lay fallow (Simms and Fagan 1992, 93). However, this fourteenth-century reference probably post-dates at least some of the medieval activity recorded on the site at Meakstown and the archaeological evidence uncovered during excavation suggests that at that time the site was part of a nucleated settlement rather than an area of open fields.

The settlement was laid out perpendicular to St Margaret's Road and the stratigraphic evidence represents three successive phases of occupation during the medieval period. The earliest settlement was characterized by the truncated remains of three structures (Structures 1–3) on the south-western end of the site and a sub-rectangular ditched enclosure with an internal stone yard, which may be described as a haggard, on the east. At a slightly later stage the site was divided into at least three property plots which were defined by two long linear ditches running perpendicular to the road. The central plot was 20m wide but the widths of the other plots were no longer evident. Occupation of the eastern plot was indicated by the presence of a slot trench, a stone-lined drain and a drainage ditch while a small gully was evident within the central plot. The third phase of medieval occupation was characterized by the remains of a timber house (Structure 4) within the eastern plot.

The structural remains were heavily truncated and it is possible that more than four structures may have occupied the site during the medieval period but that those have left no trace in the archaeological record. This is further indicated by the formal construction and distinct curvature of the Phase 2 stone-lined drain, which pre-dates the construction of Structure 4 and suggests that an earlier structure may have stood on the eastern end of the site. The linear slot trench (F21) also dates from Phase 2 and clearly represents the remains of some form of plank-built structure on this part of the site.

The excavated structural remains appear to represent three sub-rectangular buildings (Structures 1, 2, 4) and one sub-square or sub-circular structure (Structure 3). These were defined by slot trenches which are indicative of timber-framed buildings constructed on sill beam foundations. The large collection of *ex situ* nails recovered during excavation was probably derived from these or other nearby timber buildings. There was no direct evidence for the timbers used in the construction of the Meakstown structures. Although charcoal pieces were present within some of the trench fills, they were unlikely to represent structural timbers since there was no indication that any of the structures had been burned. Moreover, analysis has shown that this charcoal was from a variety of tree species which suggests that it was probably derived from material that had blown into the trench fill.

The refuse pits, drainage ditches and the gully excavated on this site are all features that would clearly have been associated with settlement and related domestic activity. The artefact assemblage is also indicative of domestic activity on site from the twelfth to the fourteenth centuries and possibly extending into the fifteenth century. These artefacts include a large assemblage (1,003 sherds) of medieval pottery and a number of metal objects. The pottery sherds were all derived from vessels that had been produced in the Dublin and/or Leinster area. The assemblage was dominated by Leinster cooking-ware of the type manufactured in the north of the province, thus suggesting that the occupants sourced their wares locally. The Dublin wares included examples of both hand-built and wheel-thrown vessels and some of the pieces were glazed. The pottery vessels represented in this assemblage include jugs and jars which would have been used for food preparation and storage. Similar ceramic assemblages comprising mainly local wares were recorded at contemporary sites in Blackcastle, Piperstown, Nangor, Merrion Road and at nearby Cappogue (Sleeman and Hurley 1987; Barry 2000; Doyle 2002; Baker 2008; McQuade 2009).

The majority of metal finds were also domestic items which include fragments of knife blades and a horse shoe. The arrowhead could have been used either for hunting or warfare. Its discovery here is not unusual since

Plate 8 French jetton obverse

Plate 9 French jetton reverse

examples of arrowheads have been recorded from medieval settlements at Piperstown, Nangor, Ardree and Cappogue (Barry 2000; Doyle 2002; Opie 2003; McQuade 2009). Of note amongst the metal items was the French jetton which dates to the fourteenth or fifteenth century (pls 8 and 9). Although it was not recovered from a sealed context, its presence is an indication that the medieval occupants of Meakstown were engaged in outside trade.

The historical sources indicate that crops were cultivated in the area and a small assemblage of highly abraded plant remains were recovered from this site. Cereal grains were present but only a few could be identified. There was one barley grain and several weeds typical of those growing on arable land. A single legume, which may have been from a cultivated variety, was also recovered. In addition to the plant remains a small assemblage of animal bone, comprising just 108 fragments, was recovered during excavation. The identifiable pieces were all from domestic species; cattle, sheep/goat, pig, horse, cat, fowl and mallard duck. There were no dog bones in the assemblage but gnawing on some of the bone pieces indicates that this species was present on the site. The variety of anatomical elements identified in this assemblage suggests that the meat-producing animals may have been slaughtered on site or somewhere nearby. The lands surrounding this site made ideal pasture and it is highly likely that livestock were kept in the environs. It is possible that they could have been housed or sheltered within the rectangular enclosure or haggard on the eastern end of the site.

Determining who occupied this site is problematic. It could have been occupied by English free tenants who were known to have lived in dispersed settlements away from the manor (O'Connor 1998, 46; after Edwards et al. 1983 and Simms 1983). The rectangular plans of structures 1, 2, and 4 compare to those of Anglo-Norman structures excavated elsewhere in Ireland (Ó Ríordáin and Hunt 1942; Cleary 1982; Sleeman and Hurley 1987; Foley 1989; O'Connor 1998; Murphy 2000; Opie 2000; Opie 2001; Fallon 2006; Clutterbuck 2007; Baker forthcoming). Alternatively the settlement at Meakstown could be that of 'betaghs' (lower-status Irish tenants living on manors) who reportedly lived in house clusters in townlands away from the main village (O'Connor 1998, 44). Gaelic houses of the period took one of two forms; sub-rectangular structures similar in size to the buildings recorded on Anglo-Norman sites, or simple oval or round structures with just one room and no window, known as a *creat* (O'Connor 1998, 95). Thus the plan form of the structures excavated at Meakstown also fits the description of betagh dwellings.

Regardless of who exactly occupied this site, the evidence for medieval occupation uncovered here is an important contribution to the data on rural settlement in the greater Dublin area during the twelfth to fourteenth centuries. The excavation of this site has uncovered evidence for property boundaries and structural remains laid out perpendicular to St Margaret's Road – indicating that it could be on the line of a medieval road. Four possible structures and associated settlement activity indicate at least three phases of medieval occupation on site. Cereal crops were cultivated in the area and livestock appear to have been slaughtered on or near the site. The medieval occupants of the site used locally-produced pottery and engaged in some outside trade.

The artefact assemblage indicates that the environs continued to be settled during the sixteenth century, although there was no evidence for on-site activity at that time. The first securely-dated evidence for on-site activity during the post-medieval period was a series of linear stone-lined drains and earth-cut drainage ditches of eighteenth- and nineteenth-century date. These features confirm the cartographic evidence for a dwelling (Meakstown House) on or near the eastern end of the site and indicate that the surrounding lands were farmed. The curving masonry wall was most probably a garden feature associated with Meakstown House.

CONCLUSIONS

The excavation carried out on this site uncovered evidence for previously unrecorded occupation dating from the prehistoric and medieval periods. This paper has focused on the medieval evidence which indicates that the site functioned as a domestic settlement around which agricultural activity was being carried out during the twelfth to fourteenth centuries and possibly extending into the fifteenth century.

There were no extant remains of the sixteenth-century Meakstown Castle (DU–014–020) on the excavation site which indicates that it was, as the cartographic evidence illustrates, located on the southern side of St Margaret's Road. The castle was located at a slight remove from the area of medieval settlement identified on the excavation site and it represents continued occuation or a slightly later reoccupation of the area. No clear evidence for Meakstown Castle (DU–014–020) was uncovered on site or during the archaeological investigations conducted on the 'site of' the castle on the southern side of the road. This suggests that the castle may have been completely demolished and its building fabric reused for later buildings or for the nineteenth-century Meakstown House that stood on the northern side of the road, close to the excavation area.

FINDS REPORTS

THE METAL FINDS

(*by Siobhán Scully MA*)

Introduction

Only a selection of the thirty-one metal objects recovered from the excavations at Meakstown (05E044ext.) are detailed in this paper. The finds are numbered according to the feature from which they were recovered, where 1 refers to items recovered from topsoil or unsealed contexts.

Metal, non-ferrous

Buckles A small, cast, single-loop buckle (05E044ext:28:31) with loped knops on the outer edge flanking transverse grooves. It measures 22mm x 19mm and is 2.5–5.5mm thick. It dates to *c.*1250–1400 (Whitehead 2003, 22). A broken double-loop oval buckle (05E044ext:11:127) has oblique lines engraved on the front of the frame and dates to the fifteenth or sixteenth century (Whitehead 2003, 52). It is *c.*47mm long x 27.5mm wide and is 3mm thick.

French jetton (05E044ext:1:43) is made of copper alloy and has a circular flan with a three-pointed crown and the legend AVE MRIA GRACIA PL on the obverse and a *fleur-de-lis* tipped cross in tressure on the reverse (pls 8 and 9). It measures 22mm in diameter and is 2mm thick. Jettons were reckoning counters which were used in trading to assist calculations. They originated in France in the medieval period and were usually made of copper and brass. The value of the jetton was calculated by its position on a chequered board (Mitchiner 1988, 17; Kenny 1997, 536). This example from Meakstown appears to be a French jetton possibly dating to the fourteenth or fifteenth century (Van Beek 1986).

Button a slightly domed livery or blazer button (05E044ext:1:44) with an eye loop and the remains of gilding, measuring 26mm in diameter and 3mm thick. It is an example of the predominant type of coat button in use during the latter half of the eighteenth century (Hume 1969, 90). On the front it shows a figure from the waist up with a key in one hand and a sword in the other. The maker's name, FOLEY & CROKER 24 COLLEGE GREEN DUBLIN, is on the back.

Metal, ferrous

Horseshoe A corroded fragment of a horseshoe heel (05E044ext:65:1) 58mm long x 20–30mm wide and 4.5–9.5mm thick. It is a straight-ended heel with a calkin in the form of an upset or 'thickened' heel. Calkins helped the shoe to grip on soft ground and they are found on medieval horseshoes. By the seventeenth century the use of calkins was declining (Clark 1995, 82).

Possible arrowhead (05E044ext:11:148) is triangular in shape and tapers to a point. A circular socket at its wider end suggests it may be a type of socketed arrowhead. It is 40mm long x 13mm wide and 10mm thick. The projectile point could have been attached to a wooden arrow shaft by pressing the wood firmly into the socketed end. Such socketed arrowheads could have been used for hunting or warfare (Jessop 1997, 2–3).

THE POTTERY
(by Niamh Doyle)

The assemblage from Meakstown consists of 1003 sherds of pottery, which includes 981 sherds of medieval pottery ranging in date from the twelfth to fourteenth century and 22 sherds of post-medieval pottery ranging in date from the sixteenth to twentieth century. The medieval pottery is all Irish in origin and includes the medieval Dublin-type wares for this period as well as Leinster cooking-ware. The post-medieval pottery consists of types manufactured in Ireland and England.

Medieval wares

Leinster cooking-ware is a hand-built ware found on numerous medieval sites in south-eastern Ireland, and ranging in date from the twelfth to the fourteenth century. The fabric is coarse and contains large plates of quartz, mica and occasionally decomposed feldspar (Ó Floinn 1988). The Leinster cooking-ware from Meakstown represented the largest group of medieval pottery at 51.2% of the medieval wares and includes a total MNR of 37 vessels. These included at least one jug, represented by a spout fragment with a simple pulled spout with incised decoration around the edge (05E044ext:31:32), as well as multiple jars or jugs represented by rim fragments. The majority of the rim types are plain everted types; there are also a number with internal lid seatings. Decorated rim types include incised patterns made with a tool or stick on the top and edge of the rim and at the rim-body join. Ó Floinn divides the forms of Leinster cooking-ware most commonly found in North and South Leinster based on morphological traits such as rim decoration. Based on this, the types found at Meakstown are those more commonly associated with Leinster cooking-ware from North Leinster (Ó Floinn 1988, 328–9).

There are several body fragments in the characteristic open fabric with frequent inclusions of mica and quartz, ranging in colour from reduced grey to oxidized orange. The assemblage contains multiple base-fragments that show the slab-built pitted bases characteristic of Leinster cooking-ware. At least three of the vessels are treated externally with a white slip, which Ó Floinn has suggested (1988) was possibly designed to imitate French cooking-wares in the marketplace.

Research on the pottery produced and consumed in medieval Dublin has provided a classification of Dublin-type pottery by fabric, form and date (Barton 1965; Papazian 1989; and McCutcheon 2000; 2006).

Dublin-type coarse-ware is a hand-built glazed ware that ranges in date from the middle of the twelfth to the middle of the thirteenth century. The fabric is micaceous with occasional quartz inclusions and varies from an orange-red exterior and grey-black core. The assemblage contains a MNR of three vessels of this type, probably jugs, represented by rim fragments. One jug has a collared rim while the other two have squared everted rims with applied frills below the rim; all three vessels represented are glazed. There is a single strap-handle fragment with an incised pattern consisting of two vertical lines, McCutcheon's type D2 (McCutcheon 2006, 49). Dublin-type coarse-ware vessels were closely modelled on contemporary Ham Green B jugs from Bristol, England (McCutcheon 2006, 68). Some partial undecorated base fragments remain.

Dublin-type is a wheel-thrown, glazed pottery produced locally that dates from the late thirteenth to the fourteenth centuries. This type superseded Dublin-type coarse-ware; it is less coarse and is heavily influenced by stylistic elements of contemporary Bristol Redcliffe wares (McCutcheon 2000, 122). The assemblage contains 264 sherds of this type, representing 27% of the medieval pottery from Meakstown, with a MNV of two and a MNR of eleven vessels, all of which are jug forms. The bodies of the vessels are decorated with the characteristic lead glaze that appears green-brown depending on the iron content of the clay. Occasional body fragments are decorated with horizontal grooving, as well as applied rosettes and applied strips in contrasting colours to the main vessel.

There is an MNR of eleven vessels, representing jugs, with one rim-handle fragment showing a strap handle decorated with an applied rosette (1:7). Handle fragments are decorated with a variety of slashes and incised patterns including McCutcheon's E4 (11:1+3) a band of diagonal slashing flanked by two incised vertical lines either side, D1 (60:2) a single incised vertical line, and one with a band of diagonal slashes down the centre (22:1); another broken handle fragment possibly represents an E1 type with a line of diagonal slashing between two vertical lines. E1, E4 and D1 types were represented in the Dublin-type wares from Wood Quay (McCutcheon 2006, 80). The jug bases are largely of a plain everted type with two examples of thumbed bases represented; several are sooted externally indicating they were used to heat their contents over a fire.

Dublin-type fine-ware is a fine, wheel-thrown type dated from the late thirteenth to the fourteenth century. This type possibly overlaps the later period of Dublin-type ware but contains much fewer inclusions and follows on from Dublin-type ware stylistically, with Bristol Redcliffe influences (McCutcheon 2000, 122). Representing 14% of the medieval pottery from Meakstown, there was an MNR of five Dublin-type fine-ware vessels in the assemblage. Body fragments are decorated with a lead glaze as typical of Dublin wares, while some fragments are decorated with applied strips glazed in contrasting colours to the main body of the vessel and occasionally also rouletted. There are also examples of applied pellets and thumbed strips; these applied decorations are influenced by contemporary Redcliffe Bristol wares.

The vessel types represented are jugs with strap handles and simple or squared rims. There is an MNV of one jug as well as an example of a pulled spout and at least two jugs with applied frills below the rim. Strap handles are fragmentary but decoration includes a single incised line, McCutcheon's D1 (2006, 49) which is well represented in the Wood Quay assemblage (McCutcheon 2006, 80) and possibly C1 with a central line of vertical slashing (McCutcheon 2006, 49). Base fragments include thumbed and plain everted types.

Dublin-type cooking-ware is an unglazed, micaceous type used to manufacture cooking and storage vessels in Dublin from the twelfth to the thirteenth century. It occurs in both hand-built and wheel-thrown forms and is contemporary with all Dublin-type wares (McCutcheon 2000, 122).

The assemblage contains a small number of these sherds, from undecorated unglazed vessels, representing only 3.4% of the medieval assemblage. A handled jar is represented by one strap handle in McCutcheon's D1 form (2006, 49) decorated with a single incised line. There is an MNR of five pots represented; two with rims that have internal lid seatings, probably to accommodate wooden lids as described by McCutcheon (2006, 83). There are also rim shapes including squared everted and flat-topped everted forms. Base fragments are all from vessels with plain sagging bases.

Table 1: Medieval pottery from Meakstown, Co. Dublin

Type	MNV	MVR	Vessel part	no. of sherds	Description of forms present
Dublin-type coarse-ware			rim		collared (1), applied frill (2)
			body	30	Glazed
			base		plain sagging
			handle		strap D2 type
			spout		
Dublin-type ware	2	1	rim	6	squared with lid seating (7), simple with applied frill below (4)
			body	227	
			base	5	11 plain everted, 2 thumbed
			handle		E4, D1
			spout		Pulled
Dublin-type fine-ware	1		rim	0	simple rounded
			body	115	applied decoration and horizontal combing
			base	4	2 plain everted, 2 thumbed
			handle	1	D1
			spout		Pulled
Dublin-type cooking-ware	0		rim		3 with lid seatings, 2 everted squared, 1 everted flat-topped
			body	27	Plain
			base		plain everted sagging
			handle	D1	
			spout		
Leinster cooking-ware		37	rim	76	with lid seating (7), decorated (9), plain everted (26)
			body	385	Plain
			base	5	sagging everted
			handle	0	
			spout		possible, decorated

Table 2: Post-medieval pottery from Meakstown, Co. Dublin

Type	Sherds	MVR	Form	Date Range	Origin
Fine black glazed red earthenware	1	1	storage jar, jug, mug	16th–18th C	English
North Devon gravel tempered ware	2	1	small bowl	17th–E18th C	English
Black glazed red earthenware	9	5	jar/mug, storage jar	18th–19th C	Irish/English
Glazed red earthenware	1	1	storage jar	18th–19th C	Irish/English
Creamware	6	2	large and small bowl	18th–19th C	English
Shell edged ware	1	1	dish/plate	m18th–19th C	English
Transfer printed ware	1	1	bowl	19th–20th C	English
Yellow-ware	1	1	bowl/ chamber pot	19th–20th C	English
Total	**22**	**13**			

THE HUMAN REMAINS

(by Jonny Geber)

A fragment of a human left femur was found in the fill of the foundation trench (F27) of a possible medieval structure. The fragment comprised of the mid-diaphysis of the bone. It had been damaged post-mortem in the ground, and was slightly eroded. The size of the bone indicates that it was from an adult individual. It was not possible to determine the sex of that individual. No degenerative or pathological changes were noted on the fragment.

THE FAUNAL REMAINS FROM MEDIEVAL LEVELS

(by Jonny Geber)

Introduction
Seven medieval features contained animal bone at a total quantity of 108 fragments and 1193g. The bones were relatively well preserved and moderately fragmented. From the

assemblage, 58% of the fragments could be identified to species which were cattle, sheep, pig, horse, cat, fowl and duck (Table 1.).

Methodology
The bones have been identified to species, skeletal element and body side with the aid of a bone reference collection (Margaret Gowen & Co. Ltd). The bones have been counted and then weighed on a digital scale with an accuracy of 0.01 grams. Measurements were taken according to von den Driesch (1976) using an osteometric board and a measuring tape with 0.50mm accuracy as well as a digital calliper with 0.01mm accuracy. The assemblage has been quantified by NISP (Number of identified specimens) and MNI (Minimum Number of Individuals). Size, side and sex charac-teristics were taken into consideration when the total minimum number of individuals was estimated. The descriptions by Boessneck and Müller (1964) and Prummel and Frisch (1986) were used to distinguish between sheep and goat when possible in caprovine remains. The estimation of age at death was done from the degree of dental attrition (Grant 1982; Benecke 1988).

The medieval assemblage
Cattle (*Bos taurus*) The majority of the bone fragments from medieval features derived from cattle, and mainly meat-poor body parts such as the skull and feet (Table 1). Dog gnaw-marks were noted on one pelvic fragment. Skeletal degeneration was noted in the metacarpal-phalangeal joint (the knee) of one animal, which could either indicate an advanced age for this individual, or that possibly cattle were used as labour animals. Up until the late thirteenth century in Ireland, oxen would have been more commonly used as a draught animal than horse (Kelly 1997, 95). Compression of the joint had led to moderate marginal osteophytic build-up on the anterior and medial and lateral portions of the proximal articulation of the proximal phalanges. No eburnation was noted.
Sheep/Goat (*Ovis aries/Capra hircus*) Bone fragments from caprovine were almost as commonly identified as cattle (Table A1.). Two fragments, one humerus and one phalanx, could with certainty be identified as sheep. Age at slaughter could be estimated from dental attrition on a left and right mandible, possibly from the same animal since both gave an age span between 4–6 years.
Horse (*Equus caballus*) Only two bones of horse were identified in the sample (F34 and F52), an anterior and a posterior proximal phalanx.
Cat (*Felis catus*) The distal ends of two left *humeri* of mature cats were found in the same medieval feature (F28). No cut marks that could indicate skinning were iden-tified. One of the humeri displayed animal gnaw-marks on the distal end.
Bird (*Aves sp.*) The distal half of a right femur of fowl *(Gallus gallus)* was identified in F34. A right coracoid from a mature domestic duck or mallard *(Anas platyrhynchus)* was identified in fill F56.

Conclusions
All the remains appear to derive from mature animals. The anatomical distribution of skeletal elements from cattle and caprovines suggests that slaughter took place on location, although the data is too small for any conclusions to be drawn on livestock economy and breeding strategy.

Table 1: Identified taxa and skeletal elements

Element	Cattle	Sheep/ Goat	Pig	Horse	Cat	Fowl	Duck	Indet.
Cranial	5	5	-	-	-	-	-	-
Mandible	1	4	-	-	-	-	-	-
Loose teeth	-	2	-	-	-	-	-	-
Atlas	1	-	-	-	-	-	-	-
Cerv.vert.	1	-	-	-	-	-	-	-
Lumb.vert.	-	-	1	-	-	-	-	-
Ribs	6	-	1	-	-	-	-	6
Scapula	-	1	-	-	-	-	-	2
Coracoid	-	-	-	-	-	-	1	-
Humerus	1	3	1	-	2	-	-	-
Radius	-	1	-	-	-	-	-	-
Ulna	-	-	1	-	-	-	-	-
Mc	-	1	1	-	-	-	-	-
Ph1Mc	2	-	-	-	-	-	-	-
Ph2Mc	2	-	-	-	-	-	-	-
Ph3Mc	1	-	-	-	-	-	-	-
Coxae	2	1	-	-	-	-	-	-
Femur	1	-	-	-	-	1	-	-
Tibia	-	-	1	-	-	-	-	-
Calcaneus	-	1	-	-	-	-	-	-
Mt	-	2	-	-	-	-	-	-
Ph1Mp	4	2	-	2	-	-	-	-
Ph2Mp	1	-	-	-	-	-	-	-
Ph3Mp	-	-	1	-	-	-	-	-
Sesamoid	-	-	-	-	-	-	-	1
Indet.	-	-	-	-	-	-	-	37
Total:	**28**	**23**	**7**	**2**	**2**	**1**	**1**	**46**
%NISP:	5.45%	0.91%	0.36%	0.82%	0.91%	0.91%	0.91%	1.82%
MNI:	1	2	1	1	2	1	1	-

WOOD CHARCOAL IDENTIFICATION

(by Susan Lyons)

Introduction
One charcoal sample was submitted for identification and analysis of the wood charcoal fragments within. The sample was taken from the fill of a medieval drainage ditch (F33).

Methodology
The sample was sieved through a bank of sieves (2mm, 1mm and 0.5mm) to separate the larger charcoal samples from the much smaller charcoal fibres, which would prove more difficult to identify.

The larger-sized charcoal fragments (>5mm) were fractured to view the three planes [transverse, radial and tangential sections] necessary for microscopic wood identification. The identifications were conducted under a binocular microscope using dark ground light and viewed at magnifications of 100x, 200x and 400x where applicable. Where possible the age and growth pattern of the wood fragments were recorded by studying the transverse section at a magnification of up to 40x.

Identifications were made using wood reference slides and wood keys devised by Schweingruber (1978) and the IAWA wood identification manuals (Wheeler, Bass & Gasson 1989).

Results
Seven wood species totalling 203 identifications were identified. While the charcoal identified represents the wood type that was burnt as fuel at the site, it is also likely to reflect some of the flora that grew in the nearby hedges, scrub and woodland in the area.

The dominant species types recorded were ash (*Fraxinus excelsior*) and apple/hawthorn/pear/whitebeam-type (*Pomoideae* spp.). Hazel (*Corylus avellana*), alder (*Alnus glutinous*) and oak (*Quercus* sp.) were also identified in lesser concentrations, while a smaller number of birch (*Betula* sp.) and blackthorn/sloe type (*Prunus spinosa*) were recorded (Table 1).

Ring growth and form The age ranges of the wood were difficult to decipher due to the fragmented nature of the material. No obvious young wood fragments were recorded, the majority of the wood pieces contained just 2–8 rings, but the absence of a pith or sapwood made ageing difficult. The general growth of the wood was relatively even. The oak, ash and alder growth rings were wider, potentially suggesting that they belonged to larger branches or the trunk of the tree. No bark or sapwood was recorded from the samples. No root material was identified.

Origin of wood species Ash was one of the dominant species identified from F33 making up 40% of the overall identifiable charcoal. Ash thrives well on nutrient-rich soils but is also a common woodland species and grows in mixed woodland with oak on damp, slightly acidic soils (Gale & Culter 2000); it is able to germinate and grow vigorously as secondary woodland and in marginal areas and hedges (Kelly 1976).

The apple/pear/hawthorn/whitebeam wood species type was also dominant within the sample making up 32% of the charcoal assemblage identified. The wood structure of these genera is very similar and only slight anatomical features separate them. They are small deciduous spiny trees or shrubs and are common to the scrubby margins of woodlands and hedgerows (Gale & Culter 2000). Hawthorn (*Crataegus* sp.) is shade-tolerant and forms understorey in ash and hazel woodland. Both hawthorn and apple-type (*Malus* sp.) produce edible fruits which would have been gathered as a foodstuff (Greig 1991). These wood types burn slow and steady and provide excellent heat with minimal smoke (Gale & Culter 2000).

Hazel values accounted for 10% of the identifiable charcoal fragments from Meakstown. This species grows on most soil types and forms a small deciduous tree or shrub. It commonly occurs in understorey of oak and/or ash woodlands, where it may grow to a height of 10m or more. In open areas or woodland glades hazel grows as a shrub. Hazel is a common species recorded from Irish archaeological sites and its widespread presence is highlighted in pollen diagrams (Caseldine 1996).

Oak accounts for 9% of the identifiable charcoal from the site. Most oak species prefer damp non-calcareous soils on lowland or montane sites at altitudes up to 4,000m (Gale & Culter 2000). It is a tall deciduous woodland tree, often growing in association with hazel and ash. Oak wood is easy to cleave both radially and tangentially and has provided one of the most important building materials since the prehistoric period (Gale & Culter 2000). When burnt, oak charcoal, and particularly the dense heartwood, has higher calorific values than most European woods. It makes for good long-lasting fuel, although oak charcoal requires good ventilation to maintain an even heat (Gale & Culter 2000).

Blackthorn/sloe (*Prunus spinosa*) accounted for 4% of the identifiable charcoal from the sample. This is a spiny shrub found in marginal woodland; it is quick to colonize clearings and rapidly forms dense thickets, particularly in coastal regions.

Alder, which made up 3% of the charcoal assemblage, is a species usually found growing close to running water, rivers or in damp woodland, often with oak in the latter. While alder makes for poor fuel, it produces good-quality charcoal (Edlin 1951)

The number of fragments identified as birch was also very low, making up just 2% of the charcoal identified. Birch grows as trees or shrubs, has a preference for light and grows well on non-calcareous soils. It is often associated with heath land and successional oak woods, but can rapidly form secondary woodland in cleared areas. Birch wood makes a hot but short-lived fuel and produces high-quality charcoal (Gale & Culter 2000).

Discussion

The presence of ash, hazel and oak, which are typical woodland species that grow in close proximity to each other, indicates that the site was located close to relatively dense woodland. While apple/hawthorn/whitebeam/pear type together with blackthorn/sloe, are common to hedgerows and the edges of woodland, they would also have colonized the marginal areas of settlement sites, such as that at Meakstown. The values for alder and birch, both species common to water-tolerant environments, such as heath lands and bog, were very low and may indicate that the site at Meakstown was primarily situated in an area of dry land, with easy access to strands of hazel and ash.

The charcoal species identified from Meakstown primarily represent a variety of wood species that was selected for fuel at the site. The absence of insect borings also suggests that it was collected fresh or indeed reused quickly for the purpose of burning. The periodic dumping of charred remains associated with occupational activity would have inevitably resulted in the mixing of wood species from different sources across the site and enter open features or become mixed with sealing deposits. The presence of such charred material within the ditch/gully (F33) is therefore likely to reflect the re-deposited or dumped remains of nearby fuelling debris.

Whether these species were selected purposely as fuel is difficult to ascertain based on such a small number of samples. It is however possible that these wood types are reminiscent of the local peripheral hedge and scrub (pomaceous woods, blackthorn/sloe, birch) that grew in and around the site, with elements of larger woodland trees (ash, oak, alder) which may have been brought to the site for other purposes.

Table 1: Wood species identified from Meakstown (F33)

Wood Species	Number of fragments	Percentage	Weight
Ash	79	40%	8 grams
Apple/hawthorn type	64	32%	6 grams
Hazel	21	10%	2 grams
Oak	19	9%	2 grams
Blackthorn/Sloe type	9	4%	1 gram
Alder	7	3%	<1 gram
Birch	4	2%	<1 gram

THE PLANT REMAINS

(by Ryan Allen)

Introduction
A sample of medieval ditch-fill (F33 S1) was analyzed for carbonized plant remains.

Methodology
A bulk soil sample was taken during excavation and was processed by flotation. The residues were collected in a sieve mesh measuring 250μm and these flots were sorted using a low-powered binocular microscope (magnification x8–x80). Identification was carried out with the aid of a modern reference collection and with reference to Berggren (1981) and Cappers et al. (2006). Owing to fragmentation of grains and seeds, only the embryo ends, the most diagnostic part, were counted. This eliminated the possibility of counting multiple pieces of the same seed/grain. Nomenclature and taxonomy generally follows Stace (1997).

Results
Due to poor preservation and abrasion, the vast majority (248) of the plant remains within F33 could not be identified. Cereal grains made up 8% (24) of the identified plants. Only one of these grains could be identified and it was barley (*Hordeum* sp.) but it was too abraded to allow for identification to a particular variety. In addition one large and possibly cultivated legume (*Fabaceae*) was present but it was not possible to determine whether it was from a crop or simply a cereal contaminate. Wild seeds were also recovered: these included a small seeded legumes, vetch (*Vicia* sp.), one seed from the Goosefoot family (*Chenopodiaceae*), and two possible cleaver seeds (*Galium* cf. *aparine*). These are all plants that grow on arable land and were most likely crop-contaminates brought on to site accidentally with the harvest. The roots of cleaver have been used in the past to produce red dye, but its low count and its presence with other contaminant plants suggests that this was not the case at Meakstown.

ACKNOWLEDGMENTS

Thanks are due to the hardworking site staff: Frank Mallon, Ciara Burke, Rachel O'Byrne, Kevin McNearny, Johnny Ryan, Frank Zack and Antoine Arekian. To those who carried out post-excavation analyses including Aimee Little whose report on the lithics has been omitted owing to constraints on the space available for this paper. Graphics were prepared by Tim Murphy, Gary Devlin and Mario Sughi. Special thanks are due to Linzi Simpson for her continued encouragement and valued advice on the preparation of this paper.

BIBLIOGRAPHY

Adams, B.W. 1881 Antiquarian notes, etc., of the parishes of Santry and Cloghran, County Dublin. *RSAI Jn.* XV, 482–98.

Baker, C. 2008 Excavations within the manor of Merrion Castle, Dublin. In Seán Duffy (ed.), *Medieval Dublin VIII*, 228–86. Dublin.

Baker, C. forthcoming Tullykane, Co. Meath: a medieval rural settlement. In C. Corlett and M. Potterton (eds), *Rural settlement in medieval Ireland in light of recent archaeological excavations.*

Ball, F.E. 1920 *A history of the County Dublin.* Dublin.

Barry, T.B. 2000 Excavations at Piperstown deserted medieval village, Co. Louth, 1987. *RIA Proc.* 100C, 113–35.

Barton, K.J. 1988 The medieval pottery of Dublin. In G. Mac Niocaill and P.F. Wallace (eds), *Keimelia: studies in medieval archaeology and history in memory of Tom Delaney,* 271–324. Galway.

Benecke, N. 1988 *Archäozoologische Untersuchungen an Tierknochen aus der frühmittel-alterlichen Siedlung von Menzlin,* Schwerin.

Berggren, G. 1981 *Atlas of seeds and small fruits of northwest-European plant species* (Part 3: Salicaceae – Cruciferae) Stockholm.

Boessneck, J. and Müller, H.-H. 1964 Osteologische Unterscheidungsmerkmale zwischen Schaf (Ovis aries Linné) und Ziege (Capra hircus Linné), *Kühn-Archiv Band,* 78. Berlin.

Bradley, J. 1998 The medieval boroughs of County Dublin. In C. Manning (ed.), *Dublin and beyond the pale, studies in honour of Patrick Healy,* 129–45. Dublin.

Birmingham, N. 2000 Meakstown, Finglas 99E0351; 1999:242. In I. Bennett (ed.), *Excavations 1999. Summary accounts of archaeological excavation in Ireland.* Dublin.

Cappers, R.T.J., Bekker, R.M. and Jans J.E.A. 2006 *Digital seed atlas of the Netherlands.* Groningen.

Caseldine, C.J. and Hatton, J.M. 1996 Early land clearance and wooden trackway construction in the third and fourth millennium BC at Corlea, Co. Longford. *RIA Proc.,* 95B, 1–9.

Clark, J. 1995 Horseshoes. In J. Clark (ed.), *The medieval horse and its equipment,* 75–123. London.

Cleary, R.M. 1982 Excavations at Lough Gur, Co. Limerick: Part II. *Cork Archaeological and Historical Society Journal.* 87, 77–106.

Clutterbuck, R. 2007 Cookstown, Co. Meath. In I. Bennett (ed.), *Excavations 2004. Summary accounts of archaeological excavation in Ireland.* Dublin.

Doyle, I. 2002 Nangor Castle 00E754. In I. Bennett (ed.), *Excavations 2001. Summary accounts of archaeological excavation in Ireland*, 136–7. Dublin.

Driesch, A. von den 1976 *A guide to the measurement of animal bones from archaeological sites*, Peabody Museum Bulletin 1, Harvard.

Edlin, H.L. 1951 *British plants and their uses*. London.

Fallon, D. 2006 Lady Castle Lower, Co. Kildare. In I. Bennett (ed.), *Excavations 2003. Summary accounts of archaeological excavation in Ireland*, 247. Dublin.

Foley, C. 1989 Excavation at a medieval settlement site in Jerpoint Church Townland, Co. Kilkenny. *RIA Proc*, 89C, 71–126.

Forde-Johnston, J. 1977 *Castles and fortifications of Britain and Ireland*. London.

Gale, R. and Cutler, D. 2000 *Plants in archaeology: identification manual of artefact of plant origin from Europe and the Mediterranean*. London.

Grant, A. 1982 The use of tooth wear as a guide to the age of domestic animals. In *Ageing and sexing animal bones from archaeological sites*, British Archaeological Reports, British Series 109, 91–108.

Greig, J. 1991 The British Isles. In van Zeist, Wasylikowa & Behre (eds), *Progress in old world palaeoethnobotany*, 299–334. Rotterdam.

Halpin, E. 1998 Holy Faith Convent, Finglas 95E0100EXT, 1997:176. In I. Bennett (ed.), *Excavations 1999. Summary accounts of archaeological excavation in Ireland*, 56. Dublin.

Hume, I.N. 1969 *A guide to artefacts of Colonial America*. Philadelphia.

Jessop, O. 1997 Medieval arrowheads. *Finds Research Group 700–1700: Datasheet 22*.

Kavanagh, J. 2007 4–8 Church Street, Finglas 04E0900, 2004:599. In I. Bennett (ed.), *Excavations 2004. Summary accounts of archaeological excavation in Ireland*, 139–40. Dublin.

Kelly, F. 1976 The Old Irish tree-list, *Celtica* 11, 107–24.

Kelly, F. 1997. *Early Irish farming. A study based mainly on the law-texts of the 7th and 8th centuries*.

Kenny, M. 1997 Coins, jetons and tokens. In M.F. Hurley and O.M.B. Scully, *Late Viking and medieval Waterford excavations 1986–1992*, 536–8. Waterford.

McConway, C. 1997 Spanish Convent, Finglas 96E130, 1996:121. In I. Bennett (ed.), *Excavations 1996. Summary accounts of archaeological excavation in Ireland*, 33. Dublin.

McCutcheon, C. 2000 Medieval pottery in Dublin: new names and some dates. In S. Duffy (ed.), *Medieval Dublin I: Proceedings of the Friends of Medieval Dublin Symposium 1999*, 117–26. Dublin.

McCutcheon, C. 2006 *Medieval pottery from Wood Quay, Dublin: the 1974–6 waterfront excavations*. Medieval Dublin Excavations 1962–81. Series B, vol. 7. Dublin.

McQuade, M. 2007 Archaeological excavation Meakstown, Finglas, Dublin 11 (Licence Ref. 05E044ext.). Report prepared by Margaret Gowen & Co. Ltd (unpublished).

McQuade, M. 2009 Archaeological excavations at the site of Cappogue Castle (RMP DU-014–027), Finglas, Dublin 11 (Licence Ref. 06E0228). Report prepared by Margaret Gowen & Co. Ltd (unpublished).

Mitchener, M. 1988 *Jetons, medalets and tokens: the medieval period and Nuremberg*. London.

O'Conor, K.D. 1998 *The archaeology of medieval rural settlement in Ireland*, Discovery Programme Monographs 3. Dublin.

Ó Floinn, R. 1988 Handmade medieval pottery In S.E. Ireland, 'Leinster cooking-ware'. In G. Mac Niocaill and P.W. Wallace (eds), *Keimelia. Studies in medieval archaeology and history in memory of Tom Delaney*, 325–48. Galway.

O'Keeffe, T. 2000 *Medieval Ireland: an archaeology*. London.

Opie, H. 2000 Ballitore, Co. Kildare 99E0202 1999:354. In I. Bennett (ed.), *Excavations 1999. Summary accounts of archaeological excavation in Ireland*, 119–20. Dublin.

Opie, H. 2002 Ardree, Co. Kildare: medieval settlement and graveyard 00E0156, 2000: 0458. In I. Bennett (ed.), *Excavations 2001. Summary accounts of archaeological excavation in Ireland*, 156–7. Dublin.

Opie, H. 2003 Ardree, Co. Kildare: medieval settlement and graveyard 00E0156ext, 2001:597. In I. Bennett (ed.), *Excavations 2001. Summary accounts of archaeological excavation in Ireland*, 174–5. Dublin.

Ó Ríordáin, S.P. and Hunt, J. 1942 Medieval dwellings at Caherguillamore, County Limerick. *RSAI Jn.* 72, 37–63.

Otway-Ruthven, A.J. 1951 The organization of Anglo-Norman agriculture in the Middle Ages. *RSAI Jn.* 81, 1–13.

Papazian, C. 1989 The medieval pottery from the Dublin Castle excavations. Unpublished MA thesis, National University of Ireland.

Prummel, W. and Frisch, H.-J. 1986 A guide for the distinction of species, sex and body side in bones of sheep and goat. *Journal of Archaeological Science*. 13, 567–77.

Schweingruber, F. H. 1978 *Microscopic wood anatomy*. Birmensdorf.

Simington, R.C. 1945 *The Civil Survey AD 1654–6: County of Dublin Vol. II*. Dublin.

Simms, A. and Fagan, P. 1992 Villages in Co. Dublin: their origins and inheritance. In F.H.A. Aalen and K. Whelan (ed.), *Dublin City and County: from prehistory to resent*, 79–119. Dublin.

Sleeman, M.J. and Hurley, M.F. 1987 Blackcastle, Co. Kildare. In R.M. Cleary, M.F. Hurley and E.A. Twohig (eds), *Archaeological excavations on the Cork-Dublin Gas pipeline 1981–82*, 101–5. Cork.

Stace, C. 1997 *New flora of the British Isles*. 2nd edn. Cambridge.

Swan, L. 1999 Meakstown, Finglas, 99E0351ext., 1999:243. In I. Bennett (ed.), *Excavations 2001. Summary accounts of archaeological excavation in Ireland*, 81–2. Dublin.

Stuijts, I. 2003/4 Appendix II: Charcoal Remains. In E. O'Donovan, A Neolithic house at Kiseoge, Co. Dublin. *Journal of Irish Archaeology*, XII–XIII, 18–21.

Sweetman, D. 1995 *Irish Castles and fortified houses*. Dublin.

Wheeler, E.A., Baas, P. and Gasson, P.E. 1989 *IAWA list of microscopic features for hardwood identification*. International Association of Wood Anatomists, Leiden, Netherlands.

Whitehead, R. 2003 *Buckles 1250–1800*. Witham.

Websites:

Van Beek, B. 1986 Jetons: their use and history.
http://www.chicagocoinclub.org/projects/PiN/juh.html viewed 14/03/2007

Negotiating authority in a colonial capital: Dublin and the Windsor Crisis, 1369–78

PETER CROOKS

The English conquest of Dublin in 1170 stands as a watershed in both the history and historiography of the city. In historical terms, 'Ireland's Hastings' brought to a close the period in which control of the city of Dublin was contested by the island's provincial kingships in their struggles for supremacy.[1] For nearly 370 years after King Henry II took the city and its environs into his hands in 1171,[2] Dublin was a bastion of English power in Ireland,[3] and suffered little in the way of an assault that threatened to dislodge it from royal control.[4] There were, of course, close encounters of several kinds. In February 1317, the Dubliners famously fired the western suburbs of the city when Edward Bruce and his brother, King Robert I of Scotland, led a Scottish army within sight of the city walls.[5] Less dramatic, but more insistent, were the raids of the Gaelic Irish, launched from the mountains to the south of the city.[6] These offensives

---

1 Seán Duffy, 'Ireland's Hastings: the Anglo-Norman conquest of Dublin', in Christopher Harper-Bill (ed.), *Anglo-Norman Studies XX* (Woodbridge, 1998), pp 69–86. For the emergence of Dublin as *de facto* capital of Ireland in the pre-invasion period, see idem, 'Irishmen and Islesmen in the kingdoms of Dublin and Man, 1052–1171', *Ériu*, 43 (1992), 93–133.   2 A.B. Scott and F.X. Martin (eds), *Expugnatio Hibernica: the conquest of Ireland by Giraldus Cambrensis* (Dublin, 1978), pp 88–9. For discussion, see Marie Therese Flanagan, *Irish society, Anglo-Norman settlers, Angevin kingship: interactions in Ireland in the late twelfth century* (Oxford, 1989), esp. pp 120–1.   3 The development of Dublin as an 'English' city is traced in Seán Duffy, 'Town and crown: the kings of England and their city of Dublin', in Michael Prestwich, Richard Britnell and Robin Frame (eds), *Thirteenth century England X* (Woodbridge, 2003), pp 95–117; James Lydon, 'Dublin in transition: from Ostman town to English borough', in Seán Duffy (ed.), *Medieval Dublin II* (Dublin, 2001), pp 128–41.   4 For the defence of the city in the period *c.*1171–1541, see James Lydon, 'Dublin castle in the Middle Ages', in Seán Duffy (ed.), *Medieval Dublin III* (Dublin, 2002), pp 115–27; idem, 'The defence of Dublin in the Middle Ages', in Seán Duffy (ed.), *Medieval Dublin IV* (Dublin, 2003), pp 63–78. For a neglected episode from 1226 in which Dublin Castle was held against the chief governor of Ireland by Theobald II Walter (d. 1230), see Peter Crooks, ' "Divide and rule": factionalism as royal policy in the lordship of Ireland, *c.*1171–1264', *Peritia*, 19 (2005), 290.   5 J.T. Gilbert (ed.), *Chartularies of St Mary's abbey, Dublin*, 2 vols (London, 1882–4), ii, p. 353; Seán Duffy, 'The Bruce invasion of Ireland: a revised itinerary and chronology', in idem (ed.), *Robert the Bruce's Irish wars: the Scottish invasions of Ireland, 1306–1328* (Stroud, 2002), pp 35–6.   6 The increasing instability of the Leinster region from the later thirteenth century is examined in Robin Frame, 'The justiciar and the murder of the MacMurroughs in 1282', in idem, *Ireland and Britain, 1170–1450* (London and Rio Grande, 1998), pp 241–7; idem, 'Two

were no trivial matter. In September 1408, Thomas of Lancaster (d. 1421), second son of Henry IV and then the king's lieutenant in Ireland, barely escaped death when the king's Irish enemies attacked the priory of St John of Jerusalem at Kilmainham, near Dublin, where he was in residence.[7] Nonetheless, Dublin remained secure in English hands to the end of the Middle Ages.[8] As J.A. Watt put it, expounding the theme of 'the making of a colonial capital':

> Dublin was to emerge from [the fourteenth century] a bit bloody, a bit bowed but tenacious, resilient and still recognizably the capital city of colonial Ireland, its Englishness ... symbolized by the grant by Henry IV to the mayor of Dublin that he might have a sword borne before him in recognition of the city's services to the English crown.[9]

The significance of the conquest of Dublin as a historiographical watershed is rather more negative. The study of 'English' Dublin – whether in terms of the city's internal political life or its role as the capital of the new English colony – remains in its infancy. The normal explanation for this neglect (the paucity of the documentary evidence) is scarcely convincing.[10] The source material is not so much exiguous as unyielding.[11] The neglect is better explained by the changed political landscape after 1171. The very certainty of English control over Dublin meant that the city seldom intruded into the arena

kings in Leinster: the crown and the MicMhurchadha in the fourteenth century', in T.B. Barry, Robin Frame and Katharine Simms (eds), *Colony and frontier in medieval Ireland: essays presented to J.F. Lydon* (London and Rio Grande, 1995), pp 155–75; J.F. Lydon, 'Medieval Wicklow: "a land of war"', in Ken Hannigan and William Nolan (eds), *Wicklow history and society: interdisciplinary essays on the history of an Irish county* (Dublin, 1994), pp 151–89; Emmett O'Byrne, *War, politics and the Irish Leinster 1156–1606* (Dublin, 2003), pp 58–102. **7** The account occurs in the chronicle of Henry Marlborough: *Bibliothèque Municipale de Troyes*, MS 1316, fo. 51; translation in Sir James Ware (ed.), *Ancient Irish Histories*, 2 vols (Dublin, 1809), ii, p. 22. The aggressors are not identified, but they were almost certainly the Irish of Leinster. Lancaster immediately proclaimed a royal service and the feudal host was instructed to meet at New Ross, Co. Wexford (Troyes, MS 1316, fo. 51; A.J. Otway-Ruthven, 'Royal service in Ireland', in Peter Crooks (ed.), *Government, war and society in medieval Ireland: essays by Edmund Curtis, A.J. Otway-Ruthven and James Lydon* (Dublin, 2008), p. 175). **8** The next great siege of the city took place during the Kildare rebellion of 1534–5 (Steven G. Ellis, *Ireland in the age of the Tudors, 1447–1603: English expansion and the end of Gaelic rule* (Harlow, 1996), pp 137–8). **9** J.A. Watt, 'Dublin in the thirteenth century: the making of a colonial capital city', in P.R. Coss and S.D. Lloyd (eds), *Thirteenth century England I* (Woodbridge, 1986), p. 157. On the civic swords of Dublin, see Claude Blair and Ida Delamer, 'The Dublin civic swords', *Proceedings of the Royal Irish Academy*, 85, C, no. 5 (1988), 87–142. **10** See, e.g., Watt, 'Dublin in the thirteenth century', p. 155: 'The evidence for the Dublin citizen is meagre'. **11** The late Philomena Connolly's examination of the early fourteenth-century mayor, Geoffrey Morton, is a superb example of the possibilities of reconstruction despite the absence of the records of the Dublin hundred court and guild merchant (Philomena Connolly, 'The rise and fall of Geoffrey Morton, mayor of Dublin, 1303–4', in Seán Duffy (ed.), *Medieval Dublin II* (Dublin, 2001), pp 233–51). Further prosopographical explorations of Dublin's leading

of high politics in the later Middle Ages, as it had done so frequently in the pre-invasion period. Yet, if the king's control over Dublin was not gravely threatened from without in the lifetime of the medieval lordship of Ireland, there is another more subtle sense in which royal authority in the city was tested from within.

From 1171, the land of Ireland was just one territory in the wider dominions controlled by the kings of England.[12] In such an extended polity, the state's capacity for routine physical coercion was severely restricted.[13] Consequently power could not be imposed unilaterally from the centre, but rather had to be 'negotiated'.[14] In colonial Ireland, the principals to these 'negotiations' were the crown's agents and the settler population, in particular the resident nobility or, in the case of Dublin, the city's ruling elites. The series of liberties and privileges conceded to the Dubliners by the kings of England from the late twelfth century onwards are the fruits of this process.[15] The present essay explores an occasion in the later fourteenth century when 'negotiations' broke down,[16] namely the controversial chief governorship of the Westmorland knight, Sir William Windsor (d. 1384).[17] The city's attitude to

families are urgently required. **12** See James Lydon, 'Ireland and the English crown, 1171–1541', in Crooks, *Government, war and society in medieval Ireland*, ch. 1; Ralph Griffiths, 'The English realm and dominions and the king's subjects in the later Middle Ages', in idem, *King and country: England and Wales in the fifteenth century* (London and Rio Grande, 1991), pp 33–54. **13** For illuminating discussions of the power of the medieval state, see Colin Richmond, 'Ruling classes and agents of the state: formal and informal networks of power', *Journal of Historical Sociology*, 10:1 (1997), 1–26; R.R. Davies, 'The medieval state: the tyranny of a concept?', *Journal of Historical Sociology*, 16:2 (2003), 280–300. In an Irish context, see Peter Crooks, 'Factions, feuds and noble power in the lordship of Ireland, *c*.1356–1496', *Irish Historical Studies*, 35:140 (2007), esp. 443. **14** Michael J. Braddick and John Walter, 'Introduction. Grids of power: order, hierarchy and subordination in early modern society', in idem (eds), *Negotiating power in early modern society: order, hierarchy and subordination in Britain and Ireland* (Cambridge, 2001). See also Jack P. Greene, 'Negotiated authorities: the problem of governance in the extended polities of the early modern Atlantic world', in idem, *Negotiated authorities: essays in colonial political and constitutional history* (Charlotsville, VA and London, 1994), pp 1–24; and Christine Daniels and Michael V. Kennedy (eds), *Negotiated empires: centers and peripheries in the Americas, 1500–1820* (New York and London, 2002). **15** See, e.g., H.B. Clarke, 'The 1192 charter of liberties and the beginnings of Dublin's municipal life', *Dublin Historical Record*, 46:1 (1993), 5–14; J.T. Gilbert et al. (eds), *Calendar of the ancient records of Dublin in the possession of the municipal corporation* [hereafter *CARD*], 19 vols (Dublin, 1889–1944), i, pp 6–24; Duffy, 'Town and crown', passim. In the period with which this essay is concerned, the most recent charter of liberties was that granted by Lionel of Antwerp at Dublin on 26 September 1363. An *inspeximus* of this charter, given under the great seal of England and dated 22 November 1363, is printed in Gearóid Mac Niocaill, *Na Buirgéisí XII–XV aois*, 2 vols (Dublin, 1964), i, pp 92–9. **16** For the vexed issues – primary among them the question of jurisdiction – that occasionally resulted in the seizure of the city's liberties into the king's hands (e.g. in 1276, 1303 and 1309), see Duffy, 'Town and crown', pp 98–100, 113–14, 116–17. **17** Sir William Windsor has generated an extensive secondary literature and relevant works are cited in the course of this essay. For brief biographies, see Philomena

Windsor is summed up by an annalist writing in Dublin, who describes the
governor laconically as a 'vigorous knight in arms, but extremely grasping'.[18]
Windsor's stormy relationship with the citizens of Dublin was by no means
exceptional: the Dublin annals are replete with poison-pen portraits of the
king's ministers.[19] The events of the period 1369–78 are, however, exception-
ally well documented and provide us with a rare insight into the relationship
between the king's ministers in Ireland and his city of Dublin.

The tale of Windsor's involvement with Dublin is a drama in three acts.
The curtain rises on 3 March 1369, when Windsor was commissioned by
Edward III to serve as the king's lieutenant of Ireland.[20] This appointment
represented a continuation of the policy of large-scale military intervention
funded by the English exchequer that had begun in 1361, when Edward III's
son, Lionel of Antwerp, was appointed lieutenant of Ireland.[21] Like most chief
governors, Windsor found it hard to make ends meet, and he sought to resolve
his financial problems by seeking subsidies from a reluctant Irish parliament
and imposing new customs in Irish ports.[22] This prompted outcry.[23] The city

Connolly, 'Windsor, William, Baron Windsor (1322x8–1384)', in H.C.G. Matthew and
Brian Harrison (eds), *The Oxford dictionary of national biography: from the earliest times to
the year 2000* [hereafter *ODNB*], 60 vols (Oxford, 2004), lix, pp 712–13; Peter Crooks,
'William of Windsor', in Seán Duffy, (ed.), *Medieval Ireland: an encyclopedia* (New York,
2005), pp 515–16. A contemporary likeness of Windsor is preserved on the 'charter roll of
Waterford', beautifully reproduced in Eamonn McEneaney and Rosemary Ryan (eds),
Waterford treasures: a guide to the historical and archaeological treasures of Waterford city
(Waterford, 2004), p. 77. For the circumstances of the creation of the Waterford charter roll
around the time of Windsor's first chief governorship, see Julian C. Walton, *The royal
charters of Waterford* (Waterford, 1992), pp 8–10; Eamonn McEneaney, *A history of
Waterford and its mayors from the 12th century to the 20th century* (Waterford, 1995), pp 71–2;
McEneaney, 'The art of diplomacy: Waterford's 14th-century charter roll', *Irish Arts
Review*, 21:1 (2004), 91–5. **18** Gilbert, *Chart. St Mary's*, ii, p. 282. For the annals in
question – commonly, but misleadingly, called 'Case's annals' – see Bernadette Williams,
'The Dominican annals of Dublin', in Seán Duffy (ed.), *Medieval Dublin II* (Dublin, 2001),
p. 152. **19** See, e.g., the hostility evinced towards Sir Robert Ufford (d. 1346); the
favourable description of Sir Thomas Rokeby (d. 1357), is exceptional (Gilbert, *Chart. St
Mary's*, ii, pp 385, 388, 392–3). For the chief governorships of Ufford and Rokeby, see
Robin Frame, 'The justiciarship of Ralph Ufford: warfare and politics in fourteenth century
Ireland', *Studia Hibernica*, 13 (1972), 7–47; idem, 'Thomas Rokeby, sheriff of Yorkshire and
justiciar of Ireland', *Peritia*, 10 (1996), 274–96. **20** H.G. Richardson and G.O. Sayles, *The
administration of Ireland, 1172–1377* (Dublin, 1963), p. 90. His powers were stipulated in his
patent of appointment (*Calendar of patent rolls 1367–70*, p. 221). For discussion of the terms
under which Windsor held office, see A.J. Otway-Ruthven, 'The chief governors of
medieval Ireland', in Crooks, *Government, war and society in medieval Ireland*, p. 81. **21** See
Philomena Connolly, 'The financing of English expeditions to Ireland, 1361–1376', in James
Lydon (ed.), *England and Ireland in the later Middle Ages: essays in honour of Jocelyn Otway-
Ruthven* (Dublin, 1981), pp 104–21. On Lionel's lieutenancy, see most recently Peter
Crooks, ' "Hobbes", "dogs", and politics in the Ireland of Lionel of Antwerp, *c.*1361–6', in
Stephen Morrillo (ed.), *Haskins Society Journal*, 16 (2005), 117–48. **22** For details of these
grants, see Connolly, 'Financing of English expeditions to Ireland', pp 113–17; H.G.
Richardson and G.O. Sayles, *The Irish parliament in the Middle Ages* (Philadelphia, 1952), pp

of Dublin was among the first communities to denounce the king's lieutenant, when an embassy of Dubliners crossed the Irish Sea to present grievances before the king in England in 1371. These remonstrations found their mark and, on 10 September 1371, the king ordered Windsor, 'to stay and altogether cease ... the levying or collecting of the sums ... unlawfully laid upon the mayor and commonalty and upon the citizens of Dublin in Ireland'.[24] The colonists also alleged that Windsor had tried to prevent them from petitioning the king in person. Consequently, Edward III ordered his lieutenant to allow 'free passage to the king's lieges who for lawful causes will come to him in England', since it was alleged that he had illegally hindered those 'who felt themselves aggrieved by the lieutenant and other the king's ministers of Ireland ... from repairing to the king for redress'.[25]

Shortly afterwards, on 10 December 1371, Edward III ordered the treasurer and barons of the Irish exchequer to stay all legal actions against the men of Dublin.[26] This was in response to further petitions from the Dubliners to the effect that Windsor was pursuing them through the royal courts for their failure to levy the subsidies to which they had agreed in parliament.[27] The fact that the order was directed to the Irish exchequer officials is significant, since it indicates that royal confidence in Sir William Windsor had been shaken. In another letter, dated 8 December 1371, the king explicitly ordered the Irish treasurer to execute his mandates, 'any command of the said lieutenant now or hereafter to them addressed to the contrary notwithstanding'.[28] Early in 1372,

80–5. The new customs were granted at the Dublin parliament that convened on 30 July 1369 (H.G. Richardson and G.O. Sayles (eds), *Parliaments and councils of mediaeval Ireland* (Dublin, 1947), no. 21). The Irish pipe rolls recorded the sums collected in Dublin from these customs, e.g., 8 Aug. 1369 to 21 Jan. 1370 – £40 9s. 7½d.; 21 Jan. 1370 to 20 May 1370 – £18 18s. 6d. The original pipe rolls are no longer extant, but these figures appear in William Betham, *The origin and history of the constitution of England and of the early parliaments of Ireland* (London, 1834), pp 310–11. **23** For complaints about the imposition of these customs, see M.V. Clarke, 'William of Windsor in Ireland, 1369–76', in L.S. Sutherland and May McKisack (eds), *Fourteenth century studies by M.V. Clarke* (Oxford, 1937), pp 186–7; *Calendar of close rolls 1369–74*, pp 256–7. Windsor naturally disputed the charge that the customs were imposed without consent (G.O. Sayles (ed.), *Documents on the affairs of Ireland before the king's council* (Dublin, 1979), no. 241). **24** *Calendar of close rolls 1369–74*, p. 246; Thomas Rymer, *Foedera, conventiones, litterae et cujuscunque generis acta publica, inter Reges Angliae et alios quosvis imperatores, reges, principes, vel communitates*, ed. Adam Clarke and Frederick Holbrooke, 4 vols in 7 (London, 1816–69), iii, part 2, p. 922. On 20 October 1371, a general order was issued to Windsor to 'stay altogether the levy of all manner of tallages, fines, ransoms, and imposts by him laid upon the people in Ireland' (*Calendar of close rolls 1369–74*, pp 256–7; Rymer, *Foedera*, iii, part 2, pp 924–5). **25** *Calendar of close rolls 1369–74*, p. 257; Rymer, *Foedera*, iii, part 2, pp 924–5. **26** *Calendar of close rolls 1369–74*, pp 265–6. The Latin text of this letter is given in Rymer, *Foedera*, iii, part 2, p. 924, where it is erroneously attributed to 10 October 1371. **27** When the community of Drogheda made a similar protest to the effect that their mayor, John Frombold, had been arrested by Windsor, we hear that 'the king [was] moved to anger' (*Calendar of close rolls 1369–74*, p. 265; Rymer, *Foedera*, iii, part 2, p. 930). **28** *Calendar of*

Edward III was forced to recall Windsor and launch an investigation into the veracity of the complaints that had been made against him.[29] In May and June 1373, the new chief governor of Ireland, Sir Robert Ashton,[30] took a series of inquisitions at various locations in Ireland,[31] including one held at Dublin on 13 June 1373, in the course of which the jury made a series of allegations concerning Windsor's mistreatment of the men of Dublin.[32]

Act two opens on 20 September 1373, when Edward III – having determined that the accusations against Windsor were largely without substance – reappointed him as his representative in Ireland, but this time with the less-exalted title of 'governor and keeper'.[33] The king granted his governor authority to collect the subsidies that he had been voted during his first term in office. The colonists, however, remained recalcitrant. Consequently, in the autumn of 1375, Edward III took the unprecedented step of summoning the commons of the Irish parliament to convene before him at Westminster, presumably in the hope that they could be brow-beaten into voting funds.[34] These elections duly took place but, almost with one voice, the communities denied their representatives full power (Lat. *plena potestas*) to grant the king any subsidies. When the mayor and bailiffs of Dublin returned the writ that had commanded to them to hold elections, they recorded that the citizens of

Dublin had 'declared, *una voce*, that they were not bound to send any one to parliaments and councils in England, yet, out of reverence for the king and saving their privileges and liberties, they … elected John Blakhorn and John White. They have granted them no power to agree to a subsidy'.[35]

A detailed account of the election in the county court of Dublin in 1375–6 is revealing of the divisiveness of Sir William Windsor's policies.[36] When the commons of County Dublin refused to grant their representatives full power, Windsor ordered the sheriff of Dublin, Reginald Talbot, to reconvene the county court. Talbot was instructed to conduct new elections, which were now to be held in the presence of two senior royal ministers, the treasurer of Ireland and the chief justice of the king's bench. Windsor further stipulated that, should the commons of County Dublin fail to grant their representatives full powers, they would be distrained in the amount of 100*s*. The result of these orders was a schism in the county court. Some 44 freeholders elected Nicholas Howth and William FitzWilliam to represent them; another 20 elected the same Nicholas Howth but, instead of FitzWilliam, returned one Richard White.[37] This deadlock doubtless reflected local rivalries within County Dublin; but it was also the product of Windsor's meddling in the electoral process. Windsor was seeking the return of a representative who would be amenable to his interests. His favoured candidate was seemingly William FitzWilliam, who had served as sheriff of Dublin during Windsor's administration,[38] and who also held the office of constable of the royal castle of Wicklow.[39] In addition, FitzWilliam held lands at Dundrum, Co. Dublin, in

present time (London, 1772), pp 444–62. **35** Clarke, 'William of Windsor', p. 236. **36** 'Documents relating to the elections in the county court of Dublin, 1375–6', in Clarke, 'William of Windsor', pp 237–41. For analysis, see James Lydon, 'William of Windsor and the Irish parliament', in Crooks, *Government, war and society in medieval Ireland*, pp 103–4. The county and city of Dublin were, of course, discrete constituencies, but the rich information on the elections in the county court is extremely valuable for reconstructing events within Dublin city. **37** When Nicholas Howth died in 1404, Henry Marlborough described him as 'a man of singular honesty' (Troyes, MS 1316, fo. 50*v*; trans. Ware (ed.), *An. Ir. Histories*, ii. 19). His career is sketched in F.E. Ball, *Howth and its owners: being the fifth part of a history of County Dublin* (Dublin, 1917), pp 8–9. **38** TNA (PRO), E 101/245/7, membrane 6; National Archives of Ireland, RC 8/30, pp 115–6, 137. **39** A writ of *liberate*, dated at Kilkenny on 20 October 1375, and witnessed by Sir William Windsor, instructs the treasurer and chamberlains of the Irish exchequer to 'pay William FitzWilliam, constable of Wicklow castle, 100*s*. arrears of his annual fee of £20 from 27 June [1375] to 17 September following, viz. a quarter year' (TNA (PRO), E 101/245/9, part 2, no. 14). This writ was issued five days before another (dated at Kilkenny, 25 October 1375) addressed to the sheriff of Dublin commanding him to cause the election of two lay persons to represent Co. Dublin before the king in England (Clarke, 'William of Windsor', p. 237) – the order that was to lead to the schism in Dublin's county court. For payments to FitzWilliam as constable, see Philomena Connolly (ed.), *Irish exchequer payments, 1270–1446* (Dublin, 1998), pp 530–31, 533–4. See also an agreement dated 25 May 1375 between the deputy treasurer of Ireland and FitzWilliam providing for the fortification of Wicklow castle, specifically that FitzWilliam shall 'complete the front wall of the castle, in length five

the archiepiscopal manor of St Sepulchre.[40] Indeed, the archbishop was soon to appoint FitzWilliam as his seneschal 'of the whole archbishopric of Dublin, to govern, hold, exercise and adjourn the archbishop's courts as often and where he thinks fit for the archbishop's advantage'.[41]

FitzWilliam's employment in the administration of the archiepiscopal estates is pertinent to this discussion because of the intimate relationship that existed between the archdiocese of Dublin and the royal administration in Ireland. In 1375, the clergy of Dublin was the only constituency to comply in full with Windsor's instructions to grant representatives full power (Lat. *potestatem de qua in dicto brevi vestro fit mentio, plenam*).[42] Professor Lydon attributed this to the fact that there was a vacancy in the archdiocese of Dublin after the death of Archbishop Thomas Mynot on 10 July 1375.[43] He might have added that, during that vacancy, the temporalities of the archdiocese were entrusted to Bishop Stephen Valle of Meath, a close ally of Sir William Windsor's who had served as treasurer of Ireland (1368–72) during the latter's first tour of duty as chief governor of Ireland.[44] As a result, Bishop Stephen became the target of several accusations made by the Irish commons.[45] Given all this, it is scarcely surprising that Windsor should have considered FitzWilliam an ally. FitzWilliam's rival in the contested election presents a stark contrast. Richard White was no friend of Windsor's. In the summer of 1376, despite the annulment of his election, White travelled to England, where he presumably remonstrated against Windsor's administration.[46]

The cacophony of complaint from Ireland coincided with mounting dissatisfaction within England about Edward III's government, grievances which ultimately exploded in the 'Good Parliament' of 1376.[47] Windsor was, by this time, closely associated with Edward III's mistress, Alice Perrers[48] – that

perches, and including three towers, with stone and cement. The wall between the towers to be 25 feet high; two towers, those above the gate and the chapel 30 feet, and the third called the Garet 27 feet' (*Calendar of ancient deeds and muniments preserved in the Pembroke Estate Office, Dublin* [hereafter *Pembroke deeds*] (Dublin, 1891), no. 64). For Wicklow castle, see Linzi Simpson, 'Anglo-Norman settlement in Uí Briúin Cualann, 1169–1350', in Hannigan and Nolan, *Wicklow History and Society*, pp 212–14.   **40** James Mills (ed.), 'Notices of the manor of St Sepulchre, Dublin, in the fourteenth century', *Journal of the Royal Society of Antiquaries of Ireland*, 4th ser., 9 (1889), 125; *Pembroke deeds*, no. 71.   **41** Charles McNeill (ed.), *Calendar of Archbishop Alen's register, c.1172–1534* (Dublin, 1950), p. 225 (a letter of notification dated 1 September 1379). For a later appointment of FitzWilliam as seneschal of the temporalities of the archbishopric of Dublin, see *Pembroke deeds*, no. 80 (26 September 1390).   **42** Leland, *History of Ireland*, pp 365–6.   **43** Lydon, 'William of Windsor and the Irish parliament', in Crooks, *Government, war and society in medieval Ireland*, p. 102.   **44** *RCH*, p. 94, no. 168; Richardson and Sayles, *Admin. of Ire.*, p. 104.   **45** Clarke, 'William of Windsor', pp 194–9.   **46** The grievances of the Irish commons presented to the king in 1376 are printed in full in Clarke, 'William of Windsor', pp 184–206.   **47** For which, see G.A. Holmes, *The Good Parliament* (Oxford, 1975).   **48** For a recent re-assessment of Alice Perrers, see W.M. Ormrod, 'Who was Alice Perrers?', *Chaucer Review*, 40:3 (2006), 219–29. See also Chris Given-Wilson, 'Perrers [*married name*

'shameless, impudent harlot', as Thomas Walsingham calls her.[49] At some point after his return to England in 1372, Windsor had secretly married Alice,[50] and his close affiliation with the king's court *covyne* made him a focus of resentment.[51] Consequently, he was recalled from Ireland in 1376, for a second time. During 1376, the citizens of Dublin were once again extremely vocal in their critique of Windsor's administration. Moreover, their representatives were rewarded for their trouble in travelling to Westminster in 1376 to present their grievances: the king ordered payment of the expenses of the Irish commons 'in coming thither [to Westminster], there abiding, and thence returning';[52] and a number of men with Dublin connections – including Nicholas Howth, Richard Plunket, the mayor and citizens of Dublin, Richard White and John Talbot – were appointed to offices in the royal administration or granted lucrative trading privileges.[53]

The third act of the Windsor crisis has previously received scant attention from historians.[54] The action begins in the aftermath of the Good Parliament and takes place in the absence of our anti-hero, Sir William Windsor. Late in 1376, orders were issued for a new investigation of Windsor's administration. These inquiries were to be headed by a courtier, Sir Nicholas Dagworth, aided by two special attorneys acting for the king.[55] These attorneys were Richard Dere and William Stapolyn, the two men who had presented the grievances of the Irish commons to the king at Westminster in the summer of 1376.[56] Dagworth's investigation would probably have got underway in the first half of 1377, but its progress was stalled by the reassertion of the interests of the

Windsor], Alice (d. 1400/01)', *ODNB*, xliii, pp 794–5.   **49** John Taylor, Wendy R. Childs and Leslie Watkiss (eds), *The St Albans chronicle: the* Cronica Maiora *of Thomas Walsingham*, i: *1376–1396* (Oxford, 2003), p. 43.   **50** The marriage may have taken place before his return to Ireland in 1374 or, at the latest, shortly after Alice's disgrace in 1376. See Ormrod, 'Who was Alice Perrers?', p. 222; Holmes, *Good parliament*, pp 97–8; Sheelagh Harbison, 'William of Windsor, the court party and the administration of Ireland', in Lydon, *Eng. & Ire. in the later Middle Ages*, pp 151–4.   **51** For an analysis of the 'court *covyne*', see Chris Given-Wilson, *The royal household and the king's affinity: service, politics and finance in medieval England, 1360–1413* (New Haven and London, 1986), pp 146–54.   **52** *Calendar of close rolls 1374–7*, p. 373; Rymer, *Foedera*, iii, part 2, p. 1059 (where this letter close is erroneously attributed to membrane 24, rather than membrane 23, of the close roll of 50 Edward III, part 2). See also Frederick Devon (ed.), *Issues of the exchequer: being a collection of payments made out of his majesty's revenue, from King Henry III to King Henry VI inclusive* (London, 1837), p. 199.   **53** *Calendar of patent rolls 1374–7*, p. 303; *CARD*, i, p. 124.   **54** Maude Clarke was aware of this 'third act' and in a footnote states her hope 'at a later date to deal with the documents of the sequel'. Sadly her premature death prevented her from revisiting the episode (Clarke, 'William of Windsor', p. 161, n. 1).   **55** *Calendar of patent rolls 1374–7*, p. 416.   **56** The roll of grievances begins: 'Ceux sont les articles mises a conseil nostre seigneur le roy en Engleterre par Richard Deere et William Stapelyn' (Clarke, 'William of Windsor', p. 184; see also *Calendar of close rolls 1374–7*, p. 368). William Stapolyn came from a Dublin family. One 'John de Stapolyn, clerk' witnessed a deed dated 14 November 1336, in which Nicholas Bishop, a citizen and merchant of Dublin, granted to Robert, son of Geoffrey Moenes, two parts of a tenement in the parish of St Audoen,

'court party' in England by the king's son, John of Gaunt (d. 1399).[57] The death of Edward III on 21 June 1377, however, caused a further shift in power. In the new political climate, it became possible to re-open the investigation.[58]

In the autumn of 1377, Sir Nicholas Dagworth received a new commission of inquiry.[59] He was preparing to set out for Ireland late in 1377, and his investigation got underway in the spring of 1378. On 8 April and 6 May 1378, he held inquisitions at Dublin.[60] His activities provoked serious disturbances. On 18 August 1378, a letter was issued in the name of the boy-king, Richard II, addressing the king's lieges of Ireland.[61] It states that the king 'has heard of the divisions among [his lieges of Ireland] and the absence of mutual good will and of any effort to provide in common for the safety of the state against the common enemy, whereat he marvels, and commands them straitly upon their allegiance to desist from mutual strife'.[62] This letter was almost certainly issued in response to news of tumultuous events in the city of Dublin during 1378. A significant number of citizens willingly assisted Dagworth by peddling damaging information about Windsor. This cost them dearly. By December 1378, tidings had reached Westminster that some forty-four Dubliners had been indicted with 'felonies and treasons whereof they are not guilty ... by malice and procurement of certain [men] who bear them ill will [for aiding Nicholas Dagworth]'.[63]

This list of forty-four Dubliners is of particular interest because it follows some sort of order of precedence. The first six men listed – Robert Stakpolle; Edmund Berle; John Passavaunt; John Beek; Walter Passavaunt the elder; and John Foylle – all hailed from important Dublin families.[64] Each member of this

Dublin (Smyly, 'Old deeds – part II', *Hermathena*, 67 (May, 1946), no. 42).   **57** *Calendar of close rolls 1374–7*, p. 469.   **58** The vicissitudes of the court party in England, and the ramifications of this for politics in colonial Ireland, are traced in Peter Crooks, 'Factionalism and noble power in English Ireland, *c.*1361–1423' (PhD, University of Dublin, 2007), pp 138–9.   **59** *Calendar of patent rolls 1377–81*, pp 27, 52, 75.   **60** TNA (PRO), E 368/157, *Recorda*, Hilary, membranes 23–4.   **61** For the continual councils that governed England in the first years of Richard II's reign, see N.B. Lewis, 'The "continual council" in the early years of Richard II, 1377–80', *EHR*, 41:162 (1926), 246–51; T.F. Tout, *Chapters in the administrative history of medieval England*, 6 vols (Manchester, 1920–33), iii, pp 326–9; Nigel Saul, *Richard II* (New Haven and London, 1997), pp 28–31; Anthony Goodman, 'Richard II's councils' in Anthony Goodman and James Gillespie (eds), *Richard II: the art of kingship* (Oxford, 1999), pp 65–6.   **62** *Calendar of patent rolls 1377–81*, p. 271. The text of this letter patent, which is written in Norman-French, is given in Rymer, *Foedera*, iv, p. 48.   **63** *Calendar of close rolls 1377–81*, pp 172, 225.   **64** The names were presumably included in a petition presented before the king's council in England in protest at their detention. The remaining thirty-eight detainees (listed in the order they appear in the records) were: Simon Hirdman; John Burley 'glover'; John Hyncle, elder; Richard Batyn; John Holdfast; Henry Waleys; John Waryn; Roger Beek; Adam Boydon; John Boydon; John Willy; Roger Morton; Richard Bertram; William Bertram; William Leyngh'; Thomas Barbour; William Bowyer; John Blossum; John Olyver; John Whyt 'smyth'; Robert Hyncle; Robert Haydon; John Babe; Walter Passavaunt, younger; William Frere; Richard Harburgh; William Wargan; Thomas Humwyn; William Hirdman; Robert Peres; John Hulle; John Holm of the

sextet had recently served as either mayor or bailiff of the city, the list opening with the incumbent mayor, Robert Stakpolle.[65] Clearly, these were not members of a Dublin rabble; rather, they numbered among the city's most eminent citizens. The last name to appear on the list of forty-four detainees is also familiar. William Stapolyn was one of the king's attorneys who had been commissioned to aid the inquiries of Sir Nicholas Dagworth.[66] It requires no great leap of imagination to see why these Dubliners should have been eager to assist Dagworth. Several of the forty-four claimed to be victims of Sir William Windsor's coercive tactics. One tale of woe must suffice. On 25 February 1371, Windsor summoned to the town of Kilkenny the mayor of Dublin (John Passavaunt), the city's two bailiffs (William Hirdman and Edmund Berle), and twelve of Dublin's better citizens, to explain why they had disregarded letters of military summons directed to them by the lieutenant.[67] Passavaunt and his fellows countered that the letters in question had in fact been addressed to men who were either out of the country, dying, or deceased, and that they themselves had received no communication from the lieutenant. Notwithstanding this defence, Passavaunt and his fellows were forbidden to leave Kilkenny until they coughed up a punitive fine of 100 marks.[68]

In light of such events, it is scarcely surprising that many of Dublin's citizens had axes to grind with Windsor. The detention of forty-four Dubliners, however, indicates that Dagworth's investigations met with formidable resistance. That opposition came from three principal sources. First, there were several members of Windsor's ousted administration who had been accused by the Dublin juries in 1378 of various misdeeds. This coterie of Windsorites included a future archbishop of Armagh, John Colton (d. 1404), then dean of St Patrick's cathedral, who had served as treasurer of Ireland during Windsor's second period as chief governor;[69] Robert Holywood, a former chief baron of the Irish exchequer;[70] and William FitzWilliam, whose election in the county court of Dublin had been disputed in 1376. These men travelled to England in

Cokstret; Richard Clerk of Tauelaghym; Walter Rede 'glover'; Robert Loghteburgh; Reynold Talbot; Richard Whit; William Stapolyn (*Calendar of close rolls 1377–81*, pp 172, 225). **65** Berry, 'Catalogue of the mayors', pp 160–1. **66** On 12 November 1377, Stapolyn and his colleague Richard Dere were reappointed as 'the king's special attorneys' in Ireland (*Calendar of patent rolls 1377–81*, p. 87). **67** All three of the civic officers here named were arrested during 1378 for aiding Dagworth (*Calendar of close rolls 1377–81*, pp 172, 225). **68** This charge was made at the inquisition held before Sir Robert Ashton in June 1373 (TNA (PRO), C 49/75, membrane 25; Clarke, 'William of Windsor', p. 230). **69** Connolly, *Irish exchequer payments*, pp 528–32. Colton was the target of a series of allegations in 1376 and 1378 (Clarke, 'William of Windsor', p. 200; E 368/157, Hilary *Recorda*, membranes 23–4). For his career, see J.A. Watt, 'John Colton, justiciar of Ireland (1382) and archbishop of Armagh (1383–1404)' in Lydon, *Eng. & Ire. in the later Middle Ages*, pp 196–213. **70** Richardson and Sayles, *Admin. of Ire.*, p. 114. Holywood was the subject of ten charges by the Irish commons in 1376 (Clarke, 'William of Windsor', pp 201–3, 207–15). His name heads the list of lay electors of William FitzWilliam in the contested election of 1375 in the Dublin county court (Clarke, 'William of Windsor', p. 239).

the summer of 1378 to rebut the charges made against them.[71] A second source of resistance came from within the incumbent royal administration. The arrest of so many of Dublin's citizens required the connivance of one of the king's ministers who was willing and able to bring judicial pressure to bear upon those who had aided Sir Nicholas Dagworth. The likely candidate is the archbishop of Dublin, Master Robert Wikeford (d. 1390). Wikeford had both opportunity and motive. He had recently been appointed chancellor of Ireland,[72] an office that enjoyed considerable judicial competence.[73] Moreover, Wikeford had a personal reason to oppose Dagworth. As a result of an inquisition taken before Dagworth in 1378, the archiepiscopal manor of Swords in north County Dublin was seized into the king's hands.[74]

The third source of resistance to Dagworth came from within the city of Dublin itself. A royal letter of 15 December 1378, addressed to the civic officers and commons of Dublin, states that the king has 'heard that strife and debate is now newly risen [within Dublin], and that certain of them are disobedient to the mayor … whereby there is no peace or good governance among them'.[75] At first sight this rift within the city's population is puzzling, since the Dubliners appear to have been of one accord in launching their salvo of accusations against Windsor between 1371 and 1378. That uniformity of opinion is, however, an illusion of the sources. Naturally, the city was made up of different interest groups. As we have seen, the proceedings of the county court of Dublin in 1375–6 reveal deep fissures within the community of County Dublin; doubtless there were similar divergences of opinion within the city of Dublin. An instructive comparison might here be made to the rancorous relationship that Richard II enjoyed with the city of London in the 1390s.[76]

---

71 Sayles, *Documents on the affairs of Ire.*, no. 263; *Calendar of close rolls 1377–81*, p. 224. **72** *Calendar of patent rolls 1377–81*, p. 27. He had previously been appointed chancellor on 18 July 1376, but the appointment did not take effect and William Tany continued in office (*Calendar of patent rolls 1374–7*, p. 300). For a biographical sketch, see D.B. Johnston, 'Wikeford, Robert (d. 1390)', *ODNB*, lviii, pp 864–5. **73** A.J. Otway-Ruthven, 'The medieval Irish chancery', in Crooks, *Government, war and society in medieval Ireland*, pp 114–15. **74** TNA (PRO), SC 8/212/10571–9. Portions of this record are printed in Sayles, *Documents on the affairs of Ire.*, no. 264 (i–iii). Other abstracts and calendars of the case may be located at: National Library of Ireland, MS 20 [Lodge abstracts], fos. 12v–16r; McNeill, *Alen's reg.*, p. 225. On Swords, see Roger Stalley, 'The archbishop's residence at Swords: castle or country retreat?', in Seán Duffy (ed.), *Medieval Dublin VII* (Dublin, 2006), pp 152–76. **75** *Calendar of close rolls 1377–81*, p. 169 (quotation); Rymer, *Foedera*, iv, pp 52–3: 'Audivimus quod debata et dissensio inter vos jam de novo est suborta, et quod quidam vestrum praefato majori inobedientes et contrariantes existunt, aliter quam secundum consuetudines et libertates civitatis praedictae [of Dublin] deberent, per quod bonum regimen, vel tranquillitas, inter vos, sicut deceret, in praesenti non habetur'. See also the minutes of a meeting of the king's council in England (Sayles, *Documents on the affairs of Ireland*, no. 257). The decisions made at this meeting, which were passed on 15 December, served as the basis for the patent letters that were drawn up and sealed on the same date. **76** A comparative exploration of the roles of Dublin and London as political capitals would

Between 1392 and 1397, the king was engaged in a protracted quarrel with the Londoners, as a result of which the city's liberties were seized into the king's hands. Not every Londoner, however, quarrelled with the king. Caroline Barron has shown that 'notwithstanding the friction between the crown and the city in these years, there was a group of Londoners, small but powerful, which supported Richard II'.[77] One famous London citizen, who turned this moment of adversity for London into a golden opportunity, was the famous Dick Whittington (d. 1423). Whittington retained the confidence of Richard II throughout the king's quarrel with London and, in 1397, the king insinuated him into the office of mayor of London, so launching the latter's glittering career.[78]

Just as Ricardian London was a diverse collectivity, so it was in Dublin in the time of Sir William Windsor. One Dubliner who can be identified positively as a supporter the Windsor administration was a citizen by the name of Nicholas Moenes. Nicholas hailed from a family, probably of Hampshire extraction, that had settled in the colony in the last decades of the thirteenth century.[79] Prominent in the financial records of that period is one William Moenes, a clerk who forged a successful career in the Irish administration between *c.*1279 and 1325, beginning as a chamberlain of the Irish exchequer in 1293 and culminating with a brief spell as chief baron in 1311–13.[80] William Moenes may have been introduced to Ireland by John Derlington, archbishop of Dublin (1279–84). He acted as executor for Archbishop Derlington after the latter's death in 1284.[81] By 1305, William Moenes was a canon of the cathedral chapter of St Patrick's, Dublin.[82] It was probably through these clerical

be useful. Such an exercise would, of course, have to allow for the vast difference in size between the two cities. For a comparative assessment of the morphological (as opposed to political or socio-economic) development of the two cities, see Howard B. Clarke, 'London and Dublin', in Francesca Bocchi (ed.), *Medieval metropolises/metropoli medievali: proceedings of the congress of the Atlas Working Group International Commission for the History of Towns* (Bologna, 1999), pp 102–25. **77** Caroline M. Barron, 'The quarrel of Richard II with London, 1392–7', in F.R.H. du Boulay and C.M. Barron (eds), *The reign of Richard II: essays in honour of May McKisack* (London, 1971), pp 198, 201. **78** Caroline M. Barron, 'Richard Whittington: the man behind the myth', in A.E.J. Hollaender (ed.), *Studies in London history presented to P.E. Jones* (London, 1969), pp 197–248; Anne F. Sutton, 'Whittington, Richard [Dick] (*c.*1350–1423)', *ODNB*, lviii, pp 770–3. **79** Ball notes that the family name originates with Meon, Hampshire (F.E. Ball, *The judges of Ireland, 1172–1922*, 2 vols (New York, 1927), p. 39). For the hundred of East Meon (spelled 'Moenis' in the thirteenth century), see William Page (ed.), *The Victoria county history of Hampshire and the Isle of Wight*, iii, (London, 1908), pp 63–81. **80** Richardson and Sayles, *Admin. of Ire.*, pp 106–7, 119. See also Patrick O'Connor, 'Hurdle making in Dublin, 1302–3', *Dublin Historical Record*, 13:1 (1952), 18–22, which includes a translation by Dr Ludwig Bieler of the account of William Moenes, appointed to provide rods for hurdles in the parts of Dublin for the crossing of horses to Scotland in 1302–3 (TNA (PRO), E 101/11/3). The translation is not, however, entirely reliable (see James Lydon, 'Edward I, Ireland and the war in Scotland, 1303–1304', in Crooks, *Government, war and society in medieval Ireland*, p. 206, n. 30). **81** M.J. McEnery and Raymond Refaussé (eds), *Christ Church deeds* (Dublin, 2001), no. 186. For Derlington's early career, see Thomas Fuller, *A history of the worthies of England*, 3 vols (new ed., London, 1840), i, p. 486. **82** Henry Cotton,

connections that Gilbert, a nephew of William Moenes, acquired lands on the archiepiscopal estates that lay to the south of Dublin city.[83] With this tenurial foothold, Gilbert soon began to cut an important figure in the local society of County Dublin. In the 1320s and 1330s, he held the constableships of the royal castles of Arklow, Balyteny (that is, Powerscourt) and Newcastle McKinegan.[84] A further sign of his status is the commission he received, on 18 July 1346, to keep the peace in the Leinster marches on the side of Dublin.[85] By the last years of the fourteenth century, the family was styling itself 'lords of Moenesrath', a fusion of the family's name and 'le Rathe', that part of the manor of St Sepulchre lying north of the river Dodder (whence Rathmines).[86] Meanwhile, another branch of the family retained its mercantile interests and became prominent in the affairs of Dublin city. This was signalled by the election of one Robert Moenes, son of Nicholas, to the mayoralty of Dublin in 1319.[87] Sometime previously, Robert had married Elena, daughter of John le Decer.[88] It was a notable match, since le Decer was the mayor of Dublin famed for building a marble cistern in the city in the early years of the fourteenth century.[89] An inventory dated 3 March 1326 shows that Robert was an affluent man, with assets worth £154 6s. 1d.[90] Robert's son and heir, John, followed in

Fasti ecclesiae Hibernicae: the succession of the prelates and members of the cathedral bodies in Ireland, ii: *the province of Leinster* (Dublin, 1848), p. 193; Newport B. White (ed.), *The 'Dignitas Decani' of St Patrick's Cathedral Dublin* (Dublin, 1957), no. 70. **83** Mills, 'Notices of the manor of St Sepulchre, Dublin', pp 36, 39–40. Notes appended to an an extent of the manor of St Sepulchre from 1326 state that, 'Gilbert … was a son of Geoffrey, and nephew of William, canon of St Patrick's' (McNeill, *Alen's reg.*, p. 172). **84** Connolly, *Irish exchequer payments*, 303, 345, 350, 357, 363, 368, 377, 383, 620–1. Powerscourt, Co. Wicklow, is identified as the site of Balyteny in Liam Price, 'Powerscourt and the territory of Fercullen', *Journal of the Royal Society of Antiquaries of Ireland*, 83 (1953), 121–2. For Newcastle McKinegan, see Goddard H. Orpen, 'Novum Castrum McKynegan, Newcastle, County Wicklow', *Journal of the Royal Society of Antiquaries of Ireland*, 38:2 (1908), 126–40. **85** Robin Frame, 'Commissions of the peace in Ireland, 1302–1461', *Analecta Hibernica*, 35 (1992), no. 26; *RCH*, p. 53, no. 93. For the significance of commissions of the peace in this region, see Christopher Maginn, 'English marcher lineages in south Dublin in the late Middle Ages', *IHS*, 34:134 (2004), esp. 122–6. **86** F.E. Ball, *A history of the County Dublin: the people, parishes and antiquities from the earliest times to the close of the eighteenth century*, 6 vols (Dublin, 1902–20), ii, pp 100–1; McNeill, *Alen's reg.*, p. 234. The archiepiscopal manor of St Sepulchre is discussed in A.J. Otway-Ruthven, 'The mediaeval church lands of Co. Dublin', in J.A. Watt, J.B. Morrall and F.X. Martin (eds), *Medieval studies presented to Aubrey Gwynn, S.J.* (Dublin, 1961), pp 57–9. That portion of the manor lying within the parish of St Peter's, Co. Dublin, included the three modern townlands of Rathmines East, South and West (ibid., pp 72–3). **87** Berry, 'Catalogue of the mayors', p. 159. Robert previously served three terms as bailiff of Dublin in 1313–14, 1315–16, and 1316–17 (ibid., pp 158–9). **88** Smyly, 'Old deeds – part II', *Hermathena*, 67 (May, 1946), no. 19 (b). This deed is a grant by John le Decer, junior, to 'Robert de Moenes and Elena his wife and sister of John'. Elena was dead before 1326 and she was buried in the Franciscan priory in the city, where Robert Moenes ordered that he himself was to be buried. See the transcript of the will of Robert Moenes (ibid., no. 26). The marriage must have taken place some years previously, since Elena bore Robert at least eight children. **89** Gilbert, *Chart. St Mary's*, ii, p. 337. **90** Smyly,

the footsteps of his father and served two terms as mayor of Dublin.[91] In 1351, another Robert Moenes – a brother of the Gilbert who held 'Moenesrath'[92] – became mayor of Dublin.[93]

It was the son of the latter Robert Moenes, Nicholas, who emerges from the records of the 1370s as an adherent of Sir William Windsor.[94] Nicholas Moenes forged his career in the law. He was paid as a justice of the justiciar's bench in 1374, towards the beginning of Windsor's second tour of duty in Ireland.[95] In 1375–6, he acted as a justice of gaol delivery within Dublin, for which service he was handsomely rewarded with five pounds.[96] His activities may have made him unpopular in the city, perhaps because his advancement to high judicial office was accompanied by a programme of personal aggrandisement. In September 1373, Nicholas acquired two properties on Winetavern Street (Lat. *in vico Tabernariorum*), one of which was situated on the grounds of the old guildhall (Lat. *vetus Gyldhalla*) of the city.[97] The guildhall, or tholsel, was a structure of considerable importance, serving as the municipal assembly hall, courthouse, and merchant headquarters.[98] Before 1305, the tholsel was moved to a new location at Christchurch Place.[99] The site it formerly occupied on Winetavern Street became redundant and, in 1311, the vacant lot was granted by the city to a Dublin citizen, Robert Bristol.[1] This was the property acquired by Nicholas Moenes in 1373. In March 1374, Moenes further consolidated his holdings on Winetavern Street by acquiring another premises bordering the site of the old guildhall.[2] These acquisitions may have brought him into

'Old deeds – part II', no. 26. For a comparable tale of upward mobility within the merchant class of Dublin, see Connolly, 'The rise and fall of Geoffrey Morton', passim.   **91** John was bailiff in 1323–4, 1326–7 and 1328–9; and mayor in 1335–6 and 1337–8 (Berry, 'Catalogue of the mayors', pp 158–60).   **92** For this Robert as the son of Geoffrey Moenes, see *Christ Church deeds*, no. 593; Smyly, 'Old deeds – part II', no. 26.   **93** Berry, 'Catalogue of the mayors', p. 159. This Robert son of Geoffrey, *c.*1326, had held the custody of two stalls owned by his cousin, Robert son of Nicholas (Smyly, 'Old deeds – part II', no. 26), an indication that the family's success was a collaborative venture.   **94** For this Nicholas as the son of Robert Moenes, see Smyly, 'Old deeds – part III', no. 92; *Christ Church deeds*, nos. 720–1.   **95** Elizabeth Dowse and Margaret Murphy (eds), 'Rotulus clausus de anno 48 Edward III – a reconstruction', *Analecta Hibernica*, 35 (1992), p. 138; *RCH*, p. 88, no. 81. See also Ball, *Judges of Ireland*, i, p. 88; Richardson and Sayles, *Admin. of Ire.*, p. 173, n. 7.   **96** Connolly, *Irish exchequer payments*, p. 537. He also received a reward of 56s. 8d. on 15 January 1375 (TNA (PRO), E 101/245/7, membrane 4).   **97** Smyly, 'Old deeds – part III', *Hermathena*, 69 (May, 1947), no. 91. For the location of the old guildhall, see Andrew Halpin, *The port of medieval Dublin: archaeological excavations at the Civic Offices, Winetavern Street, Dublin, 1993* (Dublin, 2000), pp 182–3. This report includes images (pls 1, 7) of the foundations of an impressive structure of late thirteenth-century date, which may be the old guildhall. My thanks to Dr Seán Duffy for bringing this to my attention.   **98** Duffy, 'Town and crown', p. 108; Linzi Simpson, 'Historical background', in Halpin, *Port of medieval Dublin*, p. 26.   **99** H.B. Clarke, *Dublin: part I, to 1610*, Irish Historic Towns Atlas 11 (Dublin, 2002), p. 23, s.vv. 'Guild hall, Winetavern St E., South of King's Gate'; 'Tholsel, Christchurch Place S.'   **1** *CARD*, i, pp 109–11 ('The white book of Dublin', fos. 23–23b).   **2** Smyly, 'Old deeds – part III', no. 92: 'a mesuage [*sic*] in Taverners' Street … lying between the tenement of Thomas Smothe on the north and a vacant piece of land,

competition with some of the other leading families of the city. One likely rival
was the Passavaunt family, which, as we have seen, fell foul of Windsor's
administration in the 1370s. In the years after the death of Nicholas Moenes
(which occurred no later than January 1394),[3] the Passavaunts were to acquire
the property that Nicholas had owned on Winetavern Street.[4]

It was conceivably a mixture of his affiliation to Sir William Windsor and
his entanglement in urban rivalries that brought Nicholas Moenes to the
attention of the Dagworth inquiry. In February 1378, Moenes was instructed
not to leave Ireland pending the investigations of Sir Nicholas Dagworth.[5]
Shortly afterwards, he was arrested, indicted for treasons and felonies, and
imprisoned in Dublin Castle. Despite this, the chancellor of Ireland, Archbishop
Wikeford of Dublin – the same man who may have been responsible, later in
1378, for engineering the false indictment of forty-four of Dublin's citizens –
caused Moenes to be set free.[6] No explanation for the chancellor's release of
Moenes is forthcoming. Perhaps Wikeford was prompted by personal antipathy to
the Dagworth inquiries. Perhaps he knew that the Moenes family were long-
standing tenants on the archiepiscopal manor of St Sepulchre. What is not in
dispute is that his release of Nicholas Moenes sparked a great rebellion. Amid
the turmoil, blood was spilled when Richard Dere – the second of the king's
special attorneys appointed to aid Dagworth with his investigations – was killed.[7]

The affray sparked by the release of Nicholas Moenes makes it plain that
the Dubliners were not entirely of one mind in 1378. The arrest of one of the
king's special attorneys (William Stapolyn) and the murder of a second
(Richard Dere) represent a dramatic show of defiance to the inquiries of Sir
Nicholas Dagworth. Appreciation of this enables us to reach a more nuanced
understanding of how royal authority was negotiated in the city of Dublin
during the Windsor crisis. Certainly, ministers of the crown, such as Sir
William Windsor and Archbishop Wikeford, were not afraid of using rough
tactics in pursuit of their ends; but this was not their only strategy. Another
tactic was rule through division. Such a policy may help explain some rather
cryptic memoranda in the city's custumal, the 'chain book of Dublin'.[8] The

where the old guildhall used to be, on the south; and to the said vacant piece of land where
the old guildhall used to be; and to the garden behind the said guildhall'.   3 McNeill, *Alen's
reg.*, p. 231; *Christ Church deeds*, no. 777. This latter deed, dated 19 January 1394, refers to
'William Meones, cousin and heir of Nicholas Meones'.   4 Smyly, 'Old deeds – part III',
no. 112; ibid., part IV, *Hermathena*, 70 (Nov., 1947), no. 123. See also ibid., part III, no. 87.
The fact that, as far back as the 1370s, the concerns of the Passavaunt family intersected
with those of Nicholas Moenes is shown by a deed of 1373 (*Christ Church deeds*, no. 723; see
also ibid., nos. 571, 720, 746).   5 *RCH*, p. 104, no. 69.   6 Sayles, *Documents on the affairs of
Ire.*, no. 253.   7 'Item autre brief al ercevesqe de Dyvelyn qe, com il delivera Nicholl
Moenes endites de felonies et tresouns hors du chaustell de Dyvelyn, par qel deliveraunce
grant rebelion estoit sours en pais et Richard Dier, attourne le roy, occis et plusurs autres
damages au roy faitz' (ibid.).   8 Dublin City Archive, C1/02/01 ['The Dublin city chain
book'], p. 191 [fo. 68]. The parchment of this folio was trimmed in order to allow it to be

'chain book' records that at a quarter assembly of the mayor, bailiffs, jurats and commons of the city, held after Michaelmas 1378, the commons of Dublin petitioned for the censure of certain citizens who, during a meeting of the king's council held at Naas, had caused the city's liberty to be seized into the king's hands contrary to their oaths (Fr. *faire la dite ffraunchice estre seisiz en la mayn nostre dite seignur le Roi*). The minutes of the assembly further report that the commons of Dublin demanded that legal action be taken against those citizens who were 'rebelles' to the mayor; and, finally, that the council of 48 should be elected by the commons of the city (Fr. *qe xlviij soient eluz par mesme les communes ycest [pur] conseiller le maire ovesqe les jurrez come les usages et leyes de la dite [citee] demaundent*). The last of these notes suggests a departure from the prescribed procedure for the selection of the city's outer council of 48 citizens, which was reserved to the inner council of 24 jurats.[9] An early fourteenth-century document containing the 'leys et les usages de la cyte de Diueline'[10] stipulates that:

> In addition to the mayor and bailiffs, there shall be 24 jurats to protect the city. And the 24 should elect 48 of the younger men. And the 48 should elect 96. And these 96 should guard the city from ill and from damage.[11]

At Michaelmas 1378, however, the 'chain book' records that the commons of Dublin were demanding the right to elect the council of 48.

Long ago, Robin Dudley Edwards interpreted this as a sign of urban unrest, as the commonalty of Dublin sought to wrest power from the city's ruling elite.[12] We should, however, be chary of regarding the events of 1378 as

bound with the other folios that comprise the 'chain book'. Consequently, the text along the right hand side of the folio is clipped. Gilbert's calendar of this document is very much abbreviated (*CARD*, i, p. 231). The 'chain book' is paginated with arabic numerals, which appear in ink in the top corners of the *recto* and *verso* of each leaf. When editing the 'chain book' in the late nineteenth century, J.T. Gilbert inscribed new folio numbers on the MS; these appear in pencil at the bottom of each folio. I have cited the ink pagination first, followed by Gilbert's foliation in square brackets. For a concordance these numbers with Gilbert's calendar of the 'chain book', see *CARD*, i, appendix 7, 'Collation of the leaves of the Chain Book of Dublin', pp 504–5. **9** The council of 24 is first mentioned in a document dated *c.* 22 March 1220 (see Duffy, 'Town and crown', p. 114, citing H.S. Sweetman and G.F. Handcock (eds), *Calendar of documents relating to Ireland*, 5 vols (London, 1875–86), i (1171–1251), no. 935). **10** A facsimile of the opening folio of this document appears in *CARD*, i, facing p. 204. The complete text is printed in J.T. Gilbert (ed.), *Historic and municipal documents of Ireland, AD 1172–1320, from the archives of the city of Dublin* (London, 1870), no. 68, 'Laws and usages of the city of Dublin', pp 240–69 (calendared in *CARD*, i, pp 224–32). **11** The original is in Norman-French: 'Cest a sauer qe xxiiij. iurez serrunt pur garder la cyte horspris le meyre et les baillifs. E[t] les xxiiij. deiuent eslire de ioesne gentz xlviij. E[t] les xlviij deiuent eslire iiij^{xx}. et xvj. E[t] ceus quatre vyntz et xvj. garderunt la cyte de mal et de damage' (Dublin City Archive, C1/02/01, p. 101 [fo. 53v]; Gilbert (ed.), *Historic & municipal documents*, p. 266; *CARD*, i, p. 231). **12** R. Dudley-Edwards, 'The beginnings of municipal government in Dublin', in Howard

agitation against the oligarchic rulers of medieval Dublin. Susan Reynolds has remarked colourfully that, '[u]rban society, while undoubtedly stratified, resembled a trifle rather than a cake: its layers were blurred, and the sherry of accepted values soaked through them ... it was the control of power that was the basic issue in most recorded conflicts, and misgovernment rather than discontent with the political system as such that provoked them'.[13] Reynolds's consensus interpretation is rather indulgent of the pretensions of urban governors;[14] but her assessment has the merit of alerting us to the fact that, within the municipal assembly, all those demanding to be heard were members of an elite group. If, then, the social hierarchy of medieval Dublin resembled a sherry trifle,[15] this raises the possibility that the petition for the election of the council of 48 by the commonalty, rather than by the 24 jurats, was a strategy whereby one city faction sought to enhance its power at the expense of another.[16] Furthermore, it is conceivable that those purporting to represent the 'commonalty' were encouraged in their opposition to the civic officers by members of the royal administration. Evidence in support of this suggestion comes from a petition of *c.*1378 protesting against a proposal of the mayor and bailiffs of Dublin to construct a *measonet* within the city for the keeping of 'those of whatsoever condition ... who are discovered with women in suspect places'.[17] This plan to build a prison for fornicators was allegedly being implemented contrary to the will of the majority of Dublin's citizens.[18] Significantly

Clarke (ed.), *Medieval Dublin: the living city* (Dublin, 1990), p. 151. Dudley-Edwards compares the events of 1378 to the better-documented agitation at the time of the Bruce invasion recorded in the 'white book of Dublin' (Gilbert (ed.), *Hist. & mun. docs*, pp 359–65; *CARD*, i, pp 132–5). **13** Susan Reynolds, *An introduction to the history of English medieval towns* (Oxford, 1977), pp 171, 185. See also eadem, 'Medieval urban history and the history of political thought', *Urban History Yearbook* (1982), 14–23; eadem, *Kingdoms and communities in Western Europe, 900–1300* (2nd ed., Oxford, 1997), pp 203–14. **14** Stephen Rigby, 'Urban "oligarchy" in late medieval England', and Jennifer I. Kermode, 'Obvious observations on the formation of oligarchies in late medieval English towns', both in J.A.F. Thomson (ed.), *Towns and townspeople in the fifteenth century* (Gloucester, 1988), pp 62–86, 87–106; Peter Fleming, 'Telling tales of oligarchy in the late medieval town', in Michael Hicks (ed.), *Revolution and consumption in late medieval England* (Woodbridge, 2001), pp 177–93. **15** On this issue in Ireland, see Gearóid Mac Niocaill, 'Socio-economic problems of the late medieval Irish town', in D.W. Harkness and M. Dowd, *The town in Ireland: historical studies XIII* (Belfast, 1981), pp 7–21; Colm Lennon and James Murray (ed.), *The Dublin city franchise roll, 1468–1512* (Dublin, 1998), p. xxv. For Dublin's patrician class in a later period, see Colm Lennon, *The lords of Dublin in the age of the Reformation* (Dublin, 1989), pp 64–91. **16** For a similar interpretation of events in London *c.*1376, see Pamela Nightingale, 'Capitalists, crafts and constitutional change in late fourteenth century London', *Past and Present*, 124 (1989), 19–20. **17** TNA (PRO), SC 8/109/5418; printed in Sayles, *Documents on the affairs of Ire.*, no. 261. The dating of the petition is accepted by Philomena Connolly ('Irish material in the class of Ancient Petitions (SC 8) in the Public Record Office, London', *Analecta Hibernica*, 34 (1987), p. 38). **18** There is no evidence that the project was completed, although the wording of the petition suggests that construction was at least commenced. The proposed location ('une measonet apelle Tune') is unidentified. See H.B. Clarke, 'Street life in medieval Dublin', in H.B. Clarke and J.R.S.

– in terms of demonstrating that the 'commonalty' of Dublin had supporters within the royal administration – the author of the petition was Archbishop Robert Wikeford of Dublin.

If royal ministers were indeed meddling in Dublin politics, this adds a new dimension to the resistance that the city's ruling elite offered Windsor. The most obvious explanation for the hostility of the Dubliners to Windsor is resentment at his financial exactions. Many of the charges against him are of a fiscal nature, concerning, for instance, his imposition of 'new customs', or his money-making scheme of retailing merchandise purchased from foreign merchants, to the detriment of the city's merchants.[19] Yet, Dublin also suffered another, more insidious, injury in the course of the Windsor crisis. This was the humiliation that Windsor and other royal ministers inflicted upon the select group of men that comprised the city's ruling elite. The uppermost tier of Dublin's citizenry was jealously protective of its dignity. This fact emerges clearly from the panoply of municipal regulations dating from the early fourteenth century. These set out a graduated system of penalties – ranging from amercements to mutilation and incarceration – for insubordinate behaviour, for instance insulting or assaulting the civic officers,[20] or, more generally, 'any men and women of substance [Lat. *aliquem virum vel mulierem de valore*]'.[21] Prominent citizens also cultivated their status in other ways, for instance, through acts of benevolence. The public works sponsored by the mayor, John le Decer, are a case in point.[22] Another mayor, Kenwrick Sherman (d. 1351), was a generous benefactor of St Mary's abbey in Dublin, responsible for the glazing of the great east window and erection of the belfry.[23] Acts of munificence such as these sprang from a multiplicity of motives; but among them was a desire to enhance one's standing in civic life. Windsor's mistreatment of Dublin's leading citizens threatened to undermine their self-representation as natural authority figures within the city.[24]

In such circumstances, how might the authority of the king's representative be resisted? The answer lies with the role of the chief governorship of Ireland.

Phillips (eds), *Ireland, England and the continent in the Middle Ages and beyond: essays in memory of Friar F.X. Martin, o.s.a.* (Dublin, 2006), p. 153; Clarke, *Dublin: part I, to 1610*, p. 23, s.v. 'Prison, location unknown'.   **19** See, e.g., Clarke, 'William of Windsor', p. 191: 'Item, le dit monsieur William fesoit vendre vynes a Dyvelyn a retaille, les queles il avoit achatee des estraunges marchantz … a grant damage nostre seigneur le roy et destruccion des liegez'.   **20** Dublin City Archive, C1/02/01, pp 68–9 [fo. 37*v*–38] (Gilbert, *Historic and municipal documents*, pp 244–5; *CARD*, i, 225–6).   **21** Gilbert, *Historic and municipal documents*, no. 66, 'Regulations of Dublin City', pp 232, 235; *CARD*, i, pp 219, 222.   **22** Gilbert, *Chart. St Mary's*, ii, pp 337, 342; Berry, 'Catalogue of the mayors', pp 158–9.   **23** Gilbert, *Chart. St Mary's*, ii, p. 391. See Benedict O'Sullivan, 'The Dominicans in medieval Dublin', in Clarke, *Medieval Dublin: the living city*, p. 90. Sherman served as mayor in 1339–40, 1340–1 and 1348–9 (Berry, 'Catalogue of the mayors', p. 159).   **24** See Braddick and Walters, 'Grids of power', in idem (eds), *Negotiating power in early modern society*, pp 12, 15. See also Michael J. Braddick, 'Administrative performance: the

The authority of chief governors rested on their position as representatives of the English king in Ireland. The king's subjects owed a duty of natural obedience to the crown. Consequently, forcible resistance to the king's representative could be construed as treason. Yet, the very illustriousness of the chief governorship also provided critics with their ammunition. By carefully distinguishing the office of chief governor from the incumbent of that office, complainants could protest their loyalty while simultaneously arguing that the king's representative was failing to fulfil the core responsibilities of the crown in the colony. As James C. Scott remarks in a luminous passage: 'The basis of the claim to privilege and power creates the groundwork for a blistering critique of domination ... Such a critique from within the ruling discourse is the ideological equivalent of being hoisted by one's own petard'.[25]

One forum for voicing criticisms was provided by the inquisitions taken into Windsor's misdeeds. Jury service was not simply a top-down instrument of central or local government. Rather, as Michael Braddick has written of early modern England, 'by requiring subordinates to participate in the exercise of the state's authority, [the operation of the law] also afforded them an arena and language in which to negotiate the appropriate exercise of power by their superiors'.[26] The inquisitions taken by Nicholas Dagworth in 1378, which provoked so much controversy, provide excellent examples of just such a process.[27] The jurors claimed that after Sir William Windsor returned to Ireland in April 1374, he sojourned for some seventeen weeks in the city. The Uí Bhroin of south County Dublin and modern County Wicklow were then said to be openly at war. Although Windsor was informed of the killings and felonies that were being committed, he spent the whole period idling with his retinue in Dublin Castle. Moreover, Windsor was alleged to have declared openly that, even if the whole countryside were to be burned, he would not bestir himself from the castle to resist the malice of the Irish until all the subsidies had been levied that had been granted by the Irish parliament during his first term in office.[28] The imputation here is that Windsor was neglecting the most basic duty of the crown to protect the lieges of Ireland from the king's enemies. A month later, Sir Nicholas Dagworth took a second inquisition.[29] The revelations of the jury on this occasion were still more

representation of political authority in early modern England', in ibid., pp 166–87. **25** James C. Scott, *Domination and the arts of resistance: hidden transcripts* (New Haven, 1997), p. 103. See also Joel T. Rosenthal, 'The king's "wicked advisors" and medieval baronial rebellions', *Political Science Quarterly*, 82:4 (1967), 595–618. **26** Braddick and Walters, 'Grids of power', in idem (eds), *Negotiating power in early modern society*, p. 14 (quotation). **27** TNA (PRO), E 368/157, Hilary *Recorda*, membrane 23. **28** The same charge was made in 1376, though on that occasion the record is in Norman-French: 'Item, en meisme le temps furont moultz bones gentz de la Marche ioust Dyvelyn pris et occiz, et grandz furont le rumour, cry et plente qe les lieges fesoient pur defaute deide et toutdiz le dit monsieur William gisoit en la chastelle de Dyvelyn sanz iourneye faire' (Clarke, 'William of Windsor', p. 193). **29** TNA (PRO), E 368/157, Hilary *Recorda*, membrane 23.

scandalous. They accused Windsor of conspiring falsely and contrary to his oath, and in deception of the lord king and his faithful people of Ireland, to obtain the entire land of Ireland from the king for life without paying anything for the privilege, and that he would allow his retinue to live on the king's lieges. Here was a manifest ratcheting up of the stakes. The accusation was now not just one of negligence, but of conspiracy against the crown itself. There is no need to place any credence on so wild an accusation. What is striking, however, is the success with which the civic officers of Dublin reasserted their authority. By the time the curtain fell on the Windsor crisis in December 1378, Archbishop Wikeford of Dublin had been superseded as chancellor of Ireland;[30] orders had been issued commanding that the forty-four citizens of Dublin who had suffered false indictment were to be set free;[31] and the king ordered that all the citizens of Dublin should be obedient to the mayor, who was to rule the jurats and commons in all things according to the laws, liberties and customs of the city.[32]

A cursory glance at Dublin's part in these events might lend the impression of a turbulent city, whose population was unwilling to support the king's representative in a time of dire necessity. This essay has inclined to a contrary viewpoint. Arguably, it was the actions of the king's ministers in Ireland that undermined civic order and sparked much of the turmoil. Granted, the Dubliners emerge from the records as particularly energetic rakers of muck; but this readiness to gripe about the king's ministers in no way suggests alienation from the crown itself. Rather, the city's fervent criticisms sprang from its equally fervent adherence to the crown and what it perceived as the cardinal virtues of English government. Small wonder, then, that in December 1378, the minutes of the king's council in England – without a hint of irony or incongruity – refer to the city of Dublin as the 'supreme refuge and succour of all the land [of Ireland]'.[33]

---

30 Rymer, *Foedera*, iv, p. 53. **31** *Calendar of close rolls 1377–81*, pp 171–2, 225. **32** *Calendar of close rolls 1377–81*, pp 169; Rymer, *Foedera*, iv, p. 53. **33** Sayles, *Documents on the affairs of Ire.*, no. 257. This essay was prepared during my tenure as a Past and Present Research Fellow at the Institute of Historical Research, London (2006–7). I would like to acknowledge my gratitude to the Past and Present Society and to the Institute for their support.

Some old illustrations of St Doulagh's church, Balgriffin, Co. Dublin

PETER HARBISON

In his *Observations on the ancient domestic architecture of Ireland*, published in 1859,[1] John Henry Parker described St Doulagh's church at Balgriffin, Co. Dublin, as 'a very curious mixture of the castle, dwelling house, and chapel or church, which last, in fact, forms a comparatively small part of the building'. This combination of features, and the unusual shape of the structure dictated by the conglomeration of these various elements, made St Doulagh's perhaps County Dublin's most unusual medieval church and an object of curiosity for both author and artist during the eighteenth and nineteenth centuries. In an article in *Studies* a quarter of a century ago,[2] I reproduced a number of representations of the church in order to illustrate its architectural mutations during the previous two hundred and more years. In the meantime, some more drawings have come to my attention which add further testimony to the fascination this building had for topographical artists in the decades on either side of the year 1800, and which are worthwhile assembling here for reproduction as a follow-up to my earlier paper.

The church is first known to have been drawn by Gabriel Beranger in the year 1772. His original has been lost, but a surviving watercolour copied from it[3] is probably no earlier than the 1790s.[4] Probably younger than Beranger's original, but older than his copy, is a pen and wash drawing now bearing the number 2122 TX(57) in the Cooper Collection in the Department of Prints and Drawings in the National Library of Ireland (Plate 1). This unsigned drawing is likely to have been one of those which the antiquary Austin Cooper (1759–1830) bought from the estate of William Burton Conyngham,[5] a man who had sent out artists such as Gabriel Beranger, Angelo Maria Bigari and John James Barralet to make sketches of Ireland's venerable architectural heritage. This drawing may well be from the hand of the last-named artist,[6]

1 John Henry Parker, 'Observations on the ancient domestic architecture of Ireland: in a letter addressed to the Earl Stanhope, President', *Archaeologia* 38 (1860), 158–9.   2 Peter Harbison, 'St Doulaghs', *Studies* 71 (Spring 1982), 27–42. There, I suggested a twelfth-century date for the chancel, ascribing the remainder to the later medieval period.   3 Peter Harbison (ed.), *Gabriel Beranger: the antique buildings of Ireland* (Dublin, 1998), p. 139. 4 Peter Harbison (ed.), *Beranger's rambles in Ireland* (Dublin, 2005), p. 12.   5 C.E.F. Trench, 'William Burton Conyngham (1733–1796)', *Journal of the Royal Society of Antiquaries of Ireland* 115 (1985), 40–63.   6 See Peter Harbison, '"A man of talent": John

Plate 1 A pen and wash drawing, preserved in the Prints and Drawings Dept. of the National Library of Ireland, and bearing the shelf number 2122 TX (57). Tentatively attributed here to John James Barralet and dated to around 1780, it shows a tall round-headed window in the east gable of St Doulagh's. Reproduced by courtesy of the National Library of Ireland.

though it bears no signature to identify its creator. Here, unexpectedly, the church occupies only the left-hand third of the picture, the remainder being occupied by leafy trees of various sizes and shapes, together with a three-barred gate on the extreme right. A somewhat similar composition is found in the engraving of Baggotsrath Castle on Plate 8 of the first volume of Francis Grose's *Antiquities of Ireland,* published probably in 1794, where we find the castle on the left, and a farm-cart going through a four-barred gate of similar design on the right. Because the original of this engraving was stated to have been a drawing by Barralet in the collection of the Rt Hon. W. Conyngham,[7] we may tentatively ascribe this drawing of St Doulagh's to Barralet, and the date may be around 1780, as the artist was doing much work for Burton Conyngham at about that time. Both this drawing and Beranger's depict the

James Barralet (1747–1815)', *Ireland of the Welcomes* 53(6) (2004), 18–23; idem, 'Barralet and Beranger's antiquarian sketching tour through Wicklow and Wexford in the autumn of 1780', *Proceedings of the Royal Irish Academy* 104 C (2004), 131–90.   7 Francis Grose, *The antiquities of Ireland,* vol. I (London, 1791 (1794)), p. 10. Though the engraving was published in 1794, the original drawing on which it was based was probably made a decade

ST DOULOUGH'S CHURCH co.Dublin.

Plate 2 An engraving of 1792 from the second volume of Grose's *Antiquities of Ireland* is the earliest known illustration of the spire which had been added to the tower probably not many years earlier.

church's east window as being tall and narrow, with a rounded or slightly pointed top, as opposed to the broader and definitely pointed east window in Ledwich's engraving of 1790,[8] suggesting that the present window may be a neo-Gothic version of the 1780s. The 'Barralet', however, gives a better idea of the robust size of the tower than does Beranger who makes it taller and, in proportion, more slender than it really is.

By the time an unattributed engraving was made for Plate 15 of the second volume of Francis Grose's *Antiquities of Ireland*, dated 5 November 1792 (Plate 2), the tower had been heightened by the addition of a tall spire, probably octagonal in plan, which featured in a number of subsequent representations. One of these is a soapstone engraving published in Robert O'Callaghan-Newenham's *Picturesque views* of 1830, which I had illustrated already in my 1982 paper.[9] Another example is a hitherto unpublished drawing signed by the well-known landscape painter James Arthur O'Connor (Plate 3), and now in the collection of Sheelagh, Lady Goff, who has graciously allowed me to repro-

or more earlier.   8 Edward Ledwich, *Antiquities of Ireland*, 1st edn (Dublin, 1790), Plate XII. Also reproduced in Harbison, 'St Doulagh's' (1982), 37, fig. 6.   9 Harbison, 'St Doulagh's' (1982), 38, fig. 7.

I A O Connor del

St Doloughs Church n

Plate 3 A southeast view of the church of *c*.1810–20, showing the window in the chancel as a wide gaping hole. It is signed by James Arthur O'Connor, and is reproduced by kind permission of its owner, Sheelagh, Lady Goff.

Plate 4 Captain Edward Jones's view of St Doulagh's from the south, dated 1836, shows the spire still in place, empty windows and, on the left, the western end of the eighteenth-century church which was demolished in Victorian times. The gable end of a thatched house can be seen in the right foreground. The original is preserved in the library of the Society of Antiquaries of London, and is reproduced here with the Society's permission.

duce it here. It shows the church from the southeast, and demonstrates fairly accurately the complicated interplay of window styles in the lower part of the tower which, however, is made to look even more tall and slender than in Beranger's view of 1772. The drawing is undated but, because the schematic

Plate 5 The interior view of the ground floor of the tower of St Doulagh's is described by its artist, Edward Jones, in 1836 as the 'Tomb of St Dooloch'. Now preserved in the library of the Society of Antiquaries of London, and reproduced here with its permission, it shows a medieval piscina in the foreground which is now on display in the chancel next door.

way the grass was rendered is comparable to an O'Connor sketch from his Mayo expedition of 1818,[10] a date-range of between 1815 and 1820 would be most appropriate.

   Another witness to the existence of the spire during the 1830s is a drawing numbered 12 T 14, No. 6, in the in the Library of the Royal Irish Academy which, though unsigned, may be by the famous antiquary George Petrie. It was done presumably in conjunction with the work of the Ordnance Survey but, because executed in pencil, its details, sadly, are weak, and unsuitable for reproduction. Its one advantage over all the other illustrations discussed here is that, because taken from the southwest, we are able to see details of the western end of the eighteenth-century church which was replaced by the

10 John Hutchinson, *James Arthur O'Connor* (Dublin, 1985), illustration on p. 103.

present one in Victorian times. Its west gable can be seen to have had a west doorway with a fanlight, while above it was a half-round window, the whole capped on top by a belfry.

Another aspect of the Georgian church is offered in a pen and wash drawing by Captain Edward Jones contained in an album of his work preserved in the Library of the Society of Antiquaries of London. Jones toured Ireland in 1836, exercising his pen and brush particularly on Round Towers in which he obviously had a particular interest.[11] His view of St Doulagh's (Plate 4), which is taken from the south, shows more clearly than the Petrie sketch that the western end of the eighteenth-century church had no windows in its south wall, and that the windows in the older church do not appear to have been glazed at the time. The bottom right-hand corner of the picture is taken up by the west gable of a long-vanished thatched house which lay to the south of the chancel of the old church. Jones also provides us with one of the rare nineteenth-century interior views of the church (Plate 5). This illustrates what he calls 'the tomb of St Dooloch' in a niche beneath the vaulted ground floor of the tower, which is now called 'the hermit's cell'. It also illustrates a medieval piscina, presumably one of those now preserved in the sacristy.

I am aware of only one other interior view from the nineteenth century, and that is a pencil drawing by Thomas Johnson Westropp looking eastwards in the chancel, and preserved as page 30 in his album numbered 3 A 46 in the Library of the Royal Irish Academy.

What may have been the last pictorial record of the spire is in what is probably the most attractive nineteenth-century watercolour of the church, executed in 1837 by W.F. Wakeman, Petrie's pupil and fellow artist in the Ordnance Survey office. It is on page 6 of the Royal Irish Academy's manuscript 12 T 12 (Plate 6) and gives us a more romantic view of the church from the south, though providing us with little more detail than that shown by the earlier artists mentioned above.

The presence of the spire on a number of the previously-mentioned illustrations causes a problem with an etching by Daniel Gourney which is specifically dated 1813 in a very rare volume entitled *Thirty-six etchings* dating from around 1830, of which only two copies are known to survive of the fifteen originally printed.[12] It shows the church from the southwest (Plate 7), the same angle chosen by Petrie, but giving us a closer look at the old church. The etching was copied twenty years later, though not to the same standard, in the

---

11 One wonders if Edward Jones were a brother of Col. Harry D. Jones, a Shannon Commissioner, whose long letter attempting to interest the Royal Irish Academy in researching Round Towers and other monuments along the middle stretches of the river Shannon is preserved in the minutes of the Academy's Committee of Antiquities' meeting of 8 March 1845. He is less likely to have been an Edward Jones mentioned in the same source for 15 May 1844, as being asked to tender for the fitting up of the Academy's Board Room, and the provision of chairs and tables for its museum. 12 One of these is in the

St Doulogh's Church Co Dublin.
from a sketch made upon
the spot by me in 1837
W. F. Wakeman

Plate 6 William F. Wakeman's 1837 watercolour of the church, page 6 of the Royal Irish Academy's manuscript 12.T.12, and reproduced here with the Academy's permission, is probably the last known illustration of the spire, and is one of the most attractive of the nineteenth-century views of the church.

Dublin Penny Journal of 16 February 1833. There, the accompanying article was written by Robert Armstrong, a south-side housepainter turned north-side schoolmaster in Raheny,[13] but the magazine's editor stated in a footnote that Armstrong was not the illustrator, without giving Gourney's name as the artist The problem alluded to at the beginning of the paragraph is that the drawing of 1813 does not show the spire which is shown as being present in the other illustrations ranging in date from 1792 to 1836 – unless it be that the artist of the etching wanted to show the church in its medieval pristine purity, without the modern addition of the spire, or that the drawing is much later than the caption would indicate.[14]

Library of the Royal Irish Academy.   **13** Peter Harbison, 'Ancient oratory at Ballinhollow, near Lismore, County Waterford', in William Laffan (ed.), *Painting Ireland: topographical views from Glin Castle* (Tralee, 2006), pp 27–8.   **14** Another possible explanation is that the spire may have fallen some time after 1810, when p. 296 of Patrick Lynch's *Life of St Patrick* says that 'the steeple remains still up', only to be re-erected some time after 1813.

ST DOULAGH'S CHURCH-1813.

Plate 7 Daniel Gourney's view of the church from the southwest, as seen in *Thirty-six etchings*, is dated 1813 but, curiously shows no sign of the spire, which is likely to have been extant at the time.

Plate 8 One of the earliest known photographs of St Doulagh's, dating probably from around the 1850s, is preserved as part of the Photographic Archives of the National Library of Ireland, and was featured on the invitation to its exhibition *the past in camera*, commemorating the 150th anniversary of the Photographic Society of Ireland.

We can be sure that the spire had disappeared by the middle of the nineteenth century, as witnessed by an illustration of the church in the engraved frontispiece to W.F. Wakeman's *Hand-book of Irish antiquities* published first in 1848.[15] The condition of the church shown there is similar to that seen in two photographs of around the 1850s, one in the National Library's Photographic Archives (Plate 8), and another preserved in the Eastman Collection in America, to which Dr Rachel Moss kindly drew my attention.[16] One wonders if the night of the Great Wind in January 1839 might have seen the collapse of

15 This shows the ground-floor south window of the tower as half blocked up, and a short stretch of tall cemetery wall stretching southwards from the south-eastern corner of the chancel.   16 There, the foreground is occupied by a be-hatted lady in long, dark Victorian dress. A ladder can be seen placed up against the ground-floor south window of the tower,

Plate 9 Edward Jones's pen and wash drawing of the baptistery, dating from 1836, is preserved in the library of the Society of Antiquaries of London, and is reproduced here with the Society's permission.

the spire, though I have never come across any evidence to support that suggestion.

The Royal Irish Academy preserves some further material on St Doulagh's, dating from the 1890s. It is contained in a portfolio of drawings,[17] by the amateur English antiquarian Sir Henry Dryden, who visited Ireland on a number of occasions during the years 1852 to 1860, and described St Doulagh's as 'an extraordinary jumble ... but picturesque!'. The drawings of St Doulagh's are, however, not by him, but by another man named G.G. Irvine, who presented his drawings to Dryden. Of Irvine I know nothing, but his work on St Doulagh's was obviously done in preparation for a lecture he was to give on the structure in 1898, the contents of which are briefly summarized in a report kept in an envelope in the portfolio, and seemingly in Dryden's hand. Irvine

perhaps used in removing the half-blocking seen in Wakeman's engraving of 1848.   **17** MS 3 D 2 in the library of the Royal Irish Academy.

See p.61, infra for a
small cross by the
road at St. Doulough's.

St Doulough's Well
Co Dublin.
W.F.Wakeman
1847.

Entrance to St Catherine's Pond
near St Doulough's Well
W.F. Wakeman
1847.

Plate 10 Page 7 of the Royal Irish Academy's manuscript 12.T.12, of *c.*1837, shows W.F. Wakeman's watercolour of the baptistery and the entrance to St Catherine's Pond to the north of it. Reproduced by kind permission of the Royal Irish Academy.

provides us with a hasty sketch of St Doulagh's taken from much the same angle as seen in Gourney's drawing, but his most important contribution is a detailed cross-section of the structure, together with measurements. Because done in pencil, it is, like his other drawings, sadly unsuitable for reproduction here. In addition, he provides us with a plan of the old church, which shows only two walls of the existing Victorian church, and also gives us a cross-section of the chancel, a variant of which will be familiar to students of the first volume of H.G. Leask's *Irish churches and monastic buildings.*[18]

Irvine also went to considerable trouble drawing and measuring the famous baptistery situated in a field to the northeast of the church. His pencil drawings are not suitable for reproduction, but are nevertheless of value in providing detailed plans and a cross-section of the baptistery. This monument had already attracted the attention of a number of the other artists whose work was mentioned above. Westropp did a pencil sketch of it on page 294 of his album 3 A 50 in the Library of the Royal Irish Academy. Edward Jones, too, sketched it in 1836 (Plate 9), correctly showing the stone-roofed octagonal

18 (Dundalk, 1955), p. 40, fig. 18, top.

building in a sunken courtyard, being admired and discussed by two figures, in much the same way that Beranger had represented it more than half a century earlier.[19] Wakeman also illustrated it in a watercolour on page 7 of the Royal Irish Academy's manuscript 12 T 12 (Plate 10), together with what is perhaps the only illustration of the stone doorway of St Catherine's pond which lies immediately to the north of the baptistery, and which may have enclosed the well providing the baptistery with its necessary water.

The baptistery was described by Patrick Lynch in his *Life of St Patrick*,[20] published in 1810, as a

> well of most lucid and delightful water, enclosed and arched over, and formerly embellished at the expense of Peter Fagan, brother of the late John Fagan, of Feltrim, Esq. with decorations of gildings and paintings. The descent of the Holy Ghost on the Apostles was represented on the top, with the figures of St Patrick, St Columb, and St Brigid, much after the manner they are engraved on Messingham's title page of his Florilegium Sanctorum,[21] as also of St Dolough, in a hermit's habit.

On the walls, Lynch continues, there was also a marble tablet with a Latin inscription which he quotes in full, and for which he provided the following translation in rhyming couplets:

> Bethesda's sacred pool let others tell
> With healing virtues how her waters swell,
> An equal glory shall Fingalia claim,
> Nor be less grateful for her blessed stream.
> Thy prayers, Dolachus, mounted up to Heav'n,
> Thence to the well the mighty pow'r is given.
> To drive the fiery fever far away.
> Strength to replace and rescue from decay,
> In every malady to life a stay.
> The cherub, wondrous, moves his waters there,
> The saint behold! who stirs the fountain here.
> Hail, lovely fount, if long unsung thy name,
> It hence shall rise above the starry frame.[22]

19 Peter Harbison (ed.), *Beranger's antique buildings of Ireland* (Bray, 1998), p. 137. **20** (Dublin, 1810), pp 296–7. **21** The reference to Messingham's book, which appeared in Paris in 1624, would suggest that this is a rare description of an Irish counter-Reformation fresco of the first half of the seventeenth century. For Messingham and his background, see Bernadette Cunningham and Raymond Gillespie, '"The most adaptable of saints"; the cult of St Patrick in the seventeenth century', *Archivium Hibernicum* 49 (1995), 90. **22** A slightly different version is given in Petra Skyvova, *Fingallian holy wells* (Swords, 2005), p. 46, for a copy of which I am grateful to Michael Lynch, formerly of Fingal County

Lynch also says that

> At the back of St Dolough's well (i.e. the baptistery), there is another for bathing, which is vaulted and called after St Catherine. Sir Richard Buckley brought with him after the Battle of the Boyne a party of troopers, who greatly defaced and disfigured the decorations of this well, but his prophanation escaped not unpunished, for not long before his death, which happened in April, 1710, he was strangely misled by a visionary set of people, who pretended to be prophets, and had promised to make him strait, he being a crook-backed man. His infatuations were so strong … that he designed to sell his estate among them.

However, luckily for his heirs, death intervened to prevent him from doing so, as related by Sean J. White,[23] who calls him Sir Richard Bulkeley of Old Bawn.

We should end, as we started, with John Henry Parker,[24] who describes 'St Catherine's Pond' as a small oblong chamber or bath-room, 'which has a pointed barrel-vault and a doorway, evidently of the thirteenth century' – though probably, in fact, considerably later.

ACKNOWLEDGMENTS

My thanks are due, first, to Dr Seán Duffy for having encouraged me to write this article. Secondly, I would like to express my gratitude to Sheelagh, Lady Goff, for her kind permission to reproduce the James Arthur O'Connor drawing in her collection. It was Dr Niamh Whitfield who first brought the Jones drawings to my attention and, through Bernard Nurse, the former librarian of the Society of Antiquaries of London, I was able to obtain from the Society its permission to reproduce three of them here. His assistant, Adrian James, kindly facilitated the taking of the photographs. To Siobhán FitzPatrick, the librarian of the Royal Irish Academy, I would like to express my gratitude for permission to reproduce the drawings in the Academy's collection, and to Petra Schnabel for having taken the photographs of them. Joanna Finegan, Keeper of Prints and Drawings in the National Library, was, as always, most helpful in procuring for me the illustration of the unsigned drawing then in her care, and Sandra McDermott kindly gave me the Library's permission to reproduce it. Finally, my thanks to Dr Rachel Moss, of TRIARC, and Dr Bernadette Cunningham, of the Royal Irish Academy, for help with points in the text.

Council's Parks Department.   **23** Sean J. White, 'Hermitage in the Dublin suburbs', *Irish Times*, Monday 18 September 1978.   **24** Parker, 'Observations on the ancient domestic architecture of Ireland', 159.

The Hospital of St John the Baptist in medieval Dublin: functions and maintenance

GRACE O'KEEFFE

'What should I here speake of their charitable almes, dailie and hourelie extended to the needie'

Richard Stanihurst, in describing Dublin and its citizens in the sixteenth century, believed the inhabitants of his native city to be greatly munificent. He opined that 'there are so manie other extraordinarie beggars that dailie swarme there, so charitablie succored, as that they make the whole civitie in effect their hospital'.[1] But Dubliners had been displaying a high level of social and municipal responsibility towards the needy for many years before Stanihurst's eulogistic commendation of his city. The twelfth-century saintly archbishop of Dublin, Laurence O'Toole, had himself been a provider to the poor, apparently daily feeding 'never less than thirty, often sixty'.[2] And from the late twelfth to the mid-sixteenth century, the Hospital of St John the Baptist, located outside the Newgate, in the western suburb of Dublin, mediated between those who had, and those who needed.

Although it was considered one of the duties of the church to provide for the poor, the 'institutionalization of charity was made necessary by the urgency of the need'.[3] Alleviation of the suffering of the poor required the donation of alms by the rich, either directly by feeding the poor at their door on feast days, or through the medium of the church, where the brothers and sisters of institutions such as the Hospital of St John the Baptist could decide who would benefit from the benefaction of its donors. By using the Register of the hospital, a collection of almost 600 deeds complied from original documents in the fourteenth century, an understanding of how this hospital functioned within the society of medieval Dublin can be obtained, at least to some degree.[4]

---

1 Richard Stanihurst, 'A treatise conteining a plaine and perfect description of Ireland; with an Introduction to the better understanding of the histories apperteining to that iland', in Raphael Hollinshed, *The ... chronicles of England, Scotlande and Irelande* (London, 1577), p. 34. Not everyone was as welcoming towards the swarming beggars as Stanihurst; in the late fifteenth century, resulting from a report of 'dungheaps, swine, hog-sties, and other nuisances in the streets, lanes and suburbs of Dublin', the mayor of the city was ordered to 'expel all Irish vagrants and mendicants from the city' (*Calendar of ancient records of Dublin*, eds J.T. and Lady Gilbert (18 vols, Dublin 1889–1922), i, pp 139–40). 2 L'Abbé Legris, *Life of St Laurence O'Toole* (Dublin, 1914), p. 37. 3 Michel Mollat, *The poor in the Middle Ages; an essay in social history*, trans Arthur Goldhammer (New Haven, CT, 1986), p. 50. 4 *Register of the Hospital of St John the Baptist, without the New Gate, Dublin*, ed. Eric St

There are many unanswered questions surrounding the hospital's history. This paper will investigate aspects of that history, beginning with a brief investigation of the background to the establishment of the Hospital of St John the Baptist, before examining the purpose of its foundation, how it functioned, and how it was maintained.

FOUNDATION

Several basic facts concerning the hospital are certain. Ailred Palmer was the founder. This is known from the papal confirmation given in 1188 by Pope Clement III when he confirmed the rule and possessions of the hospital and referred to Ailred as the master.[5] A small number of earlier charters in the Register refer to the hospital as specifically that which was founded by Ailred Palmer, or simply Palmer.[6] These bare facts leave as much open to speculation as they clarify. Who was Ailred? Why did he found this hospital, one which secured a significant amount of support in donations of land and rental payments? And in what sense was it a medical hospital, or is this nomenclature misleading?

St John the Baptist's was not, despite the support shown to it by the citizens, a civic-run institution. It was a religious hospital, run in accordance with a monastic Rule. In this way it conformed to the norms of contemporary hospital foundations. As Carole Rawcliffe noted:

> Generally speaking, the older, larger houses founded before 1300 either followed or took their inspiration from monastic rules, especially those of the Augustinians, which placed particular stress upon the integration of charitable work with divine worship.[7]

The efficient running of the hospital required that it adopted a Rule that would allow the brethren to maintain a presence in the wider community; for, although not mendicants, the hospital relied entirely on the support of the community in which it functioned. The Rule of St Augustine provided such a framework: in the chapter relating to the community and care of the body, it stresses that 'respect ... is to be shown for the uniqueness of each person' and

---

John Brooks (Dublin, 1936). Where a number is quoted this relates to the charter number as given by St John Brooks in his edition.   **5** Augustinus Theiner (ed.), *Vetera Monumenta Hibernorum et Scotorum Historiam Illustantia Quae ex Vaticani, Neapolis ac Florentiae Tabularis Depromsit et Ordine Chronologico Diposuit, 1216–1547* (Rome, 1864), pp 214–15. For a brief discussion of its contents, especially the grants, see *Register of the Hospital of St John the Baptist*, pp v–vii.   **6** *Register of the Hospital of St John the Baptist*, nos. 30, 38 and 41 are a small, indicative sample.   **7** Carole Rawcliffe, 'Medicine for the soul: the medieval English hospital and the quest for spiritual health', in John R. Hinnells and Roy Porter

that the sick 'should find themselves in an environment of the greatest care' where treatment would be given irrespective of their social standing.[8]

However, at some point after its foundation St John's became organized as an institution of *fratres cruciferi* (friars of the cross, or crutched friars). These were canons regular of the order of St Augustine who operated almost exclusively as hospitallers in Ireland.[9] The hospital, though, may have had religious ties which stretched beyond the Augustinians and their association with charitable care. In Francis Elrington Ball's history of the parish of Palmerstown (west County Dublin), lands which belonged to the hospital until the Dissolution, it is stated that the name Palmerstown 'has been given by the members of a religious house founded in connection with the Crusades in the Middle Ages'.[10] Also, Thomas Butler's study of the Augustinians in Dublin places Ailred Palmer in the Holy Land in 1179.[11] St John the Baptist's is not normally discussed in relation to crusading history, primarily as it was not part of the military hospitaller movement (although the *fratres cruciferi* could be called Augustinian Hospitallers).[12] In addition, studies of the hospital have tended to view it within the confines of its landholdings in Ireland, as a source for information on ecclesiastical disputes or the patronage of the english communities in Dublin and elsewhere in Ireland. But the references to the Holy Land and the Crusades suggest that St John the Baptist's should instead be viewed as part of the great wave of hospital foundation in the late twelfth and early thirteenth century,[13] and possibly as reflecting the influence of Eastern ideas brought back by religious pilgrims or military crusaders.[14]

What do we know of Ailred Palmer's career? The earliest known date for Ailred's involvement in public life is 1174, when he appeared as one of the

(eds), *Religion, health and suffering* (London, 1999), p. 318.   8 *The Rule of Saint Augustine*, trans. Raymond Canning (London, 1984), pp 68–70.   9 The precise date of the adoption by St John the Baptist's of this specific branch of the Augustinian observance is unclear, as is much about the organization of the Order of the Holy Cross, which had various, apparently unrelated, chapters across Western Europe. Studies to consult include Aubrey Gwynn and R. Neville Hadcock, *Medieval religious houses: Ireland* (London, 1970), pp 208–16; R. Neville Hadcock, 'The order of the Holy Cross in Ireland' in J.A. Watt, J.B. Morrall and F.X. Martin (eds), *Medieval Studies presented to Aubrey Gwynn* (Dublin, 1961), pp 44–53; Egerton Beck, 'The order of the Holy Cross (Crutched Friars) in England, *Transactions of the Royal Historical Society*, 3rd ser., 7 (1913), pp 191–208; *Annales Canonicorum Regularium S. Augustini, Ordinis S. Crucis*, ed. Cornelius Rudolphus Hermans (3 vols, Silvae-Ducis, 1858).   10 Francis Elrington Ball, *A history of the County Dublin: the people, parishes and antiquities from the earliest times to the close of the eighteenth century* (6 vols, Dublin, 1902–20), iv, p. 84.   11 Thomas C. Butler, *John's Lane* (Dublin, 1993), p. 12. 12 Gwynn and Hadcock, *Medieval religious houses*, p. 208.   13 Rubin, 'Development and change in English hospitals', p. 43.   14 While disagreement may exist as to the extent of the influence of the East on the development of medieval medicine in the West, some studies which investigate this phenomenon include: Piers D. Mitchell, *Medicine in the Crusades; warfare, wounds and the medieval surgeon* (Cambridge, 2004), esp Chapter 7; idem, 'The infirmaries of the order of the Temple in the medieval kingdom of Jerusalem', in Barbara S. Bowers (ed.), *The medieval hospital and medical practice* (Aldershot, 2007), pp

witnesses to a charter of Strongbow to Hamund Mac Turcaill.[15] The latter was a member of the Hiberno-Scandinavian family who had ruled Dublin before its conquest in 1170, and Ailred may also have been one of these Ostmen, although his Anglo-Saxon name may indicate an English origin. In other charters relating to the abbey of St Thomas he appears along with what are termed 'omnibus burgensibus de Dublinia (all the burgesses of Dublin)'.[16] A grant made by Laurence O'Toole as archbishop of Dublin is witnessed by, among others, an Elred Palmer (it must be dated in or before 1180, the year the archbishop left Ireland, and the penultimate year of his life).[17] This, combined with his early appearance on Strongbow's charter and his later success in attracting donations from the burgess community towards St John the Baptist's, indicates that Ailred was a burgess of some standing in the community. An Aelric Palmer of Dublin also appears as witness in a Llanthony Prima charter, again indicating that he was well integrated with the new English settlers.[18] In another charter to the same canons, we meet 'Martin, a chaplain of the hospital of the house of Palmer [and] Edred Palmer [and] Ralph Palmer', all as witnesses.[19] What, if any, is the significance of 'palmer' in relation to the foundation of the hospital?

A common descriptor for pilgrim was *peregrinus*; one who undertook a *peregrinatio*.[20] By contrast, palmer appears to have a more specific meaning. The palm was a symbol of a completed pilgrimage to Jerusalem, in the same way as the scallop-shell was for the pilgrimage to Santiago de Compostela. Men and women who undertook the pilgrimage to Jerusalem collected the palm as proof of the completion of penance:[21] William of Tyre, for example, remarks that the count of Flanders 'assumed the palm, which is with us the sign of a completed pilgrimage'.[22] In sources relating to Dublin, the surname Palmer is not confined to Ailred's family; it appears regularly in other contemporary records and in the hospital's Register, in a period when pilgrimage was extremely popular. A William de Aincurt appears as a witness to a charter of Strongbow's sister, Basilia: in this he is styled as 'palmerio Dublinensi'.[23] A William Deincurt also appears as witness to several charters relating to St Mary's abbey, but without being named as palmer, which suggests that the

225–34; Timothy S. Miller, 'The knights of Saint John and the hospitals of the Latin West', *Speculum*, 53 (1978), 709–33. **15** *Christ Church Deeds*, ed. M.J. McEnery and Raymond Refaussé (Dublin, 2001), no. 1. **16** *The Register of the Abbey of St Thomas, Dublin*, ed. John T. Gilbert (London, 1889), p. 166. **17** Ibid., p. 285. **18** To gauge how Dublin itself made the transition see, James Lydon, 'Dublin in transition: from Ostman town to English borough' in Seán Duffy (ed.), *Medieval Dublin II* (Dublin, 2001), pp 128–41. **19** Arlene Hogan, *The Priory of Llanthony Prima and Secunda in Ireland, 1172–1541; lands, patronage and politics* (Dublin, 2008), pp 242–3. **20** J.F. Niermeyer and C. Van de Kielft, *Mediae Latinitatis Lexicon Minus* (2 vols, 2nd rev. ed., Leiden, 2002), ii, p. 1026. **21** Ibid., ii, p. 985. **22** William of Tyre, *A history of deeds done beyond the sea*, trans. Emily Atwater Babcock and A.C. Krey (2 vols, New York, 1943), ii, p. 423. **23** *The Register of the Abbey of St Thomas*, p. 112.

addition of palmer was intended to indicate more than a family name.[24] Palmer, as a given name, appears in various other instances throughout the Register, not least in the name of one of the fourteenth-century priors, John. There are also various Palmers listed in the Dublin Guild Merchant Roll.[25]

Pilgrimage itself was a costly affair. In addition to the long distances covered, pilgrims had to support themselves financially, and have resources to donate alms along the route and at their final destination. Whether it was as a crusader or pilgrim, the decision to travel East carried with it great implications for those undertaking the journey. As many of the routes were dangerous, there was always the possibility that there would be no return journey, and for that eventuality a pilgrim had to arrange his affairs before departure, which for those with any possessions of value meant the making of a will.[26] Those who made a successful return from the Holy Land sometimes returned to life as it had been before their departure, while for others the journey represented the beginning of a permanent change in their life circumstances. For both pilgrims and crusaders the usual method of renouncing the world was to enter a monastery on their return.[27] It is possible then that the foundation in Dublin of a hospital for the sick and poor was inspired by the pilgrimage of Ailred to Jerusalem, for the pilgrimage or crusading experience 'created an atmosphere that enveloped rich and poor, laymen and clerics, voluntary and involuntary paupers alike'.[28]

FUNCTION

I chanced to come by a certain spital
Where I thought best to tarry a little …
As chanced to be,
The porter of the house stood also by me

… And as we gathered there at the gate
People as methought of very poor estate,
With bag and staff, both crooked, lame and blind,
Scabby and scurvy, pock-eaten flesh and rind,
Lousy and scald, and peeled like as apes
With scantily a rag for to cover their shapes.[29]

---

24 *Chartularies of St Mary's Abbey, Dublin*, ed. John T. Gilbert (2 vols, London, 1884), i, pp 111, 112 and 114. 25 *The Dublin Guild Merchant Roll, c.1190–1265*, ed. Philonema Connolly and Geoffrey Martin (Dublin, 1992). Palmers given with an English toponym include, Willelmus Palmer de Wigornia (p. 3) and one of the free citizens, a Radulphus Palmerus de Duraham (p. 113). 26 Jonathan Sumption, *Pilgrimage* (London, 1975), p. 168. 27 Ibid., p. 126. 28 Mollat, *The poor in the Middle Ages*, p. 53. 29 Robert Copland, 'The highway to the spital-house', in A.V. Judges (ed.), *The Elizabethan underworld* (2nd ed.,

Despite the sometimes idealized image of the poor as representing Christ, it is clear that those who sought alms were themselves representative of a wide and diverse social group. For the porter of the hospital of Saint Bartholomew's, London, to whom the above extract refers, deciding between the destitute presenting themselves at the door of that hospital involved separating the deserving from the undeserving. Some in medieval society (like the mendicant friars) saw merit in emulating Christ:

> 'I was hungry and you gave me food, I was thirsty and you gave me drink, I was a stranger and you welcomed me, I was naked and you clothed me, I was sick and you visited me, I was in prison and you came to me ...'. Whereupon he casts aside those who did not, saying '... as you did it not to one of the least of these, you did it not to me'.[30]

but others saw alms-giving and the support of the poor as action enough to merit their place in the Kingdom of Heaven. Thus, the élite of Dublin society were willing to patronize the Hospital of St John the Baptist, but it is likely that they were also eager that those alms be bestowed in a place where those thrown upon the mercy of society did not interfere with life within the walls: city walls, after all, were designed to protect those within from the unexpected or unwanted beyond the walls.

That is why the physical location of the Hospital of St John the Baptist within the city matters a great deal. The location of the hospital is frequently referred to in the charters, usually as a variant of 'domus Hospitalis sancti Johannnis extra Novam Portam Dublinie' ('the Hospital of St John without the Newgate, Dublin') or, in a small number of earlier charters, as being outside the West Gate of the city, this the forerunner of the Newgate.[31] This precise wording was most likely employed to avoid any confusion with the Hospital of St John of Jerusalem, run by the Knights Hospitaller in nearby Kilmainham.[32] But the emphasis on St John's setting, outside the Newgate, is not insignificant. The Newgate entrance to Dublin was one place where both provost and pauper converged. Without the presence today of the imposing city walls and Newgate, and despite the presence of the modern John's Lane church on the site of the hospital, it is difficult to imagine how impressive, and welcoming, the hospital must have been to those approaching the city. The setting was, it appears, typical

London, 1965), pp 3–5. As quoted in Nicholas Orme and Margaret Webster, *The English hospital, 1070–1570* (New Haven, CT, 1995), pp 151–4. **30** *Saint Matthew's Gospel in the Revised Standard version and the New Vulgate*, with a commentary by members of the Faculty of Theology of the University of Navarre (3rd ed., Dublin, 2005), Matthew 25:35. **31** Register of the Hospital of St John the Baptist, nos. 16, 17, 32, 33. **32** C.L. Falkiner, 'The Hospital of St John of Jerusalem in Ireland', *Proceedings of the Royal Irish Academy*, 26 (1967–7), 275–317; Gregory O'Malley, *The Knights Hospitaller of the English Langue, 1460–1565* (Oxford, 2005), pp 226–57.

of early medieval hospitals and not only of those who were built to house lepers, but of those which cared for the poor and sick within a community.[33]

The site of the hospital outside the city walls was certainly advantageous to the institution it supported. Free of the physical constraints of intramural confinement, the hospital had room to expand outside the walls. This must also have been advantageous for the health of the inmates: the proximity of habitation within the walls would not have been conducive to the improvement of the health of those who were ill. Also, located beside the Newgate, on what Howard Clarke has called 'the great artery for food and other necessities entering the city',[34] it was very visible to both visitor and citizen: this 'passing trade' may have wished, or been compelled, to donate alms as thanksgiving for a safe journey made, or in the expectation of one to come. And the proximity to St Thomas' abbey on one side and the Fair Green on the other, both places that attracted visitors and money, increased the hospital's access to alms.[35] In its later incarnation as a city gaol, Newgate itself became an even more concentrated focus for those who existed on the fringes of society, and Charles McNeill suggests that the reason for the gaol's relocation from the Werburgh Street neighbourhood to the Newgate was to give the prisoners the possibility of receiving alms from those entering and exiting through the busy gate.[36]

If the location of the hospital is to be thought of as suitable for a place of rest and recuperation, what is known of those housed within? Despite the large collection of documentation relating to the hospital in its Register, there is an unfortunate lack of material relating to those for whom it was intended. The two categories of attendee most regularly mentioned in the charters are the sick and poor, either as a collective body or in a single specification. Those patients referred to as awaiting the mercy of God were presumably facing death, though it is also possible that in light of the association of illness with sinfulness, they could have been awaiting a sign of forgiveness from God.[37] Some grantors were even more specific in the detail of their benefaction, indicating, for example, that milk was to be provided from the proceeds of their donation.[38] An even more generous donation was the grant of salmon on behalf of the citizens.[39]

33 Orme and Margaret Webster, *The English hospital,* p. 45. They point to the advantages of placing hospitals near bridges or main roads where travellers can be encouraged to part with alms.   34 Howard Clarke, *'Urbs et suburbium*: beyond the walls of medieval Dublin', in Conleth Manning (ed.), *Dublin and beyond the Pale: studies in honour of Patrick Healy* (Dublin, 1998), p. 50.   35 By 1215 the fair was of fifteen days' duration, having been extended in that year from the original eight days granted by King John in 1204: Calendar of ancient Records of Dublin, i, p. 7, (*Calendar of documents relating to Ireland,* i, p. 35).   36 Charles McNeill, 'Newgate, Dublin', *Journal of the Royal Society of Antiquaries of Ireland,* 51 (1921), p. 157. For the development of this western suburb, especially the influence of St Thomas' Abbey on this expansion, see Cathal Duddy, 'The western suburb of medieval Dublin: its first century', *Irish Geography,* 34:2 (2001), pp 157–75. For further examination of the expansion of all suburban areas in Dublin see, Clarke, '*Urbs et suburbium*: beyond the walls of medieval Dublin'. 37 *Register of the Hospital of St John the Baptist,* no. 45.   38 Ibid., nos. 56, 64, 151, 237, 317, 358, 374 are a representative sample.   39 *Calendar of ancient records of Dublin,* i, p. 170.

Indeed, the whole question of the precise nature of care has several angles from which it must be addressed. It encompasses the connection between the church and charity and the obligation of the church to provide care for the needy. But what of the notion of regular or secular clergy as medics themselves? How realistic is it to imagine cloistered monks or mendicant friars providing care for those with actual physical injuries and ailments? Lastly, it raises the question of what constituted medical care in the Middle Ages: how accessible were both physicians and the less well-thought-of barber-surgeons to anyone in society, much less those who had neither the means to pay them?[40] What of those poor and infirm who turned to the hospital as an escape from long-term vagrancy or as a temporary shelter and for provision of food? The body of work concerned with this topic, either in a broad conceptual and ideological sense, or in place-specific studies, is vast and growing, particularly in relation to England.[41] While the work of these scholars has brought about a greatly increased understanding of how hospitals functioned and how the poor were maintained in medieval society, caution must be observed in assuming that the conclusions drawn by these scholars can be easily and immutably applied to medieval Dublin and, by extension, Ireland.

Efforts to cure the sick or dying in the Middle Ages centred on two competing and mostly incompatible approaches: scholarly medicine and thaumaturgic or miracle-working beliefs, what a sceptic might call the difference between learning and luck. Those who undertook the study of medicine had to compete with the promotion of saints' relics as possessors of healing qualities.[42] Contemporaneous with the rise in hospital foundation was a marked attempt by the papacy to regulate both how closely clerics and canons might involve

---

40 Roy Porter, *The greatest benefit to mankind; a medical history of humanity from antiquity to the present* (2nd. ed., London, 1999), esp. pp 106–34 covers medicine in the Middle Ages. **41** A small selection covering this area would include: Elaine Clarke, 'Social welfare and mutual aid in the medieval countryside', *Journal of British Studies*, 33:4 (1994), 381–406, discusses how the community cares and provides for the sick within its midst and includes elements of ecclesiastical thinking on the subject; P.H. Cullum, *Cremetts and corrodies: care of the poor and sick at St Leonard's Hospital, York, in the Middle Ages* (York, 1991), especially useful as St Leonard's was probably the largest hospital in the north of England in the Middle Ages; Martha Carlin, 'Medieval English hospitals' in Lindsay Granshaw and Roy Porter (eds), *The hospital in history* (2nd ed., London, 1990), pp 21–39 provides a helpful categorization of hospitals and their functions; in the same publication, see Miri Rubin, 'Development and change in English hospitals, 1100–1500', pp 41–59 for the rise and fall of hospital creation; Nicholas Orme and Margaret Webster, *The English hospital, 1070–1570* (New Haven, CT, 1995) for a more extensive study, especially concerning areas similar to most hospitals. **42** The struggle between the secular and temporal healers was of course more than disputed theory – both sides risked losing financially to the other and for patients the choice of one over the other could literally involve risking their lives. For the opinions of one fourteenth-century surgeon, see Simone Macdougall, 'The surgeon and the saints: Henri de Mondeville on divine healing', *Journal of Medieval History*, 26:3 (2000), 253–67.

themselves in the provision of non-spiritual sustenance and how those deemed to be possessed with thaumaturgical qualities were henceforth to be assessed. This may have been nothing more than the influence of a series of 'lawyer-popes' who sought to bring cohesion across the Western church, most pronounced in the pontificate of Pope Innocent III (1198–1216), having been initiated by Pope Alexander III (1159–81). Two canons of the Fourth Lateran Council were to have a direct impact on two very different approaches of the church to the question of healing. Canon 62 dealt with the veneration of relics, the handling of which was believed to cure a pilgrim's ailment. Henceforth, this was first to be authorized by the papacy, lest the Devil deceive and Christians be found to have worshipped false gods. Before a cure was to be sought from a saint's remains, official approval had to be given that sanctity was undoubted. And in Canon 18 a more practical concern was addressed when it was decreed that no 'subdeacon, deacon, or priest shall practise that part of surgery involving burning and cutting'.[43] The concern underlying this canon appears to be the danger of death at the hands of a religious once a cut was made and blood was spilt.[44] It is apparent that as the papacy exerted more control over how the members of its church should be healed, a less intrusive but more clearly Christian method of church involvement in healing developed – the religious hospital.

The high-point of the foundation of hospitals run by religious orders matches the period during which tighter controls were placed by various popes on the whole area of church and healing. Miri Rubin described the late twelfth and early thirteenth centuries as witnessing the 'great wave of hospital foundation'.[45] In essence, institutions such as the Hospital of St John the Baptist in Dublin were a compromise between reliance on thaumaturgical healing by saints' relics, and any further involvement of monks or canons (those who, in theory, are removed from secular society) in the shedding of blood. St John the Baptist's was not then an anomaly, but clearly a product of its time. Does this apply also to the provision of physical care to those housed within the hospital? There appears to have been a parting of the ways in hospital management generally at this juncture, which led to some hospitals becoming more of a civic than a monastic or religious institution. It may even be the case that within monastic foundations the hospital became a separate entity to the priory, and almost a rival for resources.[46] Within the hospitals that

43 [http://www.fordham.edu/halsall/basis/lateran4.html, accessed 16 July, 2008]   44 Darrel W. Amundsen, *Medicine, society, and faith in the ancient and medieval worlds* (Baltimore, 1996), p. 197. Amundsen address not only papal legislation in this area but also tackles the oft-repeated claim that the church was against the practice of medicine, tracing the historiography of these claims.   45 Rubin, 'Development and change in English hospitals', p. 43.   46 *Cartulary of St Bartholomew's Hospital*, ed. Nellie J.M. Kerling (London, 1973), p. 2.

had some separation of function between religion and medicine, the appearance of physicians is better documented, whereas others, like St John the Baptist's in Dublin, in so far as we can tell, appear to have maintained the ethos of Christian charity over the development of medical theory.

The period of growth *par excellence* of the medical schools on the Continent, contemporaneous with the period which saw the increase in hospital foundation, was the thirteenth century.[47] While the spirit of learning in the field of human physiology and anatomy was flourishing, it seems, though, that there was no great rush of newly qualified physicians back to Dublin to take up positions in St John the Baptist's. It has been noted that 'much of the attention of medieval hospital historians used to be absorbed by the question of whether or not hospitals had doctors on their staff'.[48] While such confined parameters are clearly not helpful to any attempt at a comprehensive study of medieval hospitals or medicine, they are important considerations. What is a hospital if not a place where medical attention, by medical professionals, is received? If the inmates of institutions such as St John the Baptist's were not attended by doctors (such as those attending crusading hospitals would have been), should they even be considered medical centres at all? Throughout the Register, men whose occupation is given as a *medicus* do appear, though this does not prove that they had any closer professional association with the hospital than any of the other numerous professions listed.[49] In addition, the almost complete lack of sources relating to the actual inmates of most medieval hospitals results in only speculative discussion about their possible origins, either locals or 'outsiders' who found themselves thrown upon the mercy of the urban community to which they had moved. Not knowing how infirm the patients were on their entry and exit from these hospitals only confounds the lack of knowledge about direct medical intervention. Where the hospital's benefactors do specify how their donation is to help the infirm, it refers less to the provision of a physician and more to the provision of milk for the sustenance of the sick lying within the hospital.[50] Other grants refer to the work of the brothers and sisters (though the latter are less frequently mentioned), serving God and caring for the infirm, but without signifying what exactly that work entailed.[51]

By accepting that the presence of a trained *medicus*, either in a permanent position within the hospital or on a visitation basis, is probably unlikely, attention then focuses on the care given by the brothers and sisters. While this

47 Porter, *The greatest benefit to mankind*, p. 113.   **48** Peregrine Hordon, 'A non-natural environment: medicine without doctors and the medieval European hospital', in Barbara S. Bowers (ed.), *The medieval hospital and medical practice* (Aldershot, 2007), p. 140.   **49** In an undated charter, no. 257, Adam Medicus, with his wife Alice, granted land in Co. Westmeath to the hospital: *Register of the Hospital of St John the Baptist*, pp 176–7. **50** *Register of the Hospital of St John the Baptist*, nos. 56, 151, 237 are a sample.   **51** Ibid., nos. 73, 329 are again a sample.

tends to be mostly dismissed as the mere provision of food and shelter, the importance of that alone should not be underestimated. Peregrine Horden's examination of 'medicine without doctors' helps to remedy the image of medieval hospitals, like St John the Baptist's, as places where little good was achieved, and it is perhaps also useful in explaining why these hospitals were able to secure such large endowments. For instance, balancing the four humours was considered imperative to good bodily health. Horden, however, highlights that in addition to these, the *res naturales*, there existed also a belief in a balancing of the *res non naturales*, which are made up of 'ambient air, food and drink, exercise and rest, sleeping and waking, evacuation and repletion, and the *passions of the soul*'.[52] The latter he explains as emotions, in other words, negative emotions can cause illness, while positive can prevent or limit it. To a modern observer this is not surprising, nor does it need explanation. But Horden's application of it to medieval hospital care, to '*non*-doctors doctoring'[53] elevates the status of hospitals, hospices and almhouses from simply a place of religious retreat and shelter to a place where within a contemporary medieval understanding of medical care, they were in fact preventing and curing illness, of body and soul. The brothers and sisters may have been non-interventionist medics, they did not surgically treat the patient, may have administered herbal, garden-grown treatments infrequently, but by providing the six *res non naturales*, St John the Baptist's, and other hospitals like it, did provide medical care.

MAINTENANCE

The maintenance of the hospital and its patients brought together three strands of Dublin society: the marginal who were cared for, the religious who provided the care and benefactors who made it possible. Of this trio of inter-dependents, it is the patients and their carers who tend to be obscure, and of the religious it is usually only the Prior who is named in a charter, or who represents the hospital in a dispute. The benefactors fulfilled more than a simple charitable act, and secured more than prayers for themselves and their families: in the first generation of settlement following the English invasion, these benefactors used donations of parcels of this newly acquired land to establish links within communities. A cynic can easily question the motivation of donors, at least the standard refrain given in most charters, which suggests that it is purely the prayers of the religious that are being sought as reward for donation. From the graph below, it is clear that the highest number of records in the Register, as it exists today, emanated from the first twenty years after the hospital's foundation. It also indicates that, although there are obvious

52 Hordon, 'A non-natural environment', pp 134–5.   53 Ibid., p. 139.

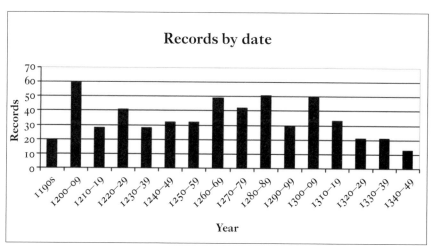

Records by date

variations in the level of donations to the hospital, in the first 150 years of its existence it was apparently well-maintained by its patrons. Although the dates of deeds in the Register continue to the late fifteenth century, from the mid-fourteenth onwards the numbers are extremely sparse. The numbers shown here are based only on those records existing within the Register, and are not confined purely to donations. There are other instances where the hospital is mentioned as a secondary recipient in a charter, and it is not included in the hospital's own collection.

There are various possibilities why the numbers peaked so early. One is that, in much the same way as St John the Baptist's was part of a trend of hospital foundation, it also shared in the 'decline in interest after a generation or two'.[54] Thus, initial fervour and desire for association with a new foundation subsided and attention moved elsewhere. Once a benefactor had done enough to provide a link between the family name and an institution, no further contact was required. But in a city which was experiencing the settlement of what had been an invading force, association with new, charitable foundations gave much more than a remembrance on death. It cannot be denied that the legitimization of conquered lands by complete or partial donation to a charitable, religious institution was part of the motivation. That St John the Baptist's was a post-invasion addition to Dublin meant that it was free from association with the native Irish and Ostman population. It was new; it was founded by a burgess with connections at the highest level of Dublin society; and, more so than donating to a monastery which might be somewhat sheltered from local society, this type of institution was a visible, active contributor to its surrounding environment.

54 Miri Rubin, 'Imagining medieval hospitals: considerations on the cultural meaning of institutional change', in Jonathan Barry and Colin Jones (eds), *Medicine and charity before the welfare state* (London, 1991), p. 21.

If by the end of King John's reign, the 'foundations of Anglo-Ireland had ... been firmly laid',[55] the establishment and support of St John the Baptist's must count as one of the, perhaps less obvious, means through which this had been achieved. The establishment of the hospital coincides roughly with John's first visit to Ireland, in 1185. Irrespective of the success or failure of that campaign for the expansion of the interests of the English crown in Ireland, the second official royal visit to Ireland was the beginning of the second wave of English interaction with Ireland. The granting of various parts of Munster by John to 'new men' created a new set of tenants and structure of ownership.[56] It is perhaps no coincidence that in a body of almost 60 charters in the Register dated to *c*.1200 (with a small margin of error on either side of that date), close to 40 are grants relating to Co. Tipperary and bordering areas of Co. Limerick. In his analysis of the reasons for the failure of John's 1185 expedition to Ireland, Gerald of Wales bemoans that 'in this new realm of ours we have not bestowed any new gift upon Christ's church'.[57] St John the Baptist's gave these new men, who held new lands, new opportunities for patronage, and a chance to bestow a gift on the Augustinians, but one that had a practical social function. Mark Hennessy, in his study of the hospital's lands in Tipperary, indicated that a large number of grants in that county can ultimately be traced back to land held from King John by Philip of Worcester.[58] A date in or around 1200 also follows quickly on the accession of John to the throne of England, the third king to hold the English throne since the hospital had been founded. The one constant from 1185 to 1199 was John's position as lord of Ireland. Throughout his tenure Ireland was settled by new tenants, who then began to search for ways to create ties within Ireland, based on more than conquest. Rather like the civil servants who run the country regardless of a change in government, these tenants continued the organization and expansion of their community irrespective of who held the English throne.

From the turn of the fourteenth century donations began a steady decline. Fourteenth-century Dublin was subjected to the impact of war and indeed famine coinciding with the years of Robert and Edward Bruce's attempts to supplant English control of Ireland with their own. St John the Baptist's, though very advantageously placed outside the Newgate, was unfortunately also in that part of Dublin which was subject to the most destruction as the Dubliners set fire to the suburbs in an effort to withstand attack by the Bruce army. In particular the churches of St John and Mary Magdalene were destroyed in the fire.[59] The combined effects of the Statute of Mortmain

---

55 James Lydon, *The lordship of Ireland in the Middle Ages* (Dublin, 2003), p. 74.   **56** Ibid., pp 61–2.   **57** Giraldus Cambrensis, *Expugnatio Hibernica the conquest of Ireland*, ed. A.B. Scott and F.X. Martin (Dublin, 1978), p. 243.   **58** Mark Hennessy, 'The priory and hospital of the Newgate: the evolution and decline of a medieval monastic estate', in William J. Smyth and Kevin Nolan (eds), *Common ground; essays on the historical geography of Ireland* (Cork, 1988), p. 44.   **59** *Chartularies of St Mary's Abbey*, ii, p. 353.

(1279), the decline in profitability of the Irish colony, the Bruce Invasion (1315–18) and the Black Death (from 1348) provide a clear distinction between the periods of growth and decline of the hospital.[60] Those who had any land or rights to rental payments were understandably more frugal with donations.

Two points should be noted about the Register, as the main source for the affairs of the hospital. Firstly, from the mid- to the late thirteenth century the business transactions of the hospital remained at the same level as in its early days, both as a benefactor itself (in its rôle as a landlord) and as recipient. In some instances, the movement of ownership of lands and rents between the hospital and an individual or family can be traced over a number of years, demonstrating how one messuage or one acre of land changed hands several times before finally being donated for the care of the sick and poor. Between 1210 and 1225, in a series of about fifteen charters, various parcels of land in Castleknock changed hands.[61] Those involved included Richard and Hugh Tyrel, Richard le Myre, his sons William, and Richard and Ingelbricht de Karmardyn. 'Colenti', 'Heruchin' and 'Alesuntrich', identified as comprising part of the land of Castleknock, were moved from Tyrel to le Myre to Karmardyn. Prominent among the witnesses to these transactions were names such as Multon, de Lyvet, de (la) Corner, de Hereford – all names which would within a few years make appearances as mayors and provosts of Dublin city. The actual size of the areas being transferred varied from fifty acres to a carucate (usually considered at 120 acres)[62] or a much smaller donation of three acres and a garden. The prior of the hospital would only have been interested in the culmination of all these into the grants of Hugh Tyrel and Ingelbricht de Karmardyn, *c.*1225, where all the land held by them in Castleknock was bestowed on the hospital, for the care of the patients lying within its walls. This one example, of which there are several in the Register, indicates the complicated story lying behind the transfer of a single piece of land. Had only the two final charters in this series been included nothing in terms of knowledge of the ownership of land by the hospital would have been lost, but an invaluable insight into the changing ownership of that land would be missing. Perhaps even more valuable is what that series yields about the interconnection between the people involved in each transaction: families who were neighbouring landowners, whose business was overseen by the same select group of burgesses and administrators, all brought together by the one final act of support for the hospital.

This leads to the second important point to be noted: the charter per transaction ratio and the categories into which the Register can be divided. As

---

60 Although the Statute of Mortmain became law in England in 1279, the exact date of its introduction to Ireland is unclear. That it was introduced is without question, but the full extent of its influence on donations to religious institutions is uncertain. For an examination of its introduction see Paul Brand, 'King, church and property; the enforcement of restrictions on alienations into mortmain in the Lordship of Ireland in the later middle ages', *Peritia*, 3 (1984), 481–502.   61 *Register of the Hospital of St John the Baptist*, nos. 271–85.   62 Joy Bristow, *The local historian's glossary of words and terms* (3rd ed., Newbury,

edited by Eric St John Brooks, the Register contains almost 600 entries. Not all of these are transfers of rents or property; some are court judgements and fines or pleas and complaints between the hospital and individuals about payments of rent.[63] More importantly perhaps, not all focus exclusively or entirely on the hospital. Of the 600, roughly 70% cite the hospital as the main intended recipient, irrespective of the nature of the benefaction. As secondary recipient St John the Baptist's features in around 7% of charters. In these, the hospital is the recipient for the rent due on the main benefaction of that charter: for example, in 1285–6, Thomas Wale, citizen of Dublin, gave Bartholomew Brek, also given as a citizen of Dublin, along with his wife Alice, land in the parish of St Audoen's, towards the Newgate; among the various recipients of the rents due on this land were the prior and brothers of St John the Baptist's.[64] Almost 13% of charters exclude the hospital as either main or secondary recipient. These encompass, as in the Castleknock case cited above, all those transactions where an eventual grant to the hospital is preceded by other charters available to the scribe at the time of the Register's compilation. As benefactor, the hospital appears in roughly 8% of charters: the majority of those concern rentals in Dublin, mostly over the twelfth and thirteenth centuries. The remaining 2% of the Register includes wills, and confirmations by archbishops and bishops concerning grants of tithes and advowson.

As the obvious main source for the affairs of the hospital, the Register is invaluable. The category division is also invaluable because, by their nature, registers and their near relatives, cartularies, are both essentially concerned with the preservation of title-deeds. Patrick Geary has pondered the preservation of original documents, in particular the curious fact that 'many institutions preserved their cartularies … with more care than they did their originals'.[65] Geary further suggests that 'neither the existence nor the purpose of such collections is self-explanatory'.[66] Despite these assertions, there is an obvious logic in assuming that a cartulary/register was wholly or at least partially created for protection and preservation of the text of original charters, especially those granting lands and rents. In the case of St John the Baptist's, if the Register was, as St John Brook suggested, compiled in the late fourteenth century,[67] it was done at a time when the numbers donating had already sharply declined. To prove legitimate claim to rent, or repel false demands of rent, would have been crucial. In addition, the longer an institution was in existence, the greater the possibility of its involvement in litigation, and, as such, the more organized the records the quicker the response to a claimant. As the hospital was closed as part of Henry VIII's Dissolution of the Monasteries, the Register had a two hundred year period in which to fulfil its legal purpose.

2001), pp 33–4.   **63** *Register of the Hospital of St John the Baptist*, nos. 70 and 71.   **64** Ibid., no. 50.   **65** Patrick J. Geary, *Phantoms of remembrance* (Princeton, 1994), p. 82.   **66** Ibid., p. 83.   **67** *Register of the Hospital of St John the Baptist*, p. xi.

Beyond that, its most enduring legacy has been to preserve knowledge of the contacts between community and carer.

CONCLUSION

The early years of the hospital not only coincided with the development of canon law and papal power, and high numbers of hospital foundations, it was also a period of great urban development and expansion, bringing people from all levels of society into closer and more immediate contact with each other. In Dublin, the Hospital of St John the Baptist was one very obvious example of these changes. It is tempting to see, in the hospital, interaction between the Three Estates: the church provides the care, the rich (nobility or merchants), through their donations ensure the continuation of this care, and the poor are the recipients of the combined efforts of both. Even a rejection of this model cannot veil the obvious dependence of each upon the other. This becomes even clearer when the fortunes of the hospital are investigated. In 1334 the hospital had responsibility for the care of 155 sick and poor persons, apart from the brothers and sisters also resident.[68] The brethren were finding it increasingly difficult to maintain these numbers, 'because their goods and possessions in the suburb of the said city and elsewhere in Ireland are greatly wasted'.[69] Just less than forty years later these numbers had fallen to 115, this number again specified as the inmates exclusively.[70] In the extent made in 1540, after the dissolution of the hospital, the area available for the care of the sick was described as

> a house in which there are 50 beds (*grabata*) for the sick, with a small parcel of ground adjoining; these of no value beyond their use for the sick'.[71]

These numbers are themselves available only because the hospital had on numerous occasions petitioned the Crown for assistance, claiming that

> their goods and possessions in the suburb of Dublin as well as elsewhere in the land of Ireland have been so destroyed by hostile attacks of the Irish that they do not suffice for the sustenance of the said brethren and paupers.[72]

St John the Baptist's clearly did not exist in a vacuum. From its foundation it was influenced by external events and trends. If Ailred Palmer brought from

---

68 *Calendar of patent rolls, 1330–34*, p. 552. **69** Ibid. **70** *Calendar of patent rolls, 1370–74*, p. 302. **71** *Extents of Irish monastic possessions, 1540–41*, ed. Newport White (Dublin, 1943), p. 55. **72** *Calendar of patent rolls, 1370–4, 1373*, p. 302.

the Holy Land the inspiration to establish a hospital, he only achieved it, to begin with, following considerable assistance from the community of the English of Ireland. So it was also for the priors who succeeded him. Without doubt it was

> ... a very well done deed
> With devotion such people to feed.[73]

73 Copland, 'The highway to the spital-house', p. 5.

Archaeological excavations at the mill-pond of St Thomas's abbey, Dublin

FRANC MYLES

INTRODUCTION

The topographical minutiae of the area generally referred to as The Liberties can perhaps best be appreciated from the seat of a bicycle. As the rider crosses from north to south, an easier contour can be negotiated across the slight ridges climbing either side of the Commons Water and through any of the imperceptible valleys which signal the presence of one of the area's many watercourses beneath. This little known three-dimensional landscape can be experienced to greatest effect further south, where the old course of the Poddle travels under the South Circular Road just to the west of Leonard's Corner.

Of more immediate interest here, another sharp rise at the western end of the Coombe ends abruptly at the junction of Ardee Street and Pimlico (the medieval Crooked Staff), with the main thoroughfare out of the city following a course to the south before continuing west again along Cork Street. This paper discusses the medieval usage of the 2.5-acre site thus avoided, bounded by Cork Street, Ardee Street, Robinson's Court and the back of the properties on the southern side of John Street South (fig. 1).

Five general phases of activity were identified over the site, of which the first and perhaps the second are of relevance to this paper. The early archaeological substrates in this area consisted almost entirely of a thick deposit of grey silty clay, up to 2.75m in depth, which initially presented as the silting up of a large pond or marsh. The deposit rested in a depression in the natural subsoil, which may have had a formal cut edge on the northern side but sloped gradually downward elsewhere. The feature has been interpreted as the remains of a millpond associated with the abbey of St Thomas and the silts were sealed by a section of the earthen defences thrown up around Dublin in the mid-1640s which in turn were later heavily truncated by brewery structures dating, in the main, to the mid-eighteenth century.

A natural watercourse, the Commons Water, bisected the site. The liberty boundary of the medieval city lay along this watercourse upstream to Dolphin's Barn and a description of its route is included in the various accounts of the Riding of the Franchises. The watercourse at this location would also appear to demarcate the urban liberty of Thomas Court from the ostensibly rural liberty of Donore to the south. The fine curving wall behind

1 Site location

the plots on Summer Street, dating from 1680 and preserved in the new development, echoes eloquently the liberty boundary today.

The eastern perimeter of the site was marked by the Abbey Stream, an artificial branch of the Poddle, created *c*.1190, which was formally defined in stone in the late seventeenth century, culverted in red brick in the early nineteenth century and channeled through a concrete pipe in the 1980s. The Commons Water passed underneath the Abbey Stream just beyond the eastern boundary of the site, an arrangement which had existed from at least 1684, if not much earlier.

The excavation was undertaken after an assessment of the site had been carried out in connection with a planning application for a mixed-use scheme, with a deep basement below the known lower level of the archaeology. An excavation licence (03E315) was issued to cover the assessment and the subsequent excavation. The latter was undertaken over two periods, the first between 22 September 2003 and 20 February 2004, the second between 20 May and 15 July 2004. The second period was mostly a monitoring phase, with a crew on site for the first week in June. All works undertaken were funded by the developer of the site, Naltmore Ltd.

THE COMMONS WATER

Introduction

The Commons Water rises to the west of the city in Drimnagh, a townland formerly part of the Commons of Crumlin (Sweeney 1991, 38). The stream extended across the centre of the site, underpinned across the millpond silts and covered over with a brick arch by Dublin Corporation *c.*1874. The evidence suggests that the underpinning partly replaced an earlier formal channelling of the stream below, which had run along its pre-2004 course at least since 1684, the date of the first lease map depicting the area. It is likely, however, that the stream originally took a course slightly further to the north and that its modern course through the site was constructed sometime after 1603, by which time the pond below had silted up. Prior to recent demolition works on the site, an overgrown strip of ground separating the eighteenth-century buildings north of the watercourse and the modern structures in Strahan's timber yard to the south provided the only evidence for the stream.

The issue of the existence or otherwise of a medieval millpond at this location has been confused with the lack of evidence for a mill, (notwith-standing the recovery of four large millstones from the foundation course of an eighteenth-century building at the south-eastern corner of the site). The presence of a millpond is, however, frequently alluded to in the sources and more particularly in the various accounts of the Riding of the Franchises and it should be borne in mind that the 'pond of St Thomas the Martyr' may well refer to a millpond at this location on the Commons Water, rather than the Watt Mill located further north along the Abbey Stream.

The topographical imperative would suggest that the Commons Water gave rise to the pond's existence at this location and the evidence put forward below thus begins with the earliest feature recorded on the site.

Gully F847

The earliest cut feature on the site was a gully extending roughly east-west in a slight arc across the northern part of the site (Plate 1). The gully cut the subsoil and its fill, F848, was sealed by the millpond silts above (F70/F802). It was not possible to establish the gully's true extent as it was heavily truncated; to the west by the machine activity of the ongoing bulk excavation and to the east by a late seventeenth-century tannery and further east again by the cut of a flood channel of the Abbey Stream. Its trajectory appeared to follow the main break of slope associated with the millpond *c.*1.5–2m to the north and was initially interpreted as being a trench cut to house a formal revetment for the northern side of the pond.

The surviving portion of the gully measured 28.7m in length and had a maximum width of 850mm and depth of 290mm. It was U-shaped in profile

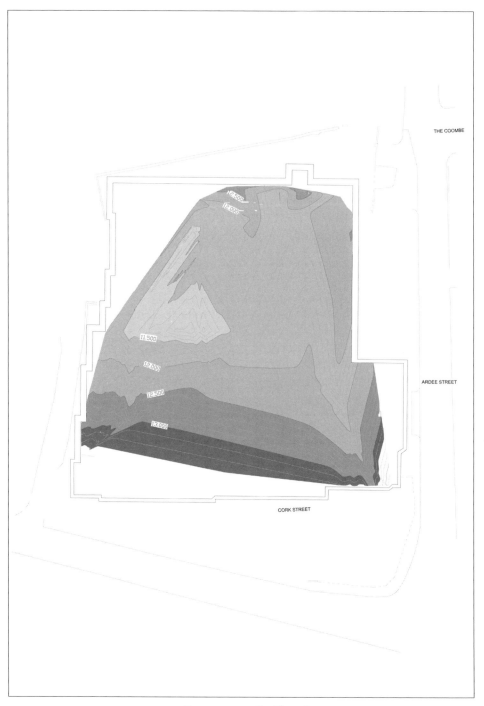

2 Contour map of millpond

Plate 1 F847 gully, looking west

Plate 2 Section through Millpond silts north of the commons water

having a sharp break of slope at the top, gradually sloping to steep sides, with a concave, slightly flattish, base. The gully snaked slightly from south to north along its east-west axis. Its width also varied from east to west, being quite narrow over the first 7m (370–550mm) then gradually getting wider along the following 10.5m (800–850mm) before narrowing again to 370–500mm along the next 3.5m and once more gradually becoming wider along the final 7.5m.

The natural subsoil sloped down to the gully from the north and there is evidence to suggest that there was a similar slope to the south, before the ground fell off again towards the base of the pond. Much of the evidence for the northward-facing slope to the south of the gully was, however, removed by machine prior to its being recorded.

At approximately 3.75m and 4.5m from where the gully was cut by the Abbey Stream, there were what appeared to be two post-holes on its northern side, measuring 250mm in diameter by 230mm in depth and 200mm in diameter by 285mm in depth respectively. In the absence of any further similar features along its extent, it is possible that they had a natural origin.

The fill of the gully was a brown to grey compact silty clay, with frequent inclusions of small shells and decayed stone (F848). There were also occasional animal bones recovered towards the centre of the fill. The fill was very wet and sticky and differed in colour and composition from the millpond silt above.

The function of the gully remains unclear. There are at least two possible scenarios: the first that the gully supported timbers forming a formal northern revetment for the millpond. There was, however, no real evidence for substantial post-holes or bracing to the north of the gully and this interpretation can probably be discounted. A second interpretation is that the gully represents a previous course of the Commons Water, truncated by scarping related to the adaptation of the topography to facilitate the pond's construction.

Whatever its original course, the fact that the millpond was fed by the Commons Water is supported by the contours of the local topography. The valley of the Coombe continues westwards across the site within the 60' contour, which follows the boundary wall to the north and runs along the centre of the (un-widened) Cork Street to the south. West of the site, the Commons Water runs closer to the northern contour, although its culverted extent within the site brings it closer to the centre of the trough. The 55' contour is evident at the western end of the Coombe, where the valley narrows slightly and drops off more sharply. The culverted extent of the Commons Water discharged out in a drain underneath Ardee Street and flowed counter-topographically to the north before following its historic course again down the Coombe to the east.

The 1874 Commons Water culvert F10

The Commons Water is depicted through the site as an open stream on Rocque's map of 1756, Brownrigg's lease map of 1793 and on editions and revisions of the Ordnance Survey up to the date of its culverting. It was referred to as 'a little Water Course Running under the Mill Stream towards the Comb' in Oliver Cheney's 1684 lease (RD 21, 104, 10898).

The watercourse would appear to have been formalized in masonry prior to 1874, some of which was retained to support the brick arch. The Victorian construction was of brick and masonry and is similar in build to other engineering works associated with public sanitation across the city. The culvert ran for 71.76m east-west across the site, with either end continuing beyond the excavated area. No earlier archaeological features were noted in the pond silts below the line of the culvert.

North side of culvert

The northern side of the culvert supported the buildings depicted on the Ordnance Survey and the maltings that replaced the earlier buildings in the early nineteenth century. It is quite likely that the buildings depicted on the northern side of the culvert on Rocque actually ran as far as the watercourse (the map depicts a gap between the southern walls and the open stream). It would appear here, however, that a brick lining was built against the earlier walls, irrespective of their condition, presumably to form a footing for the 1874 covering arch.

South side of culvert

In some areas along the southern side, the original masonry was replaced by brick down to the base of the watercourse and at the eastern end of the culvert, a cut for this activity was recorded. The cut (F354) was visible 500–800mm south of the brick lining, with the space between the edge of the cut and the culvert wall filled by a brown-grey silt-sand with inclusions of brick rubble.

The earlier walls F31 and F52 were partially brick-lined to form the southern side of the culvert. The brick arch survived intact prior to the demolition carried out over the summer of 2003 and was not recorded archaeologically. However, the arched culvert did survive demolition along the southern side of the protected structure on Ardee Street. Here, the F52 wall merged with a granite wall where there was a slight kink in the watercourse, 14m west of the opening which brought the watercourse under part of the protected structure on the street front.

The granite masonry was cut and dressed and measured some 850mm in height, over which were three courses of brick and the springers for the arch. Some of these blocks were as large as 470mm in height and 920mm in length. The granite wall cut the sluice pit but is possibly earlier than the 1874 works. It does not, however, appear to relate to any upstanding structure to the south of the watercourse.

The culvert below the protected structure

The culvert continued along the southern wall of the protected structure (in granite blocks for *c.*2.5m) and directly underneath a masonry protrusion extending out from the wall. The culvert continued out to the east under Ardee Street, where it flowed into a modern drain running north-south. A brick barrel vault, sprung from the limestone wall plates at either side formed most of the culvert's length. Elsewhere were three manholes, closed with sandstone slabs, presumably to access a previously demolished structure above. Access through the culvert was possible at a low crouch and the ceiling height never exceeded 1.5m. A constant flow of foul water ran through the culvert at a depth of between 250–300mm. This occasionally rose to 500–600mm after periods of heavy rain.

The northern continuation of the F342 arch was visible extending across the whole width and a number of slots in the side of the soffit were noted. A second arch was sprung 600mm east of the F342 arch, which lowered the height of the roof by 100mm to 1.3m for a length of 2m. An opening for a drain was noted in the southern culvert wall at a point 3.65m from the access point. It measured 1.1m across and 200mm in height and appeared to line up with the post-medieval F341 drain above.

Health and safety considerations precluded a full survey of the culvert from this point. Several features were, however, noted during a quick inspection by Steve McGlade and the writer. At approximately 6m from the entrance, a brick arch extended along over the culvert for a length of 2.7m. A second arch was sprung at the end of the first, extending the feature for a further 3.25m. A drain entered the culvert from above at a distance of 9.6m from the opening. It measured 450mm square and extended upwards for 400mm in a shaft. One of the blocked up man holes was located 11.1m from the opening.

Discussion

The dating of this activity at the eastern end of the Commons Water culvert is problematic. However, it is possible that the watercourse was channelled across the silted-up millpond to provide a more regular flow of water to the tanneries and breweries that were developing alongside its banks in the late 1600s. The sluice feature may be related to a millrace. However, the location of the mill remains elusive. Its presence suggests that the watercourse was afforded a greater importance during this period of industrial development.

Although the necessity of draining the pond area was possibly not an issue until the liberty was developed in the 1680s, it is likely that its culverted course and channelling below the Abbey Stream may pre-date this activity.

THE MILLPOND

Introduction

The millpond basin was confined by the 60' (18.3m) contour, with the main break of slope around the edges recorded at *c.*12.86mOD along the northern edge, with the silt fading out over the subsoil at *c.*13.2mOD along the south-eastern and south-western edges (fig. 2). The base of the millpond deposit was located at 11.45mOD at its deepest. All this suggests that the millpond extended to the east outside the site and had its deepest levels along a line extending from a point 9m south of the Commons Water culvert, running to the northeast to the north-western corner of the protected structure and thus out towards the top of the Coombe.

It seems therefore further likely that the original course of the Commons Water through the site followed the lowest contour along the bottom of the valley, extending from approximately 9m south of its culverted entry point towards the northeast and continuing down the Coombe. Although there was no definite evidence recovered for whatever feature blocked the watercourse, thus ponding the valley; the various possibilities are explored below.

The pond
The millpond basin presented as an oval-shaped saucer, oriented southwest-northeast, with a relatively flat bottom. At its most extensive, it measured approximately 50m (north–south) and at least 53m along the notional Commons Water axis. There was no evidence recorded along the base, with the possible exception of the gully discussed above, for erosive action indicating the course of the Commons Water through the area. The base of the culverted watercourse was, in any case, well above the base of the millpond. The only real indication that the edge of the millpond may not have been natural was towards the north, where the break in slope was less gradual than elsewhere. This, however, may be a function of the ground rising slightly more sharply at this point.

The millpond silt (F70/F802)
The area above the basin was filled with a homogeneous deposit of grey clay silt, with no inclusions except for finely crushed molluscs (Plate 2). At its deepest, the deposit was 2.75m in depth, gradually becoming shallower as it rose up the edges of the basin. No finds of any description were recovered either where the deposit was hand excavated or where it was mechanically removed (in several archaeological *sondages* and during the bulk excavation of the site).

Environmental samples of the deposit were wet-sieved by Penny Johnston and no identifiable organic remains were revealed. While there was a significant organic content evident in these sieved fractions, it is all finely comminuted. It did not, however, appear (macroscopically) to be humified, and there was no impression gained during manipulation of the soil that its structure was supported by organic matter.

Thomas Cummins examined the deposit *in situ* during the bulk excavation phase and his report appears below as an Appendix. His impression was of a 'rapidly deposited sediment, derived from fine particulate mineral and organic

Plate 3 Medieval flood channel of the Abbey Stream under eighteenth-century
brewery structures

particles, which had undergone almost no soil-development processes or
decomposition following deposition. The deposition environment was strongly
reducing and anoxic, so any organic matter that was originally deposited is
likely to have been preserved; thus the absence of such should be taken as a
positive observation'. Cummins concluded that this deposit represented a
single deposition event, considering it more likely to be an event of short
duration ('*short* being of a duration less that that required to establish bottom-
rooting or overhanging plants, so, less than a couple of years').

Milne found that the build-up of silts at Trig Lane in London could be
estimated at *c.*10–20mm per annum, although the silts in this case were
deposited by the tidal Thames (Milne 1981, 36). At its greatest extent, the
millpond deposit was 2.75m in depth, but there was no artefactual evidence
recovered to provide a *terminus ante quem* for the cessation of the sedimentation
process. Working (very roughly) on the Trig Lane model and calculating the
historical evidence for when the millpond contained water and from when it
could be crossed on planks, it should have taken approximately between 140
and 275 years to silt up. A reinterpretation of the documentary evidence
suggests that a man drowned in the millpond in 1326 and that it was possible to
traverse it on planks by 1527, two hundred years later.

The millpond silts malignly influenced the structural stability of all of those buildings constructed on the southern side of the Commons Water, where the earlier structures to the north of the watercourse were all substantially underpinned several years before their demolition.

THE RIDING OF THE FRANCHISES

Introduction

An important source for the pond is the assembly rolls of the city, calendared by Gilbert in the late nineteenth century. Of specific interest are the accounts of the Riding of the Franchises. The original grant of the city's boundaries in 1192 does not mention a pond at this location, and merely states that the western boundary extended 'from the church of St Patrick by the valley so far as Karnanclonegunethe' (*Carnán Chluana Uí Dhonchadha*, later corrupted first to Dunphy's Carn and then Dolphin's Barn). In fact the first detailed account of the boundaries of the city dates to 1326–7 (Gilbert 1889–1944, i, 157):

> On the western side of Dublin: from St Patrick's church by the middle of the valley so far as the pond of the house of St Thomas, the Martyr, leaving the south gate of Weycesthame and the Coulane towards the north on the right hand, and so equally by the centre of that pond. From the pond through the middle of the meadow extending so far as the field called the Irendam towards the north ...

Early evidence

That year saw a dispute between Richard of Swords and John Crek, the bailiffs and coroners of Dublin who claimed their rights had been diminished by the action of the king's coroner of Leinster who had 'illegally made view at the Abbey of St Thomas the Martyr of the body of William Stillman, drowned in the millpond there'. The dispute centred on whether the abbey lay without the city's boundary on royal land and the court found in favour of the city, although the king's coroner was exonerated of malice but not negligence (ibid., 155 and Davis 1987, 60). The best location of Stillman's demise is the body of water under discussion, bisected by the liberty boundary and thus a place of somewhat ambiguous jurisdiction.

By 1326 therefore, the feature is referred to as a *millpond*, well within the period after the diversion of the Abbey Stream through the area. The engineering works necessary to bring the watercourse back down towards the Double Mill at Warrenmount would have had to contend with the slight rise in ground levels evident as the watercourse passed over the southern side of the Coombe valley. Equally, there may have been an imperative to avoid restricting the flow of the Commons Water down the Coombe to the east, while maintaining levels within the millpond to the west. At no point, however, in any of the references to the procession is a mill mentioned at this location; additionally there is no mention made of the Abbey Stream, which would also have to be crossed just before the pond.

The next account of the Riding of the Franchises is from 1488, where neither the pond nor the watercourse is mentioned (Gilbert 1889–1944, i, 493). The procession continued

> over the roffe of another house and throw the gardynes till they came to the Combe, and owte at the Comb gate till they came to the Cow lane and soforth from that to Carnaclongynethe, that is bei Dolfynesberne …

The Cow Lane referred to in the 1326 and 1488 Ridings appears to have extended to the north of the southern gateway to the abbey, variously referred to as Washame's, Westchesthome or Waxamy's gate. However, it is unlikely to be an alternative name for Donour Street and may have been a laneway skirting around the northern boundary of the pond.

The route of the procession through the abbey's liberties went to arbitration in 1527 (ibid., 187). It would seem that on previous years, damage had been caused to the abbot's meadow to the west of the pond and that the abbey had petitioned for a rerouting of the procession. The court found in favour of the city and the traditional route was confirmed, with some concessions made to the abbey. The mayor, bailiffs and commons were permitted to proceed

> that they levv Waxamys gate and the hold Monastery of Seynt Thomas Court upon their right hand, and the forsayd Abbot and Convent … apon a reysonable sobmonycion … to make and preper a way over ther mylpond by Waxamys gate …

However, only the mayor, bailiffs, aldermen, sword bearer and macebearers were permitted to proceed across the millpond and through the meadow, and only then on foot without the horses, 'doyng as littill prejudes or hurtt unto the sayd medue as they can'. The remainder of the procession had to take to the nearby highway.

There appears to have been an accommodation here, where the abbey prepared a route over the millpond for the vanguard on condition that the bulk of the procession skirted the abbey grounds to the south, to rejoin the mayor further down Cork Street. This may indicate that the millpond had silted up by 1527 and that the mill, if it existed at all, had ceased to function. The pond may well have been silting up since the course of the Commons Water had been blocked by the Abbey Stream *c.*1182, its level checked by the flow of the Commons Water from the west and the porosity of the Abbey Stream works to the east.

The nature of the route over the millpond is clarified in the 1603 account of the Riding (ibid., 194). The Liberty of Thomas Court and Donore had at this stage passed into the hands of the Brabazon family, who continued the manorial administration of the liberty and the accommodation of the mayor and his retinue:

> and ther the Maior tooke horse, and rode alongst throughe the Coumbe near the houses, through Washames gate to the myll pound on the sowth syde of the smale gate, at the west end of the Cowmbe leading into St Thomas Courte, over which pound, at the east end of the meddow just against the myddest therof, called the Abbot's meddowe, ther wear plancks putt over by Sir Edward Brabazon's people for the Maior and his company to passe, over which the Maior and Swoordberrer, with many others of the company, rode through the meddowe, and in the midst of that meddowe was a great ould hathorne bonding the franches, which was lately cutt, but the roote and stocke lefte.

The next surviving survey of the city's liberties was undertaken in 1767 (Gilbert 1889–1944, xi, 490). The boundary ran from 'the House with the Sign of King William and Queen Mary', on the west side of Patrick Street and 'from thence along the Coomb, by the Water-course to Crooked-staff. From thence, over the Wall the left-hand of Crooked-staff, between the Willow-trees, and along the Water-course into the Road to Dolphin's-barn'.

This account does not tally with the layout of the structures depicted on Rocque. Apart from an entrance into the brewery yard (which spanned the Abbey Stream), there are no obvious walls that do not have buildings behind them. The pond had clearly ceased to be a feature on the landscape. However, the watercourse is presumably the Commons Water as depicted, while again Rocque is found wanting (Frazer 2004).

Discussion

The various accounts of the area agree with the presence of a pond within the excavation site from at least 1181–1212. It is referred as a millpond from 1386 to 1603, and it can probably be assumed that it had silted up by 1527, when it was possible to cross over it. While it is possible that the pond existed prior to the diversion of the Abbey Stream through the area, it is likely that the engineering works necessary for the diversion created an embankment to the east, which would probably have had the same effect. Thomas Cummins suggests below that the medieval embankment containing the latter watercourse would effectively block the Commons Water and that the balance between the inflow of water and the permeability of the Abbey Stream culvert construction would determine the water level in the pond. In any case, were the pond functioning as a millpond at this time, it would have been important to avoid interfering with its level and the mechanism of the mill and the tail race.

The construction of the Abbey Stream watercourse must also have had an impact on the natural course of the Commons Water further along the bottom of the Coombe valley. The various accounts of the Riding of the Franchises appear to ignore its culverted course, as the procession continued to the west after the Coombe, across the millpond, obviously following a straight line.

When the local topography is examined, the location of a pre-monastic millpond here should not be discounted. The Coombe valley narrows just to the east of the site at the 55' contour and there is a significant drop in level still evident as one looks down the Coombe towards the east. The initial grant to the abbey mentions a single mill and on the basis of present knowledge of the area's natural watercourses, it would appear likely that the mill was located here, on the southern boundary of the original monastic grant.

If the pond were formed incidentally by the insertion of an embankment for the Abbey Stream just to the west of the narrow 55' contour of the Coombe valley, the mill along the Commons Water may well have been decommissioned, as the new watercourse would presumably be bringing greater quantities of water through the area in a more reliable flow. One possible consequence of this may have been the construction of the Malt Mill along the Abbey Stream at this location. The Malt Mill is first mentioned in the 1544 grant to William Brabazon (*Fiants, Hen. VIII*, 547), again in 1552 (*Fiants Edw. VI*, 1055) and again in 1610 (*Cal. pat. rolls. Ire., Jas. I*, 159) but it has never been satisfactorily located. Its appearance in this location on various maps in the secondary sources may be more indicative of the presence of a maltings here during the nineteenth century.

THE ABBEY STREAM

Introduction

At some time in the late twelfth century the Poddle was diverted away from its old course at Mount Argus and brought around the western extent of the Liberties of Thomas Court and Donore to facilitate the construction of mills within the monastic estate and to formally demarcate to liberty's boundaries. The diversion was first postulated by M.V. Ronan in a 1927 article in the *Journal of the Royal Society of Antiquaries of Ireland* and more recently discussed by Linzi Simpson in the historical introduction to Claire Walsh's excavations along Patrick Street and Winetavern Street (Walsh 1997, 17–33).

Over the area under discussion, the Abbey Stream, later to be known as the Earl of Meath's Watercourse, flowed down the eastern side of the liberty along Pimlico and Ardee Street, discharging into the Double Mill further to the southeast at Warrenmount, before rejoining the old course of the Poddle behind New Row.

Previous evidence for the Abbey Stream

The date of the diversion of the Poddle to create the Abbey Stream is crucial in the interpretation of the site. Ronan suggests that the Abbey Stream dates to some time after 1244, implying that it was constructed in imitation of the city watercourse (Ronan 1927, 40). Simpson, however, has demonstrated that the Wooden Mill at Donore was constructed shortly after 1185 along the Abbey Stream watercourse (Walsh 1997, 24). To this evidence may be added a recent dendrochronological date acquired by Walsh from the site of the Double Mills on Mill Street, giving a best estimated felling date of AD1172+/−9 years or later (Q10670M C. Walsh, pers. comm.). Simpson further suggests that as the original 1178 monastic grant for the lands of Donore included 'mills and meadows', it is likely that such features existed prior to the construction of the Abbey Stream (ibid., 28). As suggested above, such a mill may well have been located along the Commons Water prior to the construction of the monastic watercourse. The association of the mill with the gate of St Kevin's could equally apply to a mill at the northern end of the lands of Donore, which are, in any case, marginally closer to St Kevin's than the Wooden Mill at Harold's Cross.

The discussion of the evidence for the Abbey Stream has been facilitated by Alan Hayden's excavation along Cork Street, immediately to the south, which uncovered similar evidence for flooding and the informal creation of flood streams to the west of the main channel. Neither excavation recovered evidence for a formal channel or revetment at this location, which was located slightly further to the east. Hayden recorded 'deposits of silt and gravel containing a small number of medieval and late medieval finds [filling] the channels and [spilling] out over the surrounding area' (Bennett 2003, 98).

Flood channels

Immediately to the north of Hayden's excavation two large trenches were opened below the early eighteenth-century brewery buildings through deposits of silts and gravels. The area was completely waterlogged after a period of heavy rain and the excavation of the lower levels of the channels had to be undertaken mechanically. A stratigraphical sequence consisting of three inter-cutting channels was recorded along the eastern boundary of the site, with a further channel recorded several metres away to the west. All of the channels extended north-south, with some evidence for slight meandering. Although the channels were deeper to the south, this was something in the order of 50–80mm over a distance of 10m.

Eastern channels

The earliest channel, F299, was excavated over a distance of 5.5m; it varied from 2.2–2.5m in width and was at least 500mm in depth (the base was not located) (Plate 3). It was found to display a slight curve back towards the northeast towards the main stream. Its fill, F300, was slightly different in the

Plate 4 Later medieval flood channel of the Abbey Stream

north of the trench, where it was a sterile mid-grey to brown clay silt, getting slightly darker further down; at approximately half way down a gravelly lens was evident. The fill to the south of the trench was a blue/grey gritty clay packed up with small stones, sand and gravel. It was identical to F291, the fill of the channel to the west.

This early channel was recorded under a low deposit of bright yellow compact gritty clay with frequent small stones, F301. It was excavated for 2m, was 1m wide and survived to 500mm in thickness. This was deposited by water coursing through F289, the next channel in the sequence. The F289 channel was excavated over a length of 9.8m and was found to be *c*.4m–5m in width and 900mm in depth. The cut was straight and regular and was not followed to the north of the two trenches. It was filled with F288, a light grey compact silty clay without any inclusions. This material was very similar to F286, the fill of the third channel in the sequence but it occurred below the F284 gravels rather than above them. This channel extended directly below a post-medieval masonry drain, F82, for most of its excavated course. One sherd of abraded medieval pottery was found in the F288 fill.

The creation of the F289 channel resulted in the deposition of a gravel bank on its western side. The bank, F284, was manually excavated over a distance of 2.4m and mechanically removed over a further 7.5m. It was between 1.8m–2.4m wide at its base and survived to 250–550mm in height. It was made up of grey gravel with lenses of yellow gravely sand and grey silty sand. At its northern extent, it appeared to be curving slightly back towards the northeast, where the main channel was located.

Sealing the gravel bank was F285, a silty deposit that consisted of a fine orange clay with frequent iron pan. It was 2.5m in length, and between 100 and 300mm in depth and the overall width was only observed in section. It was similar to the F172 material, which constituted the post-medieval defensive bank, but rather than sealing the F289 stream, this deposit was cut by the stream's latest flood channel. The F285 deposit merged with F172 to the east and may represent slippage from the bank.

Evidence for a third flood channel was recorded over the material described above. Although a cut was not recorded (but noted as F900), a linear depression was filled with F286, a light grey compact silty clay. It measured at least 10m in length, 2.3–2.5m in width and was between 200–500mm in depth. This material may represent a flood channel that was formed after the construction of the defensive bank of *c.*1664 and is therefore not medieval in date.

Western channel
Located 2.5m to the west of F289 was a fourth channel, F290 (Plate 4). This was up to 4.1m in width, U-shaped in profile, with a flat base 2m wide. Its full depth of *c.*750–800mm was excavated within the trench and the edges displayed a regular slope of 45 degrees. The channel was manually excavated for a distance of 3m within the trench and was not followed further north.

The channel was filled with two separate deposits, both of which were allocated the same number, F291. The lower fill was recorded along the entirety of the excavated channel and was a grey loose clay packed with gravels and decomposed calp limestone. The upper fill was only observed in the southern half of the excavated extent and was a compact yellow silty clay with no inclusions, which appeared to be redeposited subsoil. The F290 channel would appear to be contemporary with the F289 channel to the east.

The evidence for the early Abbey Stream was similar to that recorded by Hayden, with channels F289 and F290 corresponding both in level and location to the two channels excavated further to the south. In between were deposits of silts and gravels suggesting frequent flooding and natural recutting. The overall impression would suggest that the formal watercourse was not terribly secure at this location.

The medieval watercourse presumably ran along the extent of the seventeenth-century culvert discussed below. It must have been channeled at a level of approximately 1.5m higher than the upper level of the subsoil to the west, with an equivalent difference in level of approximately 1m to the east. There were fewer obvious flood channels present further to the north, despite the fact that the embankment for the watercourse would have been weakened by diverting the Commons Water underneath it. There is no evidence available to suggest when this might have occurred. However, it may have been as early as 1328, which is the first reference to the gate of Weycesthame (Gilbert 1889–1944, i, 157). Peter Walsh has suggested that the variants of Washams, Waxhams, Wycesthames or Whiteschams, referring to the gate just to the north of the site, may be a corruption of *withershins*, 'a word rooted in middle/high German (and found in Scots and old English) meaning counter-clockwise or in a direction contrary to the apparent course'.

This could be an indication that at this specific location, with two water-courses running in opposite directions (as was still the case until recently), the phenomenon was considered unusual enough to warrant calling the gate and adjacent meadow after the fact.

The relationship between the flood channels and the millpond edge was not established in this area. From an examination of the levels, it would appear likely that the Abbey Stream would have occasionally flooded into the millpond, the edge of which was located *c.*6m from the western channel. There would, however, have been an economic imperative to contain the watercourse to provide sufficient water to drive the Double Mills downstream at Warrenmount and it is unlikely that the channels were constantly flooded.

The evidence for the western channel, F290, suggests that it was deliber-ately backfilled. No finds were recovered with which to date this activity but it may have occurred just prior to the initial industrial development of the site in the 1680s. The flooding of the Abbey Stream was really only addressed in the 1820s when the watercourse was finally culverted (Ronan 1948). References to flooding in the general area throughout the nineteenth and twentieth centuries suggest that there was still a significant amount of water flowing through the culvert. Over the last twenty years the flow of the Abbey Stream has been diverted at several locations upstream, reducing significantly the amount of water which still flows through a concrete pipe.

Post-medieval defences
The channels were sealed by an earthen bank which continued to the north, just to the west of the Abbey Stream culvert. This feature is a section of the defences thrown up around the city in the 1640s, depicted on the Down Survey map of 1655–6. A section of the defences was recorded by Alan Hayden on the northern side of Long Lane (Bennett 2003, 98) while several street patterns in the general area are suggestive of angular seventeenth-century earthen fortifications.

The evidence from Ardee Street presents as an earthen bank located over the medieval Abbey Stream, but in front of the main channel. It may additionally have been possible to deliberately flood the area as a defensive measure by controlling the flow of the Commons Water at a sluice referred to in a contemporary account of the defences (HMC Ormond MSS, 156–7). Cork Street itself may have taken its name from the boggy area or *corcach* at its urban terminus.

Cattle hoof-marks
Set into the millpond silts, just to the west of the flood streams, was a large number of small holes or impressions in the clay (F245). These were found along both bodies of water. However, they were especially concentrated in a 1m-wide line oriented northwest to southeast, where they reached a maximum depth of 100–150mm. They have been interpreted as cattle hoof-marks. The dark material within the impressions was more organic than elsewhere, consisting of a compact black woody clay (F239) that resembled the bark-rich fill of the shallow tanning pit to the southeast (F227).

The post-medieval Abbey Stream culvert, F139
The Abbey Stream culvert ran north-south along Ardee Street, defining the eastern limit of excavation. A 28.4m section of the culvert was exposed during the course of the excavation and three separate phases of construction were recorded. There was no evidence recorded in this area for the primary course of the Stream.

First phase The first build, F321, consisted of a masonry-lined channel, with an internal width of 3.84m–3.98m and a depth of 950mm (the latter based on a measurement in the undisturbed section underneath the southern wall of the protected structure). The base of the channel was located at 13.74mOD to the north, which fell by 480mm, 70m to the south. The channel was mostly uncovered along this extent, based on the evidence of Brownrigg's 1793 lease map. Rocque depicts the Abbey Stream as an open watercourse, south of where the Commons Water appears to flow directly into it. The cut for the western wall was visible 340–480mm outside the wall. This was filled by a grey gritty sandy-silty clay, with occasional inclusions of small stones, mortar, animal bone, and charcoal (F322). The walls measured 360mm in width, faced on the inside only and were constructed from limestone blocks bonded by a creamy-white sandy mortar. The base of the culvert was lined with closely packed slate and limestone slabs set on their edges. This may have served to prevent objects getting caught along the base of the watercourse.

This phase of construction post-dates the seventeenth-century defensive bank, as the western wall of the culvert cuts it. It is likely therefore that the formal channelling of the Abbey Stream in masonry probably occurred as the area was being prepared for industrial development in the 1670s or the 1680s.

The channelling raised the level of the watercourse by at least 2m. There is no evidence as to how this affected the watercourse upstream and downstream.

However, the nature of the construction would suggest that the works were carried out over the entire length of the watercourse.

Second phase The second phase consisted of the insertion of a brick lining and arch, both inside and outside the masonry walls. The brick walls were constructed at either side of the earlier masonry walls and measured 260mm in width. They were bonded by a hard white chalky mortar with some small stone-fragment inclusions. The inner walls were built over the base of the earlier channel and the outer walls were constructed from a masonry sill on the earlier wall. The exterior crown of the brick arch was recorded in section underneath the protected structure at 14.97mOD.

At 4m from the northern edge of excavation, the culvert wall became wider by 280mm for a 3m stretch. This widened section was constructed in brick. The cut (F344) for the outer brick lining was visible for 170–200mm outside the wall. This was filled by a yellow–grey compact fine sand with inclusions of finely crushed brick (F345).

Historical evidence for this second build can be found in Ronan's second article on the Poddle published in the *Journal of the Royal Society of Antiquaries of Ireland* in 1948. Here, the frequent flooding of the watercourse is discussed along with remedial measures undertaken in the 1820s, which resulted in the Abbey Stream being completely covered over along this stretch.

Third phase The third build consisted of the insertion replacement by a concrete pipe, 600mm in diameter, which ran through the centre of the brick and stone culvert, set 400–500mm away from the sides, resting on the base of the seventeenth-century channel. The insertion of the pipe truncated the brick arch and the upper courses of masonry belonging to the first build.

Commons Water / Abbey Stream cross-over
At 15m east of the point where it flowed under the protected structure, the Commons Water culvert passed underneath the Abbey Stream. At this point the culvert base was lined with large slabs, and the only indication of the watercourse above was provided by a sudden and abrupt 250mm drop in the floor level.

DISCUSSION

The existence of a millpond at this location has been referenced in the several accounts dealing with the area. The earliest reference, preserved in the Register of St Thomas's abbey and Archbishop Alen's Register and dated to between 1181 and 1212, refers to the pond as a topographical landmark, the 'pond below St Thomas Court' (Gilbert 1889, 284; McNeill 1950, 31–2). The size of the pond located over the course of the excavation would suggest that this is the feature being referred to. The millpond is not, however, mentioned in the 1192 boundary grant of the city and one commentator inferred from this that the pond was not in existence until its first mention in an updated description of the city boundary between 1324 and 1327 (Ronan 1927, 41). A 'mill next to Donore' is, however, referenced as early as 1216 (White 1951, 38). There appear to be no other references to the pond in the Register of St Thomas's (Gilbert 1889), although the edited volume itself awaits further critical work.

To fully interpret this feature it is necessary to evaluate the primary sources, such as they are, against the evidence on the ground. In doing so, the assumption should be made that the Commons Water is a natural feature running through the area, with no known natural impediment to its fall down the Coombe valley. Thomas Cummins's assessment that the millpond silts are the result of a 'single deposition event' should also be borne in mind, along with the evidence above which suggests a *c.*200-year silting-up period.

Both the primary and secondary accounts of the medieval development of the area tend to be needlessly confusing. The latter have in the past concentrated on riverine disputes between St Thomas's, St Patrick's and the city, which refer *inter alia* to the construction of the Abbey Stream, the city watercourse and the location of various mills along the watercourse.

The first known reference to a pond at this location is in a grant by the archbishop of the parish of St James to the canons of St Thomas which delineated the boundaries of the parish from the New Gate to Kilmainham 'excepting both sides of the street in which Alelim's house stands and Donour Street *as far as the pond below St Thomas Court* in which St Patrick's church should have parochial rights' (Gilbert 1889, 284; McNeill 1950, 31–2). As already mentioned, the reference dates to between 1181 and 1212 and appears to further grant to the canons all tithes to the mills within the parish of St Patrick, as well as tithes to the arable lands, should the canons wish to let them.

The Augustinian abbey dedicated to St Thomas the Martyr was established by William Fitz Audelin in 1177 on behalf of Henry II. The grant included approximately 120 modern acres of land and a mill (although there appears to be considerable confusion about this in the secondary sources). The following year the abbey was granted one carucate of land at Donore 'with mills, meadows and other appurtenances' (Gwynn and Hadcock 1970, 172). The land was later held as a liberty free of the legal jurisdiction of the city. The Liberty of Donore extended to the south, outside of the city's limits, under the jurisdiction of the abbey. It was approached from the abbey through Donour Street, which in its present form has become Pimlico and Ardee Street.

The reference to a pond during this period strongly suggests that the Commons Water had been artificially blocked. It is, however, unclear as to whether the watercourse was ponded to provide a reservoir of water to run a mill on the Commons Water itself, or whether it had been blocked by an embankment holding the newly constructed Abbey Stream. What sort of mill would operate at this location? On the basis of the present evidence of the flow of the Commons Water, would the local topography provide a sufficient fall to turn any sort of wheel mechanism?

The grant to the abbey suggests that there were already mills in Donore, although these may have been located along the original course of the Poddle, which appears to have partly dried up after the watercourse was diverted to create the Abbey Stream. Several specific references throughout the medieval period to a mill in Donore have been thought to refer to the Wooden Mill, located along the Abbey Stream in Harold's Cross. Such a reference occurs in a 1215 confirmation of King John's grant of the church of Crumlin to St Patrick's, though Archbishop Alen inserts the note 'belongs by primitive foundation to the commons of the churches of Sts Nicholas, Brigid, Kevin, and of Cromlyn and Dunamore ecclesiastical benefices, tithes moreover of the common land of the citizens near Dunabroke and half a burgage before the gate of St Kevins and a mill near Dunnor' (McNeill 1950, 37).

The possibility exists, however, that there may have been a pond along the Commons Water prior to the creation of the Abbey Stream and therefore the 'pond below St Thomas Court' may well have been there prior to the abbey's foundation.

CONCLUSION

The archaeological evidence indicates that a large body of water constituting a mill pond or reservoir occupied the site, fed by the Commons Water which discharged down the slope at the western end of the Coombe. Its location along the boundary of the Liberties of Thomas Court and Donore would suggest that the pond was eventually under the control of the abbey of St Thomas. However, the archaeological evidence was unable to indicate whether the damming of the Commons Water occurred before or after the abbey's foundation in 1177.

It would certainly appear, however, that *the pond below St Thomas Court* was in existence between 1181 and 1212. Simpson's suggestion that the Abbey Stream was created shortly after 1185 might suggest that the construction of the new watercourse had the secondary benefit of damming the Commons Water, thus controlling the supply of water down the Coombe and toward the mills situated along the Poddle downstream. These mills as such were outside the direct control of the abbey, yet, the abbey would have exercised control over the volume of water reaching them. There are no known documentary sources identifying the pond as a bone of contention between the abbey and the city (apart from the dispute in the aftermath of Stillman's drowning), although there were extensive problems with the abbey's perceived interference with other watercourses, most notably the city watercourse.

Peter Walsh's suggestion that the variants of Washams, Waxhams, Wycesthames or Whiteschams, referring to the medieval gate just to the northeast of the site, may be a corruption of *withershins*, meaning counter-clockwise, is an attractive one; with some little effort of the imagination, the two watercourses running in opposite directions can be easily visualized at this location. Any cyclist riding south down Pimlico will be aware of the incline at the new development facing down the Coombe, and indeed the ascent beyond, now cruelly interrupted by the insertion of the Coombe by-pass.

Evidence for milling on the site was recorded in the form of six millstones, which were recovered from secondary locations and contexts. On the basis that millstones are difficult to move, it would seem likely that there was a mill in the immediate vicinity. Documentary sources locate the Malt Mill in the general area, situated along the Abbey Stream. This is first referred to as such in 1544 and is thus of relatively late construction in the scheme of things. A late seventeenth-century reference to Joseph Thomas, a well-known miller who had leased both the Double Mill at Warrenmount and the Wood Mill at Harold's Cross, would suggest that the mill, if one existed, was located in the property north of the Commons Water. The millstones recovered on site, however, came from the properties south of the watercourse and it is likely that they belonged to a post-medieval mill, wherever it was located.

The post-medieval industrial development of the site echoes the archaeology of the Liberties as a whole, with both tanning and brewing represented. The recovery of evidence for a section of the defensive bank erected around the city during the Cromwellian wars is an added bonus to our understanding of the military geography of the city and it is hoped to explore further this aspect of the site's development in print elsewhere.

ACKNOWLEDGMENTS

The writer wishes to thank the following: Antoine Giacometti, Sheelagh Conran, James Hession, Tara Doyle, Ulrika Forsman, Charlotte Comyns, Carina Erickson, Ingela Ericsson, Greg Flanagan, Fergus Grant-Stevenson, Anthony Gregory, Mark Kelly, Augusto Maecola, Steve McGlade, José Luis Siles Marino, Ray Murphy, Alex Southran, Sarah Tobin, Bella Walsh, Shane Warner, Neil Carlin, Denise Keating, Colm McCavera, Johnny Ryan, Ciara Vaughan, Jane Stradwick, Linzi Simpson, Seán Duffy, Tony Prior, Lindsay Rafter, Mario Sughi, Peter Walsh, Penny Johnston, Thomas Cummins, Antoinette Madden and Noël Siver.

SOIL NOTES

(by Thomas Cummins, School of Biology and Environmental Science, UCD)

Introduction

Excavation (03E0315) has been undertaken on a site facing the junction of Ardee Street and Cork Street in Dublin's Liberties by Margaret Gowen & Co. Ltd. At the close of the excavation, the site director, Franc Myles, requested a site visit for discussion of the remaining exposures of a millpond sediment. The site was visited briefly on 5 July 2004, during which development work was proceeding apace, and most of the excavated areas had been either buried or cleared. Unless otherwise stated, the present tense of the descriptions refers to the various features as found during excavation, rather than as directly observed during the site visit.

A previous excavation on an adjacent site now under the widened Cork Street was carried out by Alan Hayden (01E0614), revealing two main channels of the Abbey Stream, and evidence that it had overflowed its banks many times. Associated with these channels 'deposits of silt and gravel containing a small number of medieval and late medieval finds filled the channels and spilled out over the surrounding area'. Across the road, to the south of Cork Street (Site 4), 'one of [the channels] was lined with a timber revetment composed of horizontal timber planks held in place by driven posts' (Bennett 2003, 97–8).

The Commons Water and the Abbey Stream

Running east-west and roughly bisecting the site is the Commons Water. This stream is not now apparent on the surface, and has presumably been re-routed as part of the current development. As discovered in excavation, the Commons Water runs in a constructed channel. The location of this structure coincides with the same as detailed in a lease document of 1684, which document mentions the distance from the northeast and northwest corners of the site. This channel was subsequently culverted (i.e. closed over) and concealed below later fills. The course of this stream prior to its being channelled is not certain. However, a cut near the northern boundary of the site may represent an earlier location of this stream, or a period during which all or part of it was temporarily re-routed.

A second channel runs north-south inside of and parallel to the eastern boundary of the site which faces onto Ardee Street. This is the Abbey Stream, which runs in an entirely constructed waterway. The Abbey Stream is documented from the thirteenth century, though its earliest construction has not been observed in this excavation. The exact date of construction is not known, and is discussed by Linzi Simpson (1997, also citing Ronan 1927). The current culvert has two concentric structures, an outer stone channel, and a roofed brick culvert, currently surrounding the stream. The channel is a millrace which leaves the River Poddle at the Stone Boat, and follows a counter-topographic route to supply water to early mill workings within the Liberty of Thomas Court. Later mills operated at many points along its length, and may have done near this site, within the subsidiary Liberty of Donore.

The Abbey Stream crosses, but does not join, the Commons Water about midway along the eastern side of the site. At the cross-over (not a junction or confluence, since the waters do not meet), the Abbey Stream culvert is constructed directly on top of and over the constructed culvert of the Commons Water. The earliest evidence for this arrangement, with the Commons Water flowing underneath the Abbey Stream, is the documented position of the Commons Water culvert, in the position in which it was found during excavation, running east-west across the site.

The millpond deposit, F70/F802

West of the Abbey Stream, and occupying most of the centre of the site, is an extensive, continuous deposit (F70/F802), which has been identified as a sediment, corresponding to the extent of a former pond. The eastern extent of this deposit is unknown, being inaccessible to the excavation. There was a sharp break of slope defining the northern and north-western boundary, with a more gradual slope to the north along the southern and south-eastern sides; a suspicion of a sharp, 1.5–2m cut in the subsoil for a 2m extent at the south-western corner of the site strongly suggests a formal edge here, as opposed to a naturally scarped one. The lower surface of the millpond deposit is gently sloping, with its deepest position towards the east. Over much of the area, the deposit is almost flat-bottomed, which, combined with the continued low angle out to the boundary of the deposit, gives a broad, gently-sloping basin.

The upper boundary of the millpond deposit is cut by several features which are datable by association with the lease document of 1603, however it was possible to cross the millpond on planks in 1527. This provides a *terminus ante quem* for the cessation of sedimentation. The lower boundary lies on natural subsoil, with no cut features identified, so an initial *terminus post quem* for the initiation of sediment infill is no more recent than the retreat of the overlying ice.

The water supply assumed to be feeding this pond is the Commons Water, which flows across the site directly through the broadest part of the millpond sediment deposit. The culverted manifestation of this stream bisects, and overlies, the millpond deposit. This channel is constructed to flow under the Abbey Stream.

The deposit itself consists of a silty clay, with an unusual resistance to manipulation, possibly explained by an extremely uniform particle-size distribution. There are almost no coarse particles over 2mm. The soil structure appears to be massive *in situ*, with limited prismatic formation at the drying-out faces examined. There is no evidence of internal stratification or bedding within the deposit. There are occasional distinct vertically-oriented pores, presumed to be biopores, lined with an intensely-developed orange-brown coating having a smooth, metallic lustre. These pores extend through the deposit, but appear to be concentrated, wider, and more branched adjacent to the lower boundary of the deposit. While these pores may have a biogenic origin, there is no other evidence for any biomechanical action, and it may be concluded that the deposit is undisturbed by such processes. Munsell colours were not assessed in the field, and the material undergoes progressive oxidation upon exposure. Thus there is iron in reduced state within the soil material (i.e. it has not been leached). The matrix colour appears to be dark greyish brown 10YR 4/2, oxidizing on exposed surfaces and along relict biopores to yellowish red 5YR 4/6.

Examination of wet-sieved fractions by Penny Johnston revealed no identifiable organic remains. While there is a significant organic content evident in these sieved fractions, it is all finely comminuted. However, it does not appear (macroscopically) to be humified, and there is no impression gained during manipulation of the soil that its structure is supported by organic matter. It is difficult to be definite about interpreting these observations, but the impression gained is of a rapidly-deposited sediment, derived from fine particulate mineral and organic particles, which has undergone almost no soil-development processes or decomposition following deposition. The deposition environment is strongly reducing and anoxic, so any organic matter that was originally deposited is likely to have been preserved; thus the absence of such should be taken as a positive observation.

The absence of internal stratification or bedding suggests that the deposit represents a uniform deposition environment. The absence of biomechanical activity allows that this observation can be taken as positive evidence of the absence of bedding. The 'uniform deposition environment' could range between being a single short-lived event, or a long period of unchanging deposition. However, the balance of probability must tend towards a short rather than a long event, since increasing time inevitably allows a greater probability that the deposition conditions would vary.

The underlying till-like fabrics have abundant fine biopores (< 1 mm ø). Not a single artefact was observed within the millpond deposit, which was a surprise, as such deposits are typically very rich.

Combining the evidence of uniform fabric, absence of bedding, absence of coarse organic inclusions, and absence of artefacts, it seems reasonable to conclude that this deposit represents a single deposition event. Whether that event was short-lived, or due to prolonged uniform deposition conditions cannot be inferred, but the more likely explanation has to be an event of short duration (*short* being of a duration less that that required to establish bottom-rooting or overhanging plants, so, less than a couple of years).

Origin of the millpond deposit
The millpond deposit, F70, is clearly laid down in a water body lying (at least partly) to the west of the Abbey Stream culvert. The origin of this deposit is of considerable interest, and there are several alternative explanations, all with some evidence, and all having implications for the development and use of this site.

Firstly, the relationship of the underlying topography to the deposit is important. In the excavated area, clearly the underlying till deposit retains the water (this is no karstic turlough, or swallow-hole with intermittent water-holding). However, for a pond to form, there must be a topographic rise on all sides. The land falls to the east along the Coombe, but the lie of the natural subsoil surface is not clear immediately to the east of the site. Is there a natural rise here, which ponds the Commons Water? If so, then the origins of the pond are immediately post-glacial. However, if such were the case, one would expect the pond to have filled up long ago and to have ceased to be a body of open water long before the establishment of the city. Such a fill could derive from inflowing mineral sediment, or more likely from the deposition of vegetative detritus into the pond. Suffice to say, that in the climate of the area, no small permanent standing water body has remained as open water since the postglacial. On this evidence alone, we have reasonable grounds to infer that the pond has an anthropogenic origin.

The outflow of the millpond is the Commons Water, which, emerging below the Abbey Stream culvert, turns left to the north, flows north parallel to and in the opposite direction to the Abbey Stream along Ardee Street, and then takes a right turn and flows downhill along the Coombe. The counter-flow of these two streams indicates that the flow of at least one of them along Ardee Street is counter-topographic.

The Commons Water culvert lies underneath the Abbey Stream culvert. Noting the certain early origin of the Abbey Stream, likely to be in the twelfth century, we may ask what would be needed to channel the Commons Water under a pre-existing Abbey Stream. Culverting the lower watercourse would require the stoppage or local diversion of the Abbey Stream, and the dismantling and reconstruction of the Abbey Stream culvert. Alternative approaches, such as shoring the upper structure while the lower one was built, seem infeasible (though not totally impossible). Thus, the simple stratigraphic interpretation, that the lower structure is older and the upper younger, should prevail for the cross-over structures, in the absence of other information. Thus the existence of an earlier, culverted Commons Water, constructed before or at the same time as the Abbey Stream, seems the most plausible interpretation (noting that the structures imagined here are those at the initial cross-over of the two streams, not the extant culverts which are clearly later).

If such culverting predates the construction of the Abbey Stream, this would suggest that the Commons Water was already functioning as a millrace. That the pre-Abbey Stream Commons Water did indeed drive a mill has been suggested, and while there is no direct documentary or excavated evidence for this, there are indications of several mills somewhere in the area, which on current understanding are placed before the construction of the Abbey Stream.

If culverting of the Commons Water was coincident with the construction of the Abbey Stream, then a millrace function for the Commons Water seems much less likely. In such circumstances, the culverting would be seen as a protective measure for the Abbey Stream structure, to prevent its being undermined by the Commons Water.

Another alternative is that at the time of the construction of the Abbey Stream, no culvert was provided for the Commons Water, a small stream which drove no mills and did not run in any constructed watercourse. Such an approach would have caused the Commons Water to back up against the western embankment or revetment of the Abbey Stream at the point of blockage. This location corresponds to the position of the millpond deposit. In forming a pond, the water level would rise, while the still-water body created would lead to deposition of any sediment being carried. The balance between the inflow of water and the permeability of the Abbey Stream culvert construction would determine the water level. Even if the Abbey Stream channel was lined with clay (which is unknown), a supporting bank could be quite permeable. And the extensive evidence for bank collapses allows that it was built from unconsolidated earthen materials. Thus it is not necessary to see the water level of the ponded Commons Water rising to overtop the Abbey Stream.

Origin and fate of water-deposited sediment above F70

A deep, stratified, blue-grey, fine-grained deposit overlies F70 in a section to the east of the site. This section was not excavated archaeologically, but was photographed and drawn. The photographs reveal horizontal beds or layers within this deposit. The manifestation of layers may be due to preferential cracking in the exposed surface: the sub-parallel cracks observed might not correspond to individual layers, or there may in fact be no observable layering in a fresh exposure. However, the lineation may be taken to represent some structural alignment within the deposit (unlike F70, which shows no such banding, and which appeared structureless on field examination).

This appears to be a water-lain deposit of relatively uniform, fine-grained sediment, comparable in all but its apparent layering to F70. It overlies F70, and extends for several metres north-south along the exposed face. The closest opportunity to confirm its western extent was some 3m away, but the deposit was not observed at this location.

One might envisage that this deep sediment derived from the same water body as the millpond which laid down F70, that its original extent entirely covered F70, and that it has been completely removed without trace over this entire area. However, a simpler explanation would be preferable. It seems more likely that this deposit derives from water extending westwards to form a pond by leakage from the Abbey Stream, but that the pond in this case is limited in the distance it extends to the west of the Abbey Stream culvert edge. To constrain such a deep, narrow water body would require a wall or bank to have been positioned near, parallel and at a short distance from the Abbey Stream on its western side.

In some photographs it appears to be the case that the layering within this deposit is not horizontal, but that the layers are organized into a curved structure. The curve is symmetrical, with a peak above a large piece of timber which is photographed *in situ*. The trough coincides with a brick-rich feature. This appears to be a case of a structure subsiding into a soft sediment. The weight applied to the brick footing has compressed the sediment underneath, and has forced the adjoining mass upwards where less force is applied. The originally horizontal bedding planes have thus become disrupted, and are arranged as flow lines indicating the local direction of movement of the fabric due to the plastic deformation.

Table 1: Dating of deposition of millpond deposit F70

TPQ for start of deposition:

Retreating ice, 10–12,000 BP

Pre-Abbey Stream anthropogenic blocking of Commons Water
        Pond not mentioned in royal grant of Franchises, 1192
        Ponding by construction of Abbey Stream channel, *c.*1200

Date range for deposition of millpond sediment: AD *c.*1200–1324

Origin of the name which became Cork Street (corcach, a wet meadow or marsh)

Culverting of Commons Water on construction of Abbey Stream channel, c.1200
        Evidence cited by Ronan from Riding of the Franchises, 1324
        Need for boardwalk during Riding of the Franchises, 1527
        Presence of stream within culvert, 1684 lease document
        Earliest features cutting top of F70, 1684 lease document

TAQ for end of deposition

Note: this table can include contradictory evidence (poorly-associated evidence is in italics).

APPENDIX 2

A NOTE ON THE MILLPOND CONTOUR MAP (FIG. 2)

(by Franc Myles)

The contour map has been prepared on the basis of a series of levels taken on the upper surviving level of the subsoil around the site. The levels were taken at different periods during the excavation and during the bulk clearance in the early summer of 2004.

Several features are of note. The edges of the millpond are particularly sharp on the western and northern sides, which probably indicates that the Commons Water cut sharply into the subsoil in geological times. The narrow channel in the north-eastern corner indicates the previous course of the Commons Water in the direction of the Coombe, which was presumably the course taken prior to the formal culverting of the channel at some stage prior to 1756.

The slope on the southern side is much more gradual, interrupted by two anomalies. To the west, a trough indicates the presence of the F661 ditch, for which there was no dating evidence, apart from the fact that it predated the tannery activity of *c*.1680. To the southeast, the F82 drain is evident, discharging into the later course of the Commons Water.

The culverted course of the Commons Water did not impact on the subsoil and is therefore not indicated on the map.

BIBLIOGRAPHY

Primary sources

Calendar of fiants of Henry III … Elizabeth. In *Report of the Deputy Keeper of the Public Records in Ireland*, nos. *7–22* (Dublin, 1875–90). Reprinted as *The Irish fiants of the Tudor sovereigns*, 4 vols. Dublin 1994.

Gilbert, J.T. (ed.) 1889 *Register of the Abbey of St Thomas, Dublin*. London.

Gilbert, J.T. and Gilbert R.M. (eds) 1889–1944 *Calendar of ancient records of Dublin, in the possession of the municipal corporation of that city*, 19 vols, Dublin.

HMC 1895 *A breviat concerninge the perticular quartiers, posts, and ordinary centries, uppon the lyne of those five regiments which are quartered in the suburbs on this side of the river, from the Colledge to Sir William Usher's hous*. Ormond MSS, i, London.

Irish Manuscripts Commission 1966 *Irish patent rolls of James I: facsimile of the Irish Record Commissioners' calendar prepared prior to 1830*. Dublin.

McNeill, C. (ed.) 1950 *Calendar of Archbishop Alen's register c.1172–1534*. Dublin.

Registry of Deeds, RD 21, 104, 10898.

White, N.B. (ed.) 1951 *The 'Dignitas decani' of St Patrick's cathedral, Dublin*. Dublin.

Secondary sources

Barrow, L. 1983 The franchises of Dublin. *Dublin Historical Record*, 36:2, 68–80.

Bennett, I. 2003 *Excavations 2001: summary accounts of archaeological excavations in Ireland*. Bray.

Davis, V. 1987 Relations between the abbey of St Thomas the Martyr and the municipality of Dublin, *c*.1176–1527. *Dublin Historical Record*, 40:2, 57–65.

Duddy, C. 2001 The western suburb of medieval Dublin: its first century. *Irish Geography*, 34:2, 157–75.

Duddy, C. 2003 The role of St Thomas's abbey in the early development of Dublin's western suburb. In S. Duffy (ed.), *Medieval Dublin IV*, 79–97. Dublin.

Elliott, A.L. 1892 The abbey of St Thomas the Martyr, near Dublin. *RSAI Jn.*, 22, 25–41.

Gwynn, A. 1954 The early history of St Thomas abbey, Dublin. *RSAI Jn.*, 84, 1–35.

Gwynn, A. and Hadcock, R.N. 1970 *Medieval religious houses: Ireland*. Dublin.

Frazer, B. 2004 Cracking Rocque. *Archaeology Ireland*, 18, no. 68, 10–13.

Milne, G. 1981 Medieval riverfront reclamation in London. In G. Milne and B. Hobley (eds), *Waterfront archaeology in Britain and Northern Europe*, CBA Research Report 41, 32–6. London.

Ronan, M.V. 1927 The Poddle river and its branches. *RSAI Jn.*, 57, 39–46.

Ronan, M.V. 1948 The Poddle iver (1803–1829). *RSAI Jn.*, 78, 5–10.

Simpson, L. 1997 Historical introduction to the Patrick Street excavation. In C. Walsh, *Archaeological Excavations at Patrick, Nicholas & Winetavern Streets, Dublin*, 17–33. Dingle.

Sweeney, C.L. 1991 *The rivers of Dublin*. Dublin.

Walsh, C. 1997 *Archaeological excavations at Patrick, Nicholas & Winetavern Streets, Dublin*. Dingle.

Walsh, C. 2000 Archaeological excavations at the abbey of St Thomas the Martyr, Dublin. In S. Duffy (ed.), *Medieval Dublin I*, 185–202. Dublin.

From Roskilde to Dublin: the story of the
Sea Stallion from Glendalough

TRÍONA NICHOLL

INTRODUCTION

On 14 August 2007 thousands of people lined the banks of the Liffey to welcome the *Sea Stallion from Glendalough* at the end of a seven-week journey from Roskilde to Dublin. The voyage was an ambitious experimental archaeological project and the result of over fifty years of maritime archaeological research and experiment at both the National and Viking Ships Museums in Denmark, a multidisciplinary endeavour that has seen archaeologists, historians, boat-builders, craftspeople and sailors combine their efforts and skills to reconstruct and examine that most evocative of artefacts from the Viking Age, the warship.

1957–59: Underwater survey and early excavation
Folk traditions had long attested to the existence of wrecked timbers at a silted barrier on the bed of the Roskilde Fjord, a long narrow body of water running approximately 40km from the Kattegat in the north of Sjælland to the town of Roskilde at its end (fig. 1). The fjord is so shallow at this particular point, a channel called Pebberenden near the village of Skuldelev, that the timbers were often exposed at low water or after storms (Crumlin Pedersen & Olsen 2002, 23). It was not until 1956 when two amateur divers removed some timbers, bringing them to the attention of Olaf Olsen of the Medieval Department of the National Museum of Denmark that proper attention was paid to the significance of the site. Based on analysis of these timbers and the other accounts of finds from the site Olsen was confident of the existence of a wreck from the Viking Age. A two-week season of excavation began shortly afterwards in July 1957.

The first step was a survey to establish the extent of the site. The barrier was found to be circa 50m long by 10m wide and initial excavations focused on an area where fishermen had reported finding timbers during the 1920s (Crumlin Pedersen and Olsen 2002, 25). Pine planks forming part of the hull of the wreck Skuldelev 1 were quickly located. Their removal led to the discovery of a second keel lying a little further to the south of the first wreck. The recovery of associated oak planking confirmed the existence of another wreck (Crumlin Pedersen and Olsen 2002, 26).

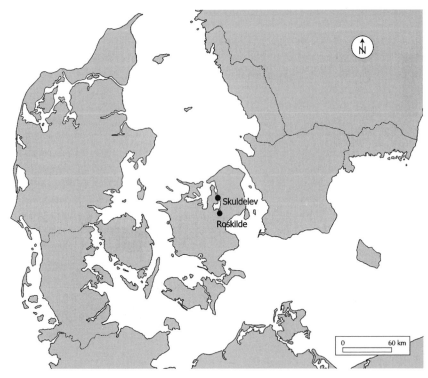

1 Map of Denmark showing the locations of Skuldelev and Roskilde.
Copyright: the Viking Ships Museum

This discovery of Skuldelev 2, the wreck on which the *Sea Stallion* is based,
led to an extended five-week season in 1958 during which a further two wrecks
were uncovered in the same area, Skuldelev 3 and 4. Skuldelev 4 was located in
the northern part of the barrier, 20m away from Skuldelev 2 (Crumlin Pedersen
and Olsen 2002, 27). The allocation of a separate name for the timbers of
Skuldelev 4 later proved to have been a mistake. The keel that was assigned to
Skuldelev 2 and the oak planking assigned to Skuldelev 4 were actually one and
the same vessel, the remains of a 30m-long warship. The distance between the
timbers of wrecks 2 and 4 had led the team to assume they were the remains of
two distinct vessels as, up to that point, no ship of such a large size had been
excavated from the Viking Age. The wreck often appears in some of the early
literature on the find as Skuldelev 4 or Skuldelev 2 and 4 (Crumlin Pedersen &
Olsen 2002, 27). Before this error was discovered, however, two further wrecks,
Skuldelev 5 and 6, were located. The wrecks therefore now number Skuldelev 1
through 6 with the original number 4 being omitted. For the purpose of clarity, all
references in this article will now be made to Skuldelev 2.

The second season of excavation also uncovered the relatively intact
remains of Skuldelev 3. The quality of preservation of this wreck – largely

2 The Skuldelev wrecks exposed in the cofferdam during the 1962 excavations.
Photo: Olaf Olsen. Copyright: the Viking Ships Museum, Denmark

down to its position deeper in the barrier – prompted a shift in focus for the investigations. The objective now became the full recovery, conservation and public display of the wreck group. The state of the timbers and the almost complete decomposition of all nails and rivets meant that attempting to raise the wreck fragments from under water would have been extremely difficult and hazardous (Crumlin Pedersen and Olsen 2002, 27). Added to this was the complication of the fact that this was now a multiple wreck site and, until the area could be properly cleared, it was difficult to gauge the exact extent of the number, size and state of preservation of the wrecks. The decision was therefore taken to construct a cofferdam around the wrecks, allowing total drainage of the site and exposure of the timbers for more secure recovery.

1962: The barrier exposed

The construction of the cofferdam enclosed an area of 2500m² that was drained and ready for excavation by 5 July 1962. The decision was made to

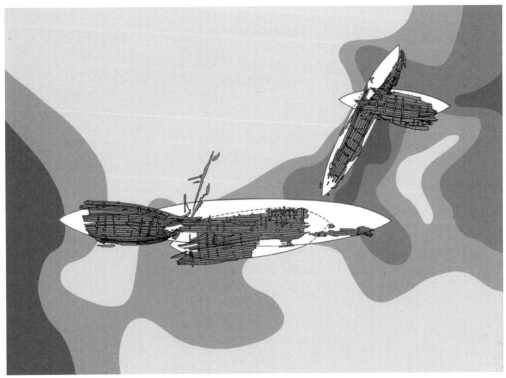

3 Illustration showing the position and remains of the five wrecks on the barrier at Pebberenden. Illustration: Jan Rilshede. Copyright: The Viking Ships Museum

gradually reduce the level of the water, thereby supporting the ships with their loads of stones for as long as possible (fig. 2). Over the course of the first month the water level was gradually reduced and sand and stones removed as they were exposed, finally leaving the five wrecks free for investigation, attracting huge interest from the Danish public with 28,000 people visiting the site during the excavation. The timbers – and the excavation team – were now being continually sprayed with water from garden sprinkler systems in order to prevent warping and disintegration of the wrecks. Under the direction of Olaf Olsen and Ole Crumlin Pedersen, a team of archaeologists and students now laboured to record and remove the wrecks as quickly as possible, completing the task by that autumn. The culmination of the excavation was the recovery of the final series of artefacts from the site – a collection of strakes that had been torn away from the wrecks over the years by wave and ice action and, crucially, the 14m-long keelson of Skuldelev 2 (Crumlin Pedersen and Olsen 2002, 41). It was this timber that would prove pivotal to the reconstruction process, allowing for an accurate estimate of the overall size and scale of the vessel.

The exact nature of the barrier could now be understood (fig. 3). At some point during the eleventh century the five ships, all well worn after years of

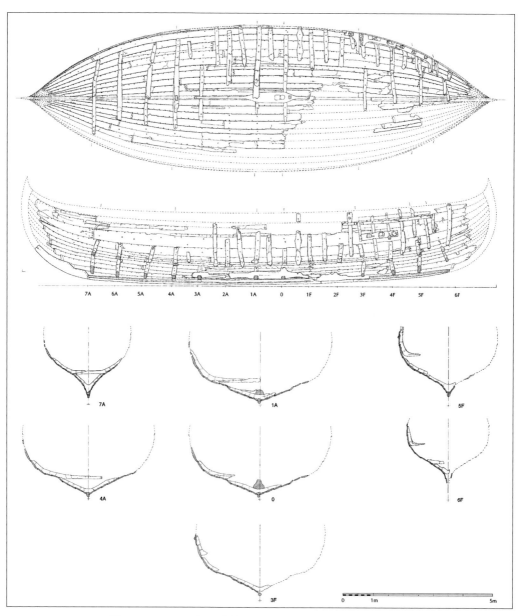

4 Torso reconstruction of Skuldelev 1. Illustration: Vibeke Bischoff.
Copyright: The Viking Ships Museum

heavy use, were taken out on the fjord, stripped of all rigging and reusable components, filled with stones and intentionally scuttled to form a blockade across the navigable channels of the Pebberenden. Following the excavation, a programme of cores and a detailed survey of the fjord bed showed the barrier to be a manmade extension to a natural bank running north-south along the channel. The ships were scuttled to block two out of the three navigable channels through the area. This was done in three separate phases, the barrier being augmented as the original ships settled and sank deeper into the fjord bed. The first phase saw Skuldelev 1, 3 and probably 5 scuttled (Crumlin Pedersen and Olsen 2002, 331). The barrier was then strengthened with the addition of piles and brushwood sections to prevent the ships sliding off their position and into the pool of Peberholmhullet located near the barrier.

Phase Two saw the scuttling of Skuldelev 2 on top of wrecks 1 and 3 that had begun to settle into the fjord bed. Skuldelev 6 was also sunk at this stage on top of Skuldelev 5. A third and final phase of construction occurred at the barrier some years later when another series of posts were inserted to prevent slippage and to hold the ships in position. This seems to have occurred quite late in the life of the barrier as the bow section of Skuldelev 2 had completely disintegrated by this stage (ibid.).

The Skuldelev ships

The results of the excavations at Skuldelev far exceeded any expectations. In all, five Viking Age wrecks were recovered from the fjord bed, ranging from a small fishing craft to a large oceangoing trader and warship. These five wrecks, originating in Denmark, Norway and Ireland, encapsulate the economy of the Viking Age with its firm focus on maritime activity across long-distance trade networks. Their remains are summarized below (figs 4–8):

Wreck name	Place of origin	Date	Ship type	Size	Function	Capacity and crew
Skuldelev 1	Western Norway	1025	Knarr	L: 16m W: 4.84m	Trading vessel	25 tons of cargo and a crew of 6–15
Skuldelev 2	Eastern Ireland	1042	Warship	L: 30m W: 4m	Transport of persons/warfare	60–100 crew
Skuldelev 3	Denmark	1040s	Coastal trader	L: 14m W: 3.28m	Trading vessel	4.5–5tons of cargo and 7 crew
Skuldelev 5	Denmark	1030s	Warship	L:17.3m W: 2.74m	Transport of persons/warfare	28 crew
Skuldelev 6	Western Norway	1030s	Phase I: Fishing boat Phase II: Small trading vessel	L:11m W: 2.3m	Inshore fishing vessel later remodelled and used as a small cargo vessel	Phase I: 2.6 tons of cargo + 10–12 crew Phase II: 4.7 tons of cargo + 5 crew

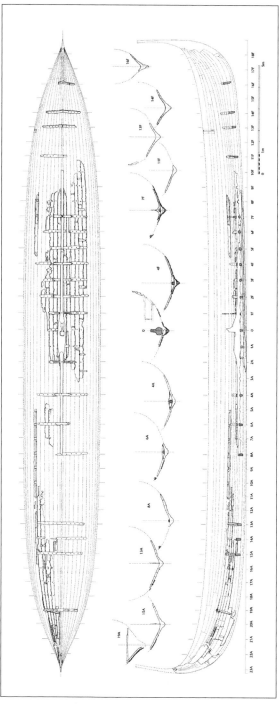

5 Torso reconstruction of Skuldelev 2, the wreck that would later
be reconstructed as the *Sea Stallion*. Illustration: Sune Willum-
Nielsen. Copyright: The Viking Ships Museum, Denmark

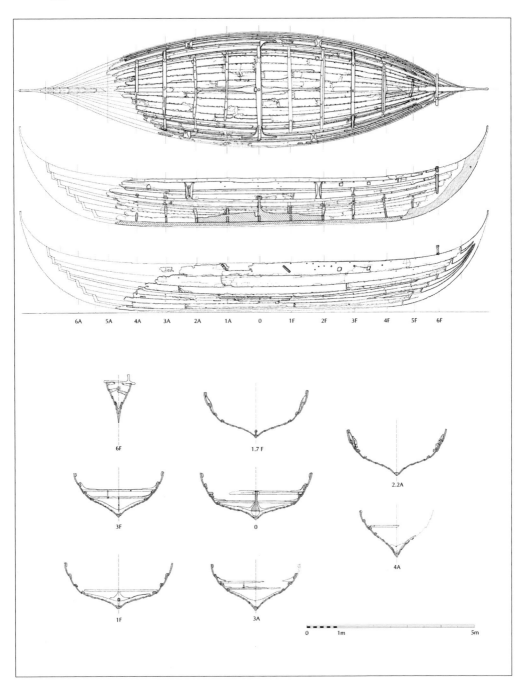

6 Torso reconstruction of Skuldelev 3, the most complete of the five wrecks.
Illustration: Sune Willum-Nielsen. Copyright: The Viking Ships Museum

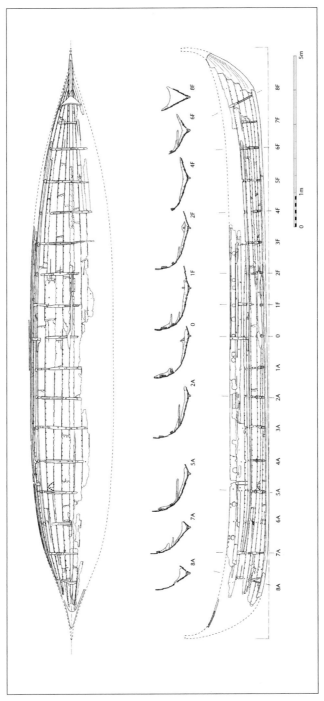

7 Torso reconstruction of Skuldelev 5. Illustration. Werner Karrasch.
Copyright: The Viking Ships Museum

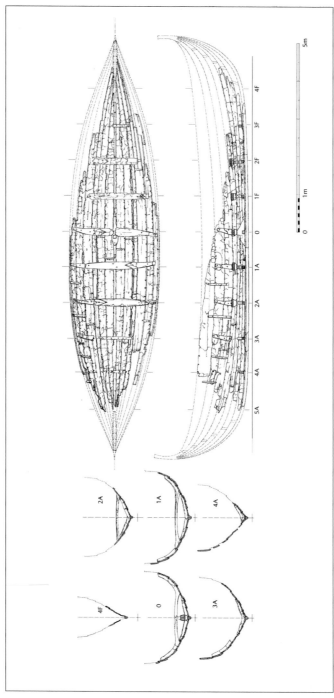

8 Torso reconstruction of Skuldelev 6. Illustration: Sune
Willum-Nielsen. Copyright: The Viking Ships Museum

Conservation, presentation, reconstruction

A number of techniques were experimented with before the final conservation methodology was decided on. Initially timbers from Skuldelev 2 and 3 were treated with linseed oil and paraffin, with eighty-seven timbers from the wreck of Skuldelev 3 conserved with alum. Neither of these methods proved satisfactory and were eventually abandoned in favour of a polyethylene glycol solution (PEG) which had at that time just been used successfully in preserving the timbers of the Swedish wreck *Wasa* (Crumlin Pedersen and Olsen 2002, 71).

By December 1975 all 50,000 timbers were fully treated and a new purpose-built exhibition hall had been constructed on the beachfront at Roskilde (Crumlin Pedersen and Olsen 2002, 75). Designed by Professor Erik Chr. Sørensen, the Ships Hall was a groundbreaking design in how the exhibition space was created to allow for the maximum visual impact of the wrecks against the backdrop of the Roskilde Fjord. In presenting the Skuldelev ships, the more traditional model of using modern timbers to 'fill in' the gaps where original components had been lost was avoided. Instead metal skeleton frames that would support the timbers of the wrecks were created to allow the viewer to see the preserved remains as well as the length, breadth and lines of the ships.

In 1982, the Viking Ships Museum brought together a multidisciplinary team of archaeologists, historians, craftspeople and sailors. Their task was to analyze the remains in a more critical way with a view to building 1:1 reconstructions of the five wrecks. By building and test-sailing accurate reconstructions it is possible to understand their capabilities, how far and how fast they can sail and under what conditions. These are issues that are central to the story of the Viking Age and the adherence to the strict principles involved in the experimental reconstructions would see the Viking Ships Museum emerge as a world leader in maritime archaeology and ship reconstruction.

These principles dictate that to obtain meaningful research results, the experiments must be based on:

- A scientific reconstruction of a well-documented archaeological shipwreck
- A well-trained crew, capable of handling the ship and its specialized functions
- Voyages and sea-trials in the seas for which the original ship was built, and under the geographical, hydrological and meteorological conditions that the vessel was designed to face
- Voyages and sea-trials using the ship's original means of propulsion – sail and oars, without the aid of a motor

(www.vikingeskibsmuseet.dk/uploads/media/Fuldblodpaahavet_Forskningsplan_nov2006_UK.pdf)

Building the Sea Stallion

Skuldelev 2 was the final ship to be reconstructed and was to be the most difficult of the five. Only 25 per cent of the ship was recovered during the excavation. Luckily, it was the crucial 25 per cent including the keel and several other key floor timbers. The reconstruction followed the same process that had been established and refined with the previous ships. All the extant elements of the ship are drawn in 1:1 followed by a highly detailed construction of a cardboard model in 1:10 (fig. 9). It is during this stage, lasting three years, that all decisions were taken about the design of the ship, as the templates from this model were expanded to act as the templates for the actual reconstruction in timber. Once the overall design has been finalized the lengthy process of locating, gathering and transporting materials to the boatyard can begin.

Construction began on the *Sea Stallion* at the boatyard of the Viking Ships Museum in September 2000 using replica Viking tools and techniques and was completed in September 2004 (figs 10 and 11). The timeframe involved in the

10 Replica Viking Age tools were used to fell the timber needed for the construction of the *Sea Stallion*. Photo: Werner Karrasch. Copyright: The Viking Ships Museum

11 This image captures the skill of the team of boatbuilders who built the *Sea Stallion*. Working by eye and with accurate replica tools they meticulously shaped each piece of theship by hand. Photo: Werner Karrasch. Copyright: The Viking Ships Museum

construction does not represent the length of time it would have taken to construct a ship in the Viking Age. The creation of the *Sea Stallion* was part of an experimental archaeological project and the boat-builders meticulously recorded every step. When procurement and processing of raw materials are also taken into account, it is estimated to have taken approximately 50,000 man-hours to build the ship. The actual construction phase lasted roughly 27,000 man-hours. Based on a thirteenth-century account of the building of a ship that describes the different craftsmen involved the breakdown of the hours is as follows:

- Master builder: 500 hours
- Stem smith: 1,000 hours
- Boat-builders: 10,000 hours
- Woodmen and assistants: 14,000 hours
- Workers to clench the nails: 1,000 hours

Søren Nielsen, head of the boatyard at the Viking Ships Museum estimates that a ship like the *Sea Stallion* could originally have been built in as little as seven months (S. Nielsen, pers comm.).

Shipbuilding and Dyflinarskiri

The construction of the *Sea Stallion* has afforded an insight into the shipbuilding industry of Viking Dublin in terms of the numbers of people, hours, and resources involved, and opens up a great many questions concerning the organization of both society and the wider hinterland surrounding the town. The table below lists the various materials involved in the construction of the different components of the ship. All diameters are estimated at chest height on the average man.

It is immediately clear from this list that woodland management within the hinterland and beyond would have been essential for the construction of ships in Dublin. The trees required for the manufacture of the different elements of these vessels would have needed specific attributes. The frames that shape the hull need to be growing in the exact curve required by the boat-builder. The mast required a perfectly straight pine with few major branches. This intimate knowledge of the woodland is a good example of the duality of movement of goods in and out of the city. We think of Viking Dublin as a thriving centre of industry and trade but rarely consider the wider network of resources and connections with the surrounding countryside that this must have entailed. Finished components such as nails, tar, sail and the time involved in their manufacture represent the collective efforts of many in terms of gathering and processing raw material beyond the walls of the city.

Component	Material	Quantity	Specific Requirements
Planks	Oak	14 oaks	8–10m high, 1m in diameter
Planks with oarports	Ash	4 ashes	10m high, 35cm in diameter
Keel, stems, keelson and mast partners	Oak	6 oaks	8–10m high, 50–70cm in diameter
Stringers	Oak	3 oaks	12m high, 60cm in diameter
Frames oak	Oak	–	285 pieces of naturally grown curved
Oars, mast, yard & spars	Pine	50 pines	5–13m high, 30–35cm in diameter
Treenails	Willow	10 willows	20–25cm in diameter
Cordage	Lime bast & horse tails	– Approximately 600 horsetails	Bast from c.4,500m of lime branches with the thickness of an arm –
Tar	Pine	18m³ pine roots and pinewood	–
Charocal (for iron smelting and smithing)	Misc. wood	130 tons of wood	–
Sail	Wool/flax or wool	200kg of flax	–

Launch of the ship and preparation for the voyage

In September 2004 the ship was launched by Queen Margrethe of Denmark who named it the *Sea Stallion from Glendalough* in tribute to the shared heritage of both Irish and Danes that the wreck represents (fig. 12). The crew could now begin to familiarize themselves with the ship and how she handled. From the outset, the objective with test-sailing the *Sea Stallion* had been to undertake the voyage from Roskilde to Dublin and back again, in order to test the ship in the waters the original was built for – the North Sea, the Irish Sea and the English Channel. This would be a long and difficult journey of almost 3,000 nautical miles through some of the most hazardous seas in Europe. A great many preparations had to be made before a crew of sixty-five people could take to the open sea in the *Sea Stallion* in safety.

12 The *Sea Stallion* was launched by Queen Margrethe of Denmark on
4 September, 2004. Photo. Werner Karrasch

Initial training with the ship was confined to the calm and sheltered waters
of the Roskilde Fjord. The first trips were solely powered by oar. Once the
skipper and boat-builders were confident with the balance and trim of the ship,
the mast, rigging and sail were installed. Short two-day training sails were
organized for the volunteer crew during which a system of organization for
both the sailing and the other practicalities of life on board was slowly
established. The difficulty with the *Sea Stallion* in this regard was that
although the principles of sailing a square rig Viking ship are well known, how
these principles could be applied and executed on a 30m-long version was not.

Every manoeuvre needed to be adapted to the larger and heavier rigging of the *Sea Stallion*. This was a slow but necessary process. For the safety of the sixty-five individuals who would take the ship to sea it was vital that all routines became clockwork and could be carried out with confidence if not ease at any time of the day or night and in any conditions.

A system of organization was also developed for the large crew. The crew of sixty-five is divided into watches and sections. A two-watch system – port and starboard – is operated on the *Sea Stallion*. This means that at any given moment while at sea and under sail, half of the crew are on duty and half are off. This changes when large manoeuvres are required such as raising or lowering the sail when all hands are needed to move the yard and sail which have a combined weight of over 1.5 tons. Watches are also disregarded when rowing as the effort involved in propelling the ship by oar is too great for just one half of the crew to sustain for any significant length of time. The watches cover a twenty-four hour period and are four hours in length excepting two short watches of two hours each, one in the morning and one in the evening. This is done so that neither half of the crew gets the shift with two watches during the night on two consecutive days. The assigning of a crewmember to either the port or starboard watch dictates many aspects of life on board, from where you will sleep and pack your personal gear to the people you will work with when on duty.

The ship is further divided into six sections; the foreship, the tack room, the midship, the drag room, the aft and the bridge. The bridge at the very rear of the ship is where the skipper and his mates are situated around the navigation and communication equipment. Decisions concerning when, where and how we sail are made here and relayed throughout the ship with the help of a repeater near the mast who shouts the commands further to the crew at the front of the ship. Each of the other five sections has two foremen and between eight and fourteen hands who very quickly become a tightly bonded unit living in close quarters and in sometimes extreme conditions. These are the people you are working with while sailing, who you eat your meals with, pack your gear next to and sleep beside; a small family at sea. Having good camaraderie within the crew as a whole is vital but having it within the individual sections is imperative. During long, often uncomfortable stretches at sea it is this bond that makes the experience so enjoyable and that helps keep anyone from getting too low.

Within their respective sections each crewmember is assigned a *rum* (pronounced 'room') after the Old Norse term for the space between two rowing benches. This *rum* is assigned to two crewmembers, one on each side of the ship and is the place where you would stow your gear and where you row when the need arises. The space allotted to each crewmember in their *rum* has been estimated at 80cm², a vast reduction on the amount of living space we are

13 Close quarters: the *Sea Stallion* is 30m long with a maximum width of 4m and carries of a crew of 60 at all times. Each of the crewmembers on the right hand side of the image are sitting in their respective *rums*, illustrating the cramped nature of the conditions on board. Photo: Werner Karrasch. Copyright: The Viking Ships Museum

accustomed to. You very quickly become used to being permanently surrounded by other people, to dressing and undressing in full view of the people around you, to constantly sitting, standing and sleeping right next to shipmates (fig. 13). The closeness of this can be difficult for some twenty-first-century people to accept: we're very used to having our own 'personal space', will choose the empty seat on the train rather than sit next to another, and expect peace and quite in our own homes at the end of the day.

This could not be further from the situation on the *Sea Stallion*. And yet it is this very closeness that is essential to the crew functioning successfully as a unit. We need to know we can rely on each other, physically, mentally and emotionally to carry out the work at hand and to see each other safely and without conflict to the end of the voyage. The ease with which the 120 standing members of the crew of the *Sea Stallion*, of all ages and from all walks of life, have integrated and come to know each other is one of the true successes of the project as it has engendered a deep and abiding enthusiasm for the ship and its voyages, something that is essential in a project manned predominantly by volunteers.

Early trial voyages
The trial voyages of the *Sea Stallion* were begun with a number of set research objectives. These were

- To test the reconstruction, the museum's hypothesis of the original ship
- To test the sailing characteristics of the reconstruction, thus also testing this type of vessel in general
- To investigate the functions, organization and logistics of the ship and her crew (http://www.vikingeskibsmuseet.dk/uploads/media/Fuldblodpaahavet _Forskningsplan_nov2006_UK.pdf).

The summer of 2005, one year after the launch of the ship, the *Sea Stallion* went on its first experimental voyage, a two-week trip from Roskilde to the Isefjord on Sjælland. This trip was primarily about familiarizing the crew with the ship and also each other in the context of a longer time together at sea and on land. The ship was blessed with sunshine and fine weather with light winds, making it a good – though slightly unrealistic – introduction to life on the *Sea Stallion*. That autumn and the following spring saw further specific training back on the Roskilde Fjord before a longer four-week voyage during the summer of 2006 from Roskilde, along the coast of Sweden to Oslo. The route home headed further west along the coast of Norway before swinging close to the North Sea on the return to the west coast of Denmark. This would potentially be the most difficult stretch of the voyage – almost two days straight at sea, open to the swells from the North Sea. But it was not to be. The good weather that had dogged the ship in 2005 continued for the entire summer voyage in 2006. The crossing from Norway to Thyborøn on the west coast of Denmark was like sailing on a lake. Although this made for very pleasant conditions for the crew it created problems for the project as a whole. The following summer we would take the ship out on a trip of 1,000 nautical miles through what we could be certain were difficult conditions and yet we had never really experienced what it was like to sail the *Sea Stallion* for many days in the cold and rain and in high seas. However we would very quickly become all too familiar with what that was like during the voyage to Dublin in 2007.

Life on board the Sea Stallion *from Roskilde to Dublin*
Sailing an open ship across the North Sea, around the northern tip of Scotland, through the Western Isles and across the Irish Sea to Dublin during one of the wettest summers on record proved both physically and mentally challenging for the ship and her crew (fig. 14). These waters include some of the most hazardous sailing conditions in Europe with exposure to current and tide from the Atlantic and the North and Irish Seas. The ship contended with force 9 winds, racing tidal streams, broken rudders, waves up to 8m high and the constant, relentless rain that fell on all but five days out of the seven-week voyage. There is no shelter from the elements, no space below deck to retreat to when it gets too wet, too cold, too exhausting. All life on board is conducted in the open, night and day, from working, sleeping and eating to telling stories,

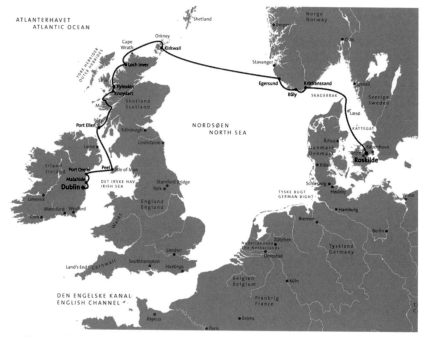

14 Route of the *Sea Stallion*'s voyage from Roskilde to Dublin. Illustration: Mette Kryger. Copyright: The Viking Ships Museum

passing the time with bad jokes that get progressively worse and progressively funnier the longer you sail. Waterproofs and wet woollen blankets provided the only barrier between you and the weather. The voyage to Dublin tested both the ship and crew beyond anything we had experienced before, beginning with the first thirty-six hours sailing.

Roskilde to Kristiansand

Watched by a crowd of 10,000 well-wishers and during a rare spell of sunshine the *Sea Stallion* and her eager and excited crew left Roskilde on Sunday July 1 to begin her seven-week voyage to Dublin. Joined by a large flotilla of every kind of watercraft from kayaks to traditional boats the ship made her way up the Roskilde Fjord, heading for the sea and for Kristiansand 240 nautical miles away on the southwest coast of Norway. The good humour and excitement of the day would continue; the sunshine would not. Before the first night at sea was over, the rain had come and it was to stay with the ship the entire way to Norway. Constant driving rain presents many challenges when onboard the *Sea Stallion*; we have very little space in which to move around and so being permanently wet makes it difficult to stay warm. The ropes and sail become very heavy as they absorb the water and trying to move around on the slippery deck timbers as the ship pitches and rolls with the swell can be an acrobatic feat.

In situations like this the crew rely on each other, stoicism and volumes of chocolate and coffee. But there is also a kind of comfort to be had in the regimen of life on board. The division of the day into the various watches means that there is rarely a long stretch of tedium. You know your day will be neatly subdivided, punctuated by events such as breakfast, lunch and dinner that take on whole new levels of fascination when there is little else to distract. Your focus and your world narrows to consist of only this ship, the people within it and the job you are there to do and so your perception of what equates as being normal begins to shift. Tasks such as taking on an extra layer of clothes, for example, can take up much of your time; first you consider at length whether or not this is the right time to do so as there is always a need for extra layers as night falls and the temperature drops. Then you have to judge the right moment and spot in which to execute this change, keeping yourself sheltered from the rain as much as you can. The actual action itself must be carried out quickly and so a procedure is established in your mind – open time-consuming zips and buttons, have jumper the right way around, remove life jacket and so on until finally the task is complete and you can sit back in slightly warmer satisfaction. It might still be raining but you have just whiled away a good ten minutes of a wet, cold day. There is also a strange sort of calm that comes from having all major decisions about your time and how you spend it decided by someone else. And so as the tally of sea miles increases, the crew and the ship slip into their own little – figuratively – insulated world.

The ship arrived at Bragdøya, near the town of Kristiansand on the coast of Norway at 0300 on Tuesday morning, with the crew cold, wet and in need of sleep. A total of four crewmembers were moved from the ship over the course of the two days, three of these due to extreme cold or seasickness and one due to a fall which aggravated an old knee injury. All four were taken to Cable One, the support ship assigned to follow the *Sea Stallion*, given treatment and returned to the *Sea Stallion* the next day. Cable One was there to provide backup in situations such as these when people could not receive adequate medical attention from the nurse on the *Sea Stallion*. It was also charged with our rescue should the ship capsize or suffer major structural damage as well as transport of provisions and equipment that due to lack of space could not be fitted on the *Sea Stallion*.

The use of Cable One for these purposes is a good example of the fundamentals of the *Sea Stallion* project; it is the ship and its sailing capabilities that are being tested, not the crew, and so we make no attempt to sail like 'Vikings'. We wear modern sailing clothes, have a full complement of navigation and communications equipment and have strict safety standards. The project has often been criticized for this – the public forum on the website the BBC created to follow the voyage contained lengthy criticism of everything from the use of life jackets to the presence of women on board. Analyzing how far, how

15 The closeness of the rowing benches on the *Sea Stallion* mean that rowing with 60 oars requires a short, sharp stroke which must be powered by the arms alone. This method cannot be sustained over a long period. Photo. Werner Karrasch. Copyright: The Viking Ships Museum

fast and how efficiently the ship sails will not be in any way compromised by the use of modern equipment. On the contrary, these questions cannot be answered *without* using navigation and GPS tracking systems, as it is necessary to plot and transmit data concerning the exact position of the ship in order to make these analyses.

And it was the data from these systems that showed that the sailing from Roskilde to Bragdøya had been one of the fastest the *Sea Stallion* had ever had. The 240 nautical miles had been covered in just thirty-five hours giving an average speed of 7 knots. It was a great start to the voyage but the speed with which the ship had eaten up those first miles was going to become a distant memory as the *Sea Stallion* made its way along the south-western coast of Norway.

Sailing west and waiting
From Bragdøya the route was to take the ship further west along the coast in preparation for the crossing of the North Sea to Scotland. The crossing is best attempted from the west coast of Norway where the distance between the two coastlines is shortest. However the wind was not with the ship and it made slow progress along the coast, often resorting to rowing for hours at a stretch. Propelling the *Sea Stallion* by oar requires a huge expenditure of energy on

16 When longer periods of rowing are required, every second oar is used. This allows for the rotation of two crewmembers to each oar and the increased amount of space means that the crew can use their back and stomach muscles much more effectively allowing us to continue rowing for hours at a time. Photo: Werner Karrasch. Copyright: The Viking Ships Museum

the part of the crew and unless it is part of a specific testing process, is limited to occasions when lack of wind leaves no other option. The rowing benches in Skuldelev 2 were found to be only 72cm apart, on average 20cm closer together than on most other Viking ships. The effect of this was to reduce the length of the rowing stroke while increasing the number of crew who could be on board. There is provision for sixty oars on the *Sea Stallion* though early rowing trials quickly demonstrated that it is more effective to use just half or even one third of these. When all sixty are in use, the lack of distance between rowers means a very short, sharp rowing stroke must be used which requires the rower to primarily use their arms rather than their backs (fig. 15). As the oars on the *Sea Stallion* are 4m long and weigh approximately 10kg this becomes tiring quite quickly. It also means that there is no chance to rest as every crewmember is already working, so there is no one to provide relief. Normally rowing with every oar is restricted to occasions when we want to make a good impression – leaving and entering harbours and so on – or when conducting comparative trials to test the efficiency of rowing teams and techniques.

When a long period of rowing is called for, we use every second or every third oar. This means that there is much more room to take a larger stroke with the oar (fig. 16). The crew of the *Sea Stallion* have developed our own peculiar rowing style that involves using your back and stomach muscles much more than your arms, allowing for far greater endurance. The handle of the oar is brought forward and the blade dropped into the water. The blade is then dipped as far as you can, raising your arms upwards as you pull the oar through the water by leaning backwards until almost horizontal and allowing the counterbalancing weight of the water against the blade to keep you from falling. You then sit up again as the oar is brought out of the water, an unorthodox but effective method which means that we can keep rowing at an even tempo for far longer than if we were using our arms alone. This is further helped by the rotation of two to three crewmembers to the one oar, meaning you row for half an hour then rest for either thirty minutes or an hour.

By this method the *Sea Stallion* made its way slowly to Båly, a small fishing harbour on the south coast. The rowing had some pleasant interludes though, such as the arrival by rib of freshly baked cakes from the ever-obliging Peter, cook on the Cable One. This was the first of nine days the ship would spend in this small harbour as westerly after westerly forced the *Sea Stallion* to wait for a change in the weather. This can be immensely difficult for the crew. You live from weather forecast to weather forecast, hoping all the time for a change in the wind direction. Twice daily meetings at breakfast and dinner bring the latest reports and you live in a state of limbo never knowing how long you will stay in one place. Added to the frustrations of this is the fact that even with all of this free time, there is nowhere to go. Båly is a tiny fishing harbour surrounded by nothing but countryside. The consensus among the crew is that if it weren't likely to land them in jail, a bit of raiding and pillaging would have been just the ticket to dispel the pall of boredom that was beginning to settle on Båly and its recently increased population as the westerly winds and non-stop rain continued.

Half in jest though the idea was, there is a truth to the suggestions about raiding and pillaging. In the Viking Age as now, sailors were just as much at the mercy of the weather and could easily get pinned down on that stretch of the coast waiting for a favourable wind to take them over the North Sea. Warships like the *Sea Stallion* have such limited storage facilities on board that the maximum amount of supplies that can be carried would be exhausted after only five days, leaving them with nothing on which to fuel the crew on the energy-sapping journey over to the British coast. The crew would then have to replenish their stocks honestly or by more nefarious methods. Either way, no ship could attempt to cross the North Sea with an under-stocked store and so provision of food and water would have been a central concern for every one of the countless thousands of ships that would have followed that same route.

17 The rudder was to prove the weak point during the voyage to Dublin.
This is the broken rudder strap which gave way off the coast of Norway.
Photo/Copyright: The Viking Ships Museum

The stay in Båly was a difficult lesson in patience and self-discipline for a crew that had spent three years training for this voyage and despite best efforts were becoming bored, frustrated at being on land and increasingly out of pocket thanks to the price of Norwegian beer. The project leaders had attempted to keep morale up through activities such as safety drills with Cable One, a memorable day spent acting as escort to the Danish Queen as she attended the celebration of the birthday of Queen Sonja of Norway, and organizing trips to local sights. All the same, no-one was sorry when the order was finally given to prepare the ship to move further up the coast.

First faults and knotted ropes
The leg from Båly up to Egersund followed the same weather pattern that had been established so far on the voyage; it rained most of the time but the wind was good, with the ship making 10 knots at times. The trip was not to be a quiet one though. While making good speed the command to lower the sail came from Carsten the skipper. The leather strap that attaches the rudder to the side of the ship had broken, leaving the ship rudderless until a replacement could be fitted (fig. 17). In this situation it is imperative to drop the sail as quickly as possible and to stabilize the rudder to prevent the ship going broadside to the swell and

18 Immediately after the rudder had been repaired, one of the reef lines on the sail got entangled. This meant the sail could not function properly, a hazardous situation on a ship with no engine. Here one of the crew members can be seen crawling out on the yard to try to free the rope while sea water begins pooling dangerously in the sail on the opposite side. Photo: Morten Nielsen. Copyright: The Viking Ships Museum

increasing the risk of capsizing. The strap was replaced quickly and the sail raised again. The problems were not over however. When the yard was hoisted back into position it became clear that one of the small reef ropes had got knotted with another and the sail was bunched together on the starboard side. The order to drop the sail came again and with more urgency this time.

The gravity of the situation meant that there was no time to take the yard inside the shrouds as normal; instead it was lowered across the midship with the crew endeavouring to keep the sail out of the water. Edgar, an experienced rigger, donned his survival suit and crawled out across the yard to try to free the rope (fig. 18). While he was lying along the yard the ship, now with no forward propulsion, had again started to turn with the waves so that the swells were coming from the side. She began to pitch from side to side, raising Edgar, who was struggling with the ropes at the end of the yard, ten or fifteen feet above the water while the opposite end of the yard dipped beneath the waterline, the sail dangerously scooping up thousands of litres each time. The weight of this actually cracked the top strake on the port side where the water was gathering. Eventually the decision was made to cut the rope, Edgar crawled back inside the ship and the sail could finally be raised.

The event was a wake-up call for many of the crew. It was the first time a vital component of the ship had failed and also the first time the crew had been in a potentially dangerous situation with the *Sea Stallion*. It served to focus people's attention and to highlight the reality of what we were doing here – this was an open ship where things can go wrong very quickly and we had to be prepared to cope with that at all times. But still no-one doubted the ship or its capabilities. We had had a problem and had dealt with it well. With characteristic understated humour, Carsten the skipper decided that it was a very good thing that the rudder strap had broken that day as he'd much rather it happened there than on the North Sea. The rest of the passage to Egersund was problem-free and the *Sea Stallion* was once again in waiting but this time for the big one, the crossing of the North Sea.

Over the North Sea by line and by sail

The summer of 2007 saw a series of westerly winds sweeping across the North Sea towards the Norwegian coast. The *Sea Stallion* needed an easterly and time was beginning to get a little tight. This was a volunteer project and all of the crew had jobs and families to go back to: this was not a venture that could continue indefinitely. Therefore a seven-week limit was set for the voyage with an end date in Dublin on August 14. Added to this was the necessity of a stay of a number of days in the Hebrides where the conditions with tide and current were perfect for the test-sailing that was central to the project. At last, on 19 July the ship made ready to cross the North Sea. Just after midnight, the *Sea Stallion* was rowed quietly out of the harbour at Egersund and away from the coast. After a number of hours the oars were put away and the sail was raised in expectation of the forecast wind. But it never arrived. The ship was drifting at about 0.1 knots and a swell meant that it was now impossible to row to increase the speed. Then a further blow: the latest news from the Met Service warned that a severe gale was due in the area in the next few hours. Carsten was now faced with a tough decision. Either go back to the Norwegian coast, potentially getting pinned down for days if not weeks and miss the opportunity to carry out the test-sailing in Scotland, or take a tow from Cable One, sacrificing the North Sea crossing but in the knowledge that it could be reattempted in 2008 when the ship returned to Roskilde. Reluctantly, the decision to tow was made and a disappointed crew lowered the sail and prepared the ship to accept the towrope.

When under tow there is little that needs to be done by the crew. Tents were set up to provide as much shelter as possible from the cold and wet and people

19 Crewmembers sleeping on a 'bed' made by rolling out the oars on the windward side of the ship. Their close proximity is due to the lack of space on board but also serves to create much-needed body warmth when crossing the open sea at night.
Photo: Tríona Nicholl

passed the time as they could, sleeping being one of the key pastimes. When sailing with a steady wind the sleeping quarters are relatively comfortable by *Sea Stallion* standards. The oars are laid out on the rowing benches on the windward side of the ship to create a bed to lie on. We have thirty foam mattresses and thirty woollen blankets for the half of the crew who are off duty. Those who have a free watch settle down on the bed and try to sleep while the rest of the crew work around them. When it rains, we lay a long tarpaulin over the sleeping crew to try and keep out the worst of the wet. Warmth is provided by the blankets, tarps and the proximity of the other crewmembers; the limited amount of space available means that it is not unusual to see ten or fifteen people neatly spooned together beneath the grey blankets (fig. 19).

Those who could not sleep passed the time talking, listening to music or playing cards and trying not to think about their situation. After twenty-four hours and one hundred sea miles the wind picked up and the towline was cast away. The *Sea Stallion* could now complete the remaining 250 sea miles of the journey to Kirkwall on Orkney.

20 When on land the crew sleep in the relative comfort of these tents. The main challenge lies in trying to find enough space in small harbours to erect them.
Photo: Tríona Nicholl

Island life and testing times

From Kirkwall the *Sea Stallion* made its way without incident along the Scottish coast stopping in at Loch Inver in the northwest before putting into Kyleakin on the Isle of Skye. The sailing around Scotland is remembered by most of the crew as some of the finest times we have spent on the ship. The rugged beauty of the coastline, even in the grey and the mist of that dismal summer, kept all of us entranced. Normally, we have quite an introspective view: we focus on what is happening in the ship and tend not to notice the seascapes around us. In Scotland it was the opposite and the ship became calm and peaceful as we spent hours just sitting looking out over the side of the ship at the amazing scenes slipping by. The stopover at Skye also had some practical motivations. The ship was to be reprovisioned and some of the crew would be changed. From Skye we sailed south through the ever-present rain to Knoydart and then further on down through the Hebrides, along coastlines devoid of any sign of life except sheep.

Our destination was Islay, an island with 4,000 people and eight whisky distilleries. We arrived into the harbour at the Lagavulin Distillery, just outside of the main town of Port Ellen on July 30. This was to be our home for the next

21 The cooking facilities on the *Sea Stallion* consist of two gas rings and two large pots, the only equipment available to the cook who is charged with providing food for 60 hungry crewmembers. Photo: Werner Karrasch. Copyright: the Viking Ships Museum.

seven days as the ship and crew carried out a series of test-sailings in the waters just outside the harbour. The accommodation for the crew on the island was fairly rudimentary by most standards but habitable by ours. We were offered space to pitch our tents on an open area next to distillery harbour. When on land we have five large tepee tents, one for each section since every night one section will stay on the ship as the anchor watch (fig. 20). These tents can hold up to twelve people and quickly become crowded and cosy as wet clothes are hung up to dry and people build small nests with thermarests, sleeping bags and an assortment of woolly jumpers, revelling in the comparative comfort of sleeping on land.

The cooking facilities on Islay were the same as when at sea. The ship is equipped with two gas rings located in a wooden box in the aft (fig. 21). On these two rings it is the responsibility of the chef and the steward to produce enough food to fill the bellies of sixty permanently hungry crewmembers. The amount of energy expended in trying to keep warm while sailing in an open boat means that the quantities of food we need to consume are far above what we would eat at home. Breakfast consists of porridge to which we add

22 The toilet facilities on the *Sea Stallion* are simple but effective. Here head boatbuilder Soren Nielsen can be seen repairing the toilet – a seat which is rests on two rowing benches with a bucket underneath. A small tent provides a modicum of privacy. Photo. Tríona Nicholl

everything from jam and peanuts to maple syrup and dried fruit in an attempt to make it palatable. Lunch consists of sandwiches made from long-life Danish rye bread with either tinned fish or smoked sausage and as much fresh fruit and vegetables as we can have on board. Dinner is always a hot meal, generally potatoes, pasta or rice in one pot and some kind of meat or stew in the other. Outside of these main meals we also consume vast quantities of sweets, biscuits, chocolate, peanuts and raisins, anything that will give you an energy boost, particularly when on night watch.

Sadly, the toilet facilities on Islay were also going to be the same as when at sea. On the *Sea Stallion*, we have our euphemistically named toilet that consists of a bucket with a detachable toilet seat, enclosed by a small tent (fig. 22). When you have used the toilet, the contents go over the side and the bucket and seat are cleaned and disinfected. It was largely the same on Islay. During the day, the distillery manager kindly granted us access to the staff toilets but after 5p.m. each day we were on our own. This is something that we accepted with little complaint and it demonstrates how quickly you can become removed from normal standards of living when on a ship like the *Sea Stallion* – something which makes you eternally grateful for the small things we all take for granted when you finally get back home to your flushing toilet, shower and mattress.

Our stay on Islay was punctuated with visits from the islanders, endless acts of generous hospitality on their part in the form of hot showers, lifts in and out of town, use of washing machines and the odd glass of whisky or two and a series of test-sailings in Lagavulin Bay. This meant we had short days on the *Sea Stallion* where we would repeat a number of set manoeuvres such as rowing or tacking into the wind over and over. The data gathered during these and other test-sailings is currently being analyzed and will be published as part of the Viking Ship Museum's monograph series, *Ships and Boats of the North*.

Time was now moving on, and again we were coming under pressure to continue further along our route. At the evening meeting on 5 August Carsten announced that a storm was due the following day and so we would stay at least another twenty-four hours on Islay. The next morning though the forecast had changed, as the storm had moved further north. We were woken up at 6a.m., told we would be having no breakfast and to break camp and prepare the ship to leave as quickly as possible.

STORMY MONDAY

That day was to be the most dramatic the *Sea Stallion* and its crew have ever had. We set off from Islay and began to make our way down through the North Channel, headed for the Isle of Man. Carsten had warned that conditions in the North Channel could be tricky and that this was probably not going to be a calm and easy day's sailing. After an hour we lowered the sail so that the rope attaching the rudder to the ship could be tightened. The constant pressure it was under had caused it to stretch, making steering increasingly difficult. With that task complete, the sail went up again and we sailed on. The wind continued to strengthen and it was down with the sail once more for the first of many reefs, reducing the amount of sail to slow the ship through waves that were growing higher. The storm that had been forecast to go north had obviously not gone far enough.

That afternoon we were ordered into our survival suits for the first time. These are one of the key pieces of safety equipment on board and each crewmember has their own tailor-made suit, designed to keep you afloat and insulated from the freezing waters should the ship go down. On Stormy Monday as it became known we were ordered into the suits as a precaution. We were in no immediate danger but, in an open boat like the *Sea Stallion*, safe is most definitely better than sorry. With the wind now at 15m/sec and waves of over 4m, there came a frantic command from the bridge – we were to drop the

23 Stormy Monday as it's now known saw the rudder system fall again, this time in a force 9 gale on the Irish Sea. Here the crew, all in survival suits, have lowered the sail across the ship in an attempt to prevent a potential capsize due to lack of steering capability while the rudder is repaired once more. Photo: Werner Karrasch. Copyright: The Viking Ships Museum

sail immediately and take the yard across the midship. The rudder-strap had failed again.

This time the situation was far more serious. Carsten ordered us to detach the yard from the parrell and try to get it as far inside the ship as possible to prevent seawater from filling the sail as had happened in Norway (fig. 23). The shout came out to make all survival suits fast, justifying Carsten's caution in ordering us into them that morning. As the boat-builder and mates worked to repair the rudder and the crew in the midship reefed down the sail, the rest of the crew had to just wait and look incredulously over the side at the seas that had begun to rise around us and to provide care for an increasing number of seasick shipmates. We were now rudderless in the middle of a force 9 gale.

With no propulsion and no rudder to steer, the powerful swell pushed the ship sideways so that we were now sitting broadside to the waves, exactly where you do not want to be. The mast of the ship was swinging from side to side like a 20m metronome as the ship was rolled dangerously from port to starboard and back again. This was a nervous time for the crew – if the length of the wave pattern was to change the ship would not have time to right itself again before the next wave came sweeping in over the rail. We could potentially be swamped by thousands of tons of water in a matter of seconds. But as the

24 With the rudder repaired the *Sea Stallion* sails out of danger in winds so strong the sail had to be reduced to its smallest possible extent, Photo. Werner Karrasch, Copyright: The Viking Ships Museum

minutes passed we began to understand just how stable the *Sea Stallion* actually was. A shout would come out, 'Hold fast! Big wave coming!' and everyone would hunker down and find something to hold on to but just as the side ship rode up the face of the wave and the crest should have broken over the rail the opposite happened. The majority of the waves rolled under the keel without breaking over the deck. Certainly, many did break over the ship that day, drenching us and filling the bilges below deck but, overall, the ship rode gently sideways over the waves and we slowly learned to adjust our balance to this unfamiliar and thoroughly unexpected motion.

Twenty minutes later, the rudder was repaired, the reefing complete and we raised the sail once again to sail out of there. Our sail had been reefed down as far as possible and was now only 18m² instead of the usual 112m² and we were still making 9 knots (fig. 24). Looking at our support ship, a smaller Scottish vessel that had taken over from Cable One, we could see that the shape of the *Sea Stallion*'s hull actually allowed us to ride these large waves more effectively than a modern vessel. The narrow entry and shallow draught of the vessel means that the *Sea Stallion* slices through rather than crashes into the waves and the sailing down from Islay to the Isle of Man gave us all a whole new insight into the incredible balance and sophistication of Viking ship design. These were conditions that any vessel would have had trouble in and, broken rudder-straps aside, the *Sea Stallion* was riding over these waves with ease.

Although it was not a situation anyone would intentionally have sailed into, in terms of the project and our understanding of how these ships sail and what they can handle, Stormy Monday was an incredibly useful and informative experience. It gave both crew and boat-builders an increased confidence in their ship and what it could cope with and helped to cement the already strong bond amongst the crew. We had proved ourselves capable of reacting to danger with speed and efficiency and Stormy Monday has now become the stuff of legend among the wider network of people involved with the *Sea Stallion*.

The rest of the leg down to the Isle of Man passed without incident. We were tired but still full of adrenalin and constantly discussing over and over what had happened that day. After a meal of dehydrated food, as the conditions were still too rough to cook safely, and still in our survival suits, it was a different crew that lay down to sleep that night, a more focused, determined and proud one.

Over the Irish Sea to … Clogherhead

Two days of rest and relaxation with some much-needed sunshine on the Isle of Man had recharged all of our batteries and our increasing proximity to Ireland was starting to send a ripple of excitement through the crew. We were getting closer to our goal at Dublin. We left the harbour at Peel at 8a.m. on 9 August and set out across the Irish Sea. The sailing was fantastic – sunshine and good wind and there was much speculation as to where we would make land in Ireland. Having no engine, the *Sea Stallion* is at the mercy of the wind direction and there were many potential landing points from Carlingford to Drogheda proposed and then discarded as we gained on the Irish coast. Eventually, in true *Sea Stallion* fashion, we arrived into the harbour at Clogherhead, Co. Louth at 4:30a.m. Two hours later we were to realize how effective the *Sea Stallion* media machine was.

From the outset, one of the key objectives of the project had been to successfully disseminate the story of the project, not just to the academic world but to the wider public. To that end the website, www.seastallion.dk had been developed and used to great success. We had also engaged a number of media partners such as RTÉ and the BBC who carried regular news updates of our progress en route. One of the other strategies had been to target local newspapers and radio stations, but never with such good effect as at Clogherhead. From 7a.m. on the morning we arrived until we left the harbour the following night the quayside was constantly thronged with cars and hundreds of people coming to visit the ship. The scale of the interest of local people in the ship was incredible and matched only by their generosity in offering transport, food, showers and laundry services and a very warm welcome in the local pubs. As the only Irish person on board at the time, I was quietly proud of the reception that Ireland had given the *Sea Stallion*.

25 During the final moments of the voyage the *Sea Stallion* sails through the Eastlink Bridge on the Liffey, propelled by an uncharacteristically perfect wind. Photo: Werner Karrasch. Copyright: The Viking Ships Museum

To Malahide by the light of the moon

The last night at sea that summer saw us rowing out of Clogherhead at 10p.m. on our way to Malahide, the last port of call before Dublin. Since arriving in Ireland you could almost feel the energy on board and amongst the crew. Normally at night people focus on sleeping and the ship is silent but for the noise of the wind and waves. That night, there was a low but persistent murmur of chat and laughter as almost all the crew forsook sleep in favour of experiencing our last night for almost 12 months on board our ship. The sail was lowered and we rowed into Malahide harbour at 5a.m. the next morning, eating a quick breakfast on the quayside before finding somewhere to sleep at last. The next days were a flurry of activity as the ship was prepared for its arrival at Customs House Quay in three days' time. All the luggage and extra equipment was emptied, counted and stored and the ship cleaned from top to bottom.

A warship on the Liffey

We left Malahide on the 14th and spent a sunny morning tacking back and forth in Dublin Bay surrounded by other sailing craft. As the ship finally entered the mouth of the Liffey, the full extent of the interest and support for this maritime archaeological experiment was revealed. From the lighthouse that marks the entry to the river, people stood three and four deep to see the ship sail past, waving Danish and Irish flags and holding banners bidding us welcome.

Church and cathedral bells rang out, the sirens of every ferry, ship and moving vehicle in the docklands blasted from bank to bank and still the crowds grew larger. The noise reached such a crescendo that Carsten's orders could no longer be heard from one end of the ship to the other and one of the ship's mates was assigned the duty of scurrying back and forth to relay commands. We sailed on, through the raised arms of the Eastlink Bridge under full sail before the order to lower the sail was given for the final time that summer (fig. 25). The oars were brought out and after some manoeuvring through the Sean O'Casey Bridge we docked at Customs House Quay. Amidst the speeches, cheers and music from the quayside, smiles, laughter and not a few tears broke out amongst the crew as the realization sank in: we had done it.

The voyage had been an overwhelming success on many levels. The data gathered during the test-sailings would help to establish a deeper practical understanding of how these ships sailed and what impact this would have had on maritime strategies during the Viking Age. The varied conditions in terms of both the weather and the types of seas we sailed through allowed us to test the ship from every conceivable angle; the *Sea Stallion* had been through days of no wind, days with far too much wind, surging tidal streams and the powerful currents of the Atlantic Ocean and the North and Irish Seas. The crew too had been pushed to their limits, both mentally and physically, and they had excelled. The winter months would see the *Sea Stallion* move into the National Museum at Collins Barracks where the ship was displayed outside in Clarke Square while inside an exhibition told the story of the ship and its construction. In 2008, the ship would go back on the water once again to sail a southerly route through the English Channel, across the North Sea and back home to Roskilde, creating a whole new chapter in the story of this historic vessel.

BIBLIOGRAPHY

Crumlin-Pedersen, Ole and Olsen, Olaf (eds) 2002 *The Skuldelev Ships I*. Viking Ships Museum. Roskilde.

Viking Ships Museum 2007 *Welcome on board! The Sea Stallion from Glendalough: a viking longship recreated*. Viking Ships Museum. Roskilde.

Kastoft, Henrik 2007 *På vikingetogt med Havhingsten – et krigsskib vender hjem*. Forlaget Sohn. Copenhagen.

http://www.vikingeskibsmuseet.dk/uploads/media/Fuldblodpaahavet_Forskningsplan_no v2006_UK.pdf, accessed 10 December 2008.